The Future of U.S. Politics
in an Age of Economic Limits

Also of Interest

World Economic Development: 1979 and Beyond, Herman Kahn

A Westview Special Study

The Future of U.S. Politics
in an Age of Economic Limits
Bruce M. Shefrin

This study of the future of U.S. politics begins with an in-depth examination of the political, social, and economic dynamics of the present. Dr. Shefrin demonstrates that economic growth has been a key element in maintaining political stability by diverting the attention of materially deprived groups away from disruptive political activity. Examining the interaction of technological and political forces in the physical and social environment, he argues that an expectation of economic limits is reasonable—and perhaps undeniable—and focuses on the changes in the political system that can be anticipated in a no-growth or slow-growth society. Dr. Shefrin employs a nondeterministic "social choice" approach to reach the conclusion that, because the shape of the future is of major political significance, it will be the focus of intense political conflict. The four scenarios he presents reflect the major alternative directions possible for U.S. society, according to current social theory. Dr. Shefrin feels that the conflict among supporters of these alternatives will constitute the politics of the future.

Bruce M. Shefrin, assistant professor of political science at LeMoyne College and adjunct professor in the Civil and Public Service Program at Onondaga Community College, has also taught at Muskingum College and the University of Massachusetts.

The Future of U.S. Politics in an Age of Economic Limits

Bruce M. Shefrin

Westview Press / Boulder, Colorado

A Westview Special Study

Published in 1980 in the United States of America by
    Westview Press, Inc.
    5500 Central Avenue
    Boulder, Colorado 80301
    Frederick A. Praeger, Publisher

Library of Congress Cataloging in Publication Data
Shefrin, Bruce M.
    The future of U.S. politics in an age of economic limits.
    (A Westview special study)
    Bibliography: p.
    1. United States—Economic policy—1971- 2. United States—Politics and government—1945- I. Title.
HC106.7.S365   338.973   79-26575
ISBN-0-89158-770-5

Printed and bound in the United States of America

To Lillian and Albert Shefrin
With Pride, Gratitude, and Love

Contents

Preface

This book is in part a plea for multidisciplinary research. Scholarly inquiry has all too frequently been influenced by narrow academic loyalties and has thus served to perpetuate parochial perceptions of human experience. Compounding this bias, the economics of the publishing industry compels most authors to target their material toward the traditional course offerings found in institutions of higher education. In short, departmental demarcations and market considerations dictate research directions. Yet, it is clear to me that our energy would be best spent investigating themes that bring out the complex interaction among varied and interrelated topics. This book could not have been written in any but a cross-disciplinary manner. But what was a consequence of content for me ought to be the result of intent for others. Themes that focus on broad questions of social concern are apt to *demand* the most from us but also to *return* the most to us.

This work is also a call for a more realistic approach to futures research. Many futurists attempt to develop assumptions and methodologies they feel are appropriate to their unique subject matter. The historical debates of social science are deemed irrelevant to their discussions of the future. The uncertainties of present social analysis have no place in their study of events to come. The politics of choice, the role of self-interest, the conflict among diverse values, perspectives, and objectives—all are barely given a mention in many discussions in this field. It seems to me that the "humanness" of our future is often overshadowed by a concern with technical accuracy and a tendency to isolate the "future" from the continuous flow of human history. So, my perhaps ironic conclusion is that one must get a firm grip on the present if one wants to gain insight into the future.

Finally, this book is personal proof of the existence of limits for procrastination. My self-doubts and delaying tactics were overcome by the aid and encouragement of those who wanted this *thing* finished. Thanks are due Professor Glen Gordon, who helped me in the initial stages of the manuscript and who guided my transition from graduate student to teacher. I could not have hoped for a better role model. I acknowledge, too, the financial support of LeMoyne College for part of this project. I wish also to thank my children, Elise and Amy, who lovingly interrupted my labors and who happily ignored my protests. My brother, Arthur, was an effective (and affectionate) thorn in my side, for which I am (possibly) grateful. And to my wife, Maxine, a very special note of appreciation. She gave me motivation (in her fashion) and comfort, without which this enterprise would have quickly folded. The fact remains, however, that the writing of this book was a lonely, painful, one-person endeavor for which I accept both credit and criticism.

Bruce M. Shefrin

The Future of U.S. Politics
in an Age of Economic Limits

1
Introduction

It has been said that those who do not heed the past are condemned to repeat it. Might it not also be claimed that those who do not wonder about the future are destined to be its victims? Speculation on the future of politics in the United States is a necessary and appropriate focus of political research. Its academic legitimacy is aptly defended by Bertrand de Jouvenel:

> Forecasting would be an absurd enterprise were it not inevitable. We have to make wagers about the future; we have no choice in the matter.
> . . . The proof of improvidence lies in falling under the empire of necessity. The means of avoiding this lies in acquainting oneself with emerging situations . . . before they have become imperatively compelling.[1]

We are living in a time in which events in environmental, social, and economic systems threaten or promise to bring about vast changes in our political system. Past studies of political behavior did not often take into account such nonpolitical factors as the gradual depletion of natural resources or the psychological tensions of modern living. This omission indicates the basic security that their authors had in an immutable present. Today that security no longer can be assumed. Current patterns of political conflict are being undermined. If we are not to be overwhelmed by the changes and decisions facing us, we must discuss the future whenever we seek to describe a dynamic present. These are inextricably interrelated endeavors.

The topic of this book should be considered in light of the foregoing. One general question directs my research: What will be the effect of a severe decrease in the rate of economic growth on U.S. political attitudes and behavior? It is my contention that our ability to sustain growth at the levels and in the manner we have been used to is questionable. The factor of a high and steady rate of economic growth, which many social scientists had taken to be a fixed moderating influence on political conflict, has suddenly become a dynamic variable. This being the case, it behooves us to contemplate the shape of the political future insofar as it is a consequence of the economic future. We cannot expect current political structures to survive the coming economic upheaval.

The current political structures on which I focus are those that reduce conflict over economic inequality. The fact is that U.S. politics is uniquely nonpolarized and nonideological. Though the price of industrial development has been harsh and unevenly paid, despite a violent history of labor strife and against the present backdrop of inequality and deprivation, the issues of relative shares and the distribution of wealth have rarely arisen. Unlike other Western democracies, we have neither a strong radical tradition nor a major Socialist party. Chapter 2 explores this seemingly anomalous situation and the political-ideological processes—labeled "consensus politics"—by which it is maintained. Other writers have recognized, often with pleasure, the ability of the political system to prevent the rise of a powerful structural critique of stratification. Specific demands for economic redistribution rarely see the political light of day, being suppressed, ignored, deflected, or transformed by the procedural and conceptual biases of consensus politics. Actual conflict over economic benefits and burdens often approaches (as an ideal type) a self-perpetuating cycle of limited demands carried forward by limited strategies resulting in limited and nonredistributive concessions. That some temporary improvement in the status of disfavored groups is often gained by this process encourages its continued application, leaving the fact and the structure of inequality, which gave rise to the original demand, an unacknowledged and unchallenged part of the political culture. In two distinct areas of conflict—party politics and labor-management relations—combatants are locked into patterns of thought and action that perpetuate the structures of stratification. Chapter 2 concludes by showing that both radical and establishment explanations of these phenomena depend upon a common element—economic growth.

Chapter 3 argues that economic growth underpins the operation of consensus politics and thereby insulates the economic system from structural criticism. My initial interest centers on public awareness of this nation's material success. The perceptual context that helps to define the concept of success determines the types of demands placed on economic and political institutions, and it provides criteria by which to evaluate the ability of society to deliver. Within this context the system seems to function well. Most groups believe that some improvement in their standard of living will occur or already has occurred. And this improvement can take place without the prolonged and intense struggles that foster individual frustration, class consciousness, irreconcilable positions, and ideological criticism. This expectation of incremental and peaceful progress rests on a continuation of economic growth. In the absence of growth, one group can demand material progress for itself only at the expense of some others; more income or opportunity for disadvantaged classes necessarily involves attacks upon the possessions and privileges of the economic elite. The stratification system itself must then become the visible reason for relative deprivation and the visible obstacle to advancement. Economic growth avoids the divisive consequences of redistributive conflict by providing two system-supportive outlets for economic demands. First, growth increases rates of upward mobility by creating positions for individual advancement. Therefore, pressures for a higher standard of living are effectively channeled into demands for more opportunity. In addition, since growth appears to make upward mobility possible without a comparable amount of downward mobility, the political system is spared the resentment of those groups that otherwise would have been displaced. Second, growth allows most parties to gain from a shared prosperity, thereby deflecting attention from the issue of relative shares. As long as the future holds out the promise of mutual progress, disadvantaged groups are less inclined to challenge the inequities of the present. In both cases, economic growth promotes the types of demands and the levels of participation that are in line with consensus politics.

The major thrust of Chapters 2 and 3 is to establish what is often conceded and then as often ignored in most research and debate about the future. The forces maintaining stability, the foundations of the past, must be understood in order to anticipate the changed shape of the future. The success of consensus politics at reducing the tensions of inequality is the premise upon which stability rests. Only by appreciating the social energy now directed toward growth can we realize the strength of the tensions that may be released upon the decline of growth. It is vitally important, therefore, to recognize that the U.S. economy does indeed parcel out material resources very unequally and that such economic stratification is the major variable in the distribution of every other desirable social value. The viability of current political arrangements hinges on the ability of the economy to turn our attention away from that objective fact, to cloud that reality, by directing our strivings toward growth and its promises.

Under these circumstances, discussions about the limits to economic growth must raise serious questions for political analysts. Public policies, market mechanisms, and advanced technologies may to some extent ease the impact of economic slowdown or even prolong our belief in the permanence of national material progress. However, increasing numbers of studies are putting into doubt the capacity of the economy to expand at the rates and in the directions it traditionally has. A reckoning with limits cannot be indefinitely postponed. Chapters 4 and 5 explore debates over no-growth and slow-growth hypotheses. The major theme here is to weigh the strengths and weaknesses of the contending arguments in light of the three central variables in the debate: politics, technology, and time. While no definitive judgments on this multi-faceted question can be laid down, I do mean to show that limits-to-growth positions have a substantial basis. Thus, speculation about the future of politics under the assumption of limits becomes a vital enterprise.

Chapter 6 examines possible consequences of economic slowdown on political behavior. The future is, of course, not predetermined. Social choice in a context of political conflict must be accepted in any assessment of future possibilities. Not surprisingly, the way in which we identify these choices—that is, the types of political scenarios that we imagine and desire—is the product of our social and ideological perspectives. Liberals, emphasizing regulation and opportunity, would tend to promote policies that centralize economic planning without centralizing ownership and that open up the class system without changing its basic structure. Radicals would hope that economic slowdown might bring about the creation of a massive Socialist constituency demanding changes in the stratification system. Authoritarian forces would seek to shift power to established elites under the guise of protecting democracy from internal and external threats. Classic conservatives would preach a traditional conservative position—that lower classes lessen their economic expectations and accept their station in a more static social system. Thus, we have four sets of values, strategies, and policies, each designed to deal with future economic realities. Whether a strategy will be effective in garnering support, whether a scenario will be believable, depends on a host of interrelated conditions: the actual extent of decreased growth and how different groups are affected by the decline; the presence of crosscutting or status-reinforcing foreign and domestic issues; the capability and inclinations of leadership; the role of the media; the extent of coercion employed in the face of dissent; the evolution of values; and so on. Thus, the politics of the future will remain political; choices will still have to be made between competing alternative images of the future. A futurology that stresses imperatives rather than options has ignored the political nature of social history.

We determine the shape of tomorrow by what we do today. "The future is not an overarching leap into the distance; it begins in the present."[2] Recent headlines concerning natural resources, pollution, international economic competition, social breakdown, and the like reflect and justify past work that has been done on these topics. Present research has the object of anticipating the implications of these headlines for the U.S. economy. Political science must take notice of the train of events that moves from one subsystem of society to another. Change will not stop at the door of a discipline that chooses to ignore its own future—or its own past. Knowing what to expect is not essentially or even primarily an exercise in soothsaying. The crystal ball looks backward as well as forward. As I have already implied, past and future, history and forecasts, ought to be employed in any account of present political trends. It is to this objective that this book is directed.

2
Consensus Politics

A Taxonomy of Conflict Management

The U.S. economy provides a vast diversity of goods and services to the consumer-citizen. Some of these have had an enormous influence on social attitudes and behavior, especially in the communications and transportation fields. But of all the outputs (products and by-products) of the economy, economic stratification has had the most long-term impact on our lives. The fears and wants of the majority of citizens are in large measure shaped by their place in the stratification system. Income and wealth are primary determinants in the distribution of almost every other valued personal attribute, from mental health and job satisfaction to educational attainment and leisure time. Given this situation, we might anticipate political battles over redistributive policies, tense struggles of self-interest between mobilized economic groupings, or theoretical critiques of and justifications for the economic status quo. But the issues of relative shares, generalized deprivation, and the rules of the stratification system rarely, if ever, animate our political processes. The institutions of government seem isolated from those pressures and inequities that debilitate our personal relationships and weaken our social fabric. On the contrary, these issues get transformed as they enter the political arena into demands of a nonideological and nonstructural character. The policies that they call forth often satisfy immediate demands without meeting the underlying need that the expressed demands should reflect. The pattern of conflict that has evolved in this country to deal with the contradictions of economic inequality is not uniquely American, but it is sharply distinguishable from other types of political confrontation and other models of democratic industrialized polities.

This chapter examines those elements of the political system that cause the submergence of redistributive issues. Initial reference is made to a four-cell taxonomy that frames a comparison among different modes of dealing with such issues. Our approach, termed "consensus politics," is then analyzed as to the nature of the economic demands that are advanced and the political constraints confronting those economic demands. The structural mechanisms described are further illuminated by investigating two arenas where conflict over economic inequality conceivably might arise but in fact rarely does—party politics and labor relations. As a style of conflict-management, consensus politics is the starting point in this study's exploration of the direction of future economic and political change.

Table 1 classifies divergent ways in which conflict over inequality is expressed in the political system. Numerous variables could have been used for this purpose. I have chosen to stress two characteristics that seem most central for delineating differences in styles of political conflict in the United States and in similarly developed countries. The first factor is the intended consequences of the economic policy demands that are brought up for political debate. The dichotomy offered is between structural and reformist demands. The second factor highlights the level of intensity with which these demands are sought—high versus low intensity. Each of the resulting cells refers to a pattern of political conflict that is more or less divisive and to a set of political strategies that is more or less threatening to the stability and continuity of the system.[1]

The four models thus presented are not necessarily permanent or stable approaches—movement from one to another cell is possible and perhaps likely within a given set of circumstances; nor is

Table 1
Models of Political Conflict Over Redistributive Issues

Level of Intensity	Intended Consequences	
	Structural	Reformist
High	1	2
Low	3	4

it assumed that a society exemplifies the same ideal type on all issues—some areas of conflict are bound to be more intense and the positions taken more destabilizing than would be true for other matters of policy. The hope is that, in contrasting consensus politics with other models of conflict, the distinctive nature of our system will be emphasized.

Cell 1, the politics of polarization, represents those societies in which conflict rages over basic values. The actual rules of the distribution system are directly challenged at either or both of the following points: an alternative set of rules on the distribution of economic shares may be presented against which the system of inequality is compared and in light of which it will be modified; and/or policies for the alleviation of generalized deprivation are demanded that consciously and necessarily involve basic attacks on the structure of stratification itself. A high level of emotional involvement plus a narrowed time frame impart to these demands an immediacy with which most governmental processes cannot cope. Thus, confrontations of this type often involve strategies of mass mobilization and countermobilization with both sides holding positions that require basic concessions from the other. The stability of such a system is usually dependent upon the sometimes tenuous ability of status quo forces to check the power and popularity of the party seeking change.

This pattern of political conflict, so alien to our own experience, is not irrelevant to the histories of other industrialized democratic states. The series of confrontations between Communist and National Socialist forces in Weimar Germany is in some respects an example of this style of politics. Modern-day Japan exhibits many of the qualities of political polarization, especially during those times when crucial issues come to the fore and allow various radical groups to mobilize opinion against the established business ideology. All situations in which there is potential for revolutionary change through electoral means can be placed with some validity into this category.

The politics of politicization (2) involves the highly intense pursuit of minor changes. Though general support for or acquiescence in the justifications and values of the stratification system exists, specific improvements relating to one's particular economic situation are demanded. Often, these proposed adjustments are incremental in scope and reformist in character and can easily be

accommodated within the present structure of benefits and burdens. However, demands of this type (more jobs, higher wages,
better social services) are made with such an uncompromising
intensity that immediate political fulfillment is difficult, often due
to the resistance of other groups in society. The strategies discussed
with respect to the preceding ideal type are somewhat relevant
here, but the focus of mobilization is on specific, structurally
isolated issues that subside once resolution is achieved. The possibility exists that continual frustration will lead to permanent
lines of combat with the need for ideological supports that go beyond the original narrow issue. More likely, this pattern of political
conflict is the product of manipulation by group elites who sense
the usefulness of *controlled intensity.* An escalation of the level of
debate may have a number of strategic advantages over subtler
and more easily ignored forms of confrontation. For instance,
groups gradually gaining power and importance will seek to transform their new status into economic improvements. But first they
must prove themselves, as it were, by demonstrating their own
increased determination, unity, and strength or by revealing the
weakness of countervailing interests. A show of force (sit-ins,
marches) would not be lost on political and economic leaders. The
development of industrial unionism, reflected in a bitterly fought
battle over relatively reformist objectives, represents an excellent
example from U.S. history of such a modus operandi (although
the inference should not be drawn that this conflict was purely a
fabrication of union organizers).

Cell 3 symbolizes the most common pattern of confrontation in
industrial democratic society: the politics of evolutionism. Mass-
based organizations representing disadvantaged economic (or regional or cultural) groups band together, more or less united in
their support of a party or movement whose expressed aims involve
a basic reshaping of the distributive system. Antireformist in its
ultimate intent, this party or movement may propose policies that
appear incremental and system supportive but that, taken in total,
are consciously designed to change rather than make more bearable the rules of stratification as they currently operate. The critique of inequality put forth interrelates the economic injustices
of the various nonelites in the society. Thus, solutions are generalized and structural (e.g., nationalize heavy industry, control
investment capital, redistribute wealth) rather than isolated and

reformist. But these demands are not made with the same intensity and immediacy, nor do they lead to the same level of mass involvement as is the case in the first two ideal types. Instead, the leadership tries to work within the boundaries of traditional political processes in order to gradually and peacefully promote a more egalitarian society. A long time-frame allows supporters of this position to deal with temporary electoral setbacks without the divisive and unbending attitudes characteristic of the politics of polarization or politicization.

Countries with a strong democratic Socialist party seem to typify this pattern of political conflict. But the resemblance could be rather superficial, for the politics of evolutionism are difficult to sustain. This is so, first, because the party's leaders, unpressured and isolated from a nonmobilized membership, may gain more from preserving the present structure than from working toward an egalitarian alternative. As Robert Michels demonstrates, elites who head supposedly conflicting groups have a closer proximity of interests than do those whom they represent.[2] The piecemeal and reformist nature of the policies that comes out of elite accommodation is often masked behind ideological rhetoric and public relations flourishes. Secondly, evolutionism is a precarious political stance because the essence of the egalitarian alternative requires a redistribution of power as well as wealth and an increase in personal choice as well as in popular control. A worker who sits on the political sidelines until told to march (or strike or vote) by his union's leaders is not being allowed to participate in his own restructuring and growth. If inequality is such a critical feature of U.S. society and life, then it is only logical that an individual's political involvement on economic issues should reflect that degree of importance. This is not to say that evolutionism is not viable, but it is vulnerable to pressures that push the movement into a reformist mold. The partial Americanization of party conflict in England and West Germany (to mention two nations with democratic Socialist parties) is indicative of this shift.

As for examples closer to home, it may be argued that Martin Luther King tried to establish a civil rights movement that would press for basic changes in race relations with a calm, single-minded determination. It should be obvious from the last example that conflict of this type can intensify (Model 1) if people get frustrated with the slow pace or absence of basic change. Thus, pressures of a reformist and polarizing nature combine to make the stability of evolutionism suspect.

An analysis of the final ideal type—the politics of consensus—follows, but some prior remarks are in order. First, there is a distinction that must be made between consensus politics and consensual societies. Our reference here is to a political system that structures out issues, demands, and policies of an ideologically divisive nature. This situation in some cases may be the result of a basic value agreement with respect to distributive issues, but this is not necessarily true. Indeed, all systems exhibit some of the manifestations of consensus politics on most issues. However, it is rare to find an industrialized society that reflects its basic features as accurately as does our own. It is a major achievement to have a political system in which economic demands are presented in a form that allows them to be so easily accommodated within the ongoing pattern of stratification.

But we should be clear as to the nature of the relative political peace accompanying consensus politics. The peace does not imply that a deep unanimity of opinion supporting the value and legitimacy of the stratification system exists; neither is it the outwardly calm sign of a repressive state. The political peace of consensus politics is real in that it stems from *self-imposed* restraints on a citizen's thoughts and behavior at every point in the political process. The structure protects patterns of inequality by circumscribing how individuals define their political interests and how they participate (or do not participate) in politics. Internalized ideological prohibitions discouraging the formation of redistributive demands, coupled with a policymaking process designed to thwart those redistributive demands that do surface, explain the safety and stability of inequality.

The most striking characteristic of consensus politics as it operates in the United States is that social pressures originally stemming from redistributive needs and desires are somehow modified and transformed before entering the political arena. The resulting political demands, without ideological or structural import, reflect a narrow and easily accommodated range of choices. Indeed, to label these inputs as "demands" is a misnomer, since the strategies associated with political conflict in the United States do not involve the degree of intensity or depth of commitment that is implied by the term "demand." The extent of political mobilization and consciousness raising entailed by these strategies is often minimal. Thus, there is not even an organizational or attitudinal potential for threatening or seriously disruptive political behavior on behalf of economic objectives. On the contrary, limited aims pursued through limiting procedural channels result in the limited conflict typical of consensus politics: the nature of economic demands and the means by which they are promoted reinforce rather than undermine the biases of the political system. Past power relationships among elites and between elites and publics are maintained by this pattern of conflict. More importantly, the resulting public policies often strengthen these relationships despite the rhetoric of the political battles that might suggest otherwise. The economic concerns of lower-income groups are perceived as and transmitted to the political process in the form of symptomatic wants; that is, they are transformed into policy requests that skirt the structural roots of problems and instead focus on their superficial manifestations. The system, if it responds at all, will not incur more conflict than is necessary to ameliorate the situation. Thus, somewhat superficial programs will be offered. But precisely because of the nature of the political demands and political strategies, these symptom-related programs have been acceptable. Whether one believes that this acceptance is akin to appeasement or to satisfaction, the political peace that is its consequence is the central feature of consensus politics.

Demand Formation

It is generally agreed that the pattern of economic demands, political strategies, and institutional responses encompassed by consensus politics in the United States has effectively defused inequality as a divisive issue. Louis Hartz in his study, *The Liberal Tradition in America,* claims that the lack of class conflict or redistributive political pressures has been a major distinguishing feature of the U.S. social system.[3] Christopher Jencks supports the contention with this account of political inactivity:

> Almost none of the legislation passed during the 1960s tried to reduce disparities in adult status, power, or income in any direct way. There was no significant effort, for example, to make taxation more progressive, and very little effort to reduce wage disparities between highly

paid and poorly paid workers. . . . Nor was there much effort to reduce
the social or psychological distance between high- and low-status
occupations.[4]

Jencks's statement, essentially an updated corroboration of Hartz's
observation on the U.S. historic nature, has not since been refuted
by any massive shifts in public consciousness or legislative action.
But if existing economic relationships and institutions are beyond
the pale of popular political challenge, what then is the sum and
substance of the economic demands currently being made by disadvantaged groups? What is the context of their desires for a materially better life that explains why these desires are compatible
with the economic status quo?

Primary in that context is a bipartisan anticommunist perspective that "has had dramatic and for the most part conservative
effects upon liberal politics. . . . More than any other single factor
perhaps, it accounts for the demise of political radicalism in the
United States following World War II."[5] The open and cultivated
identification of egalitarian demands with socialism and of socialism
with un-Americanism and communism removed many potential
redistributive desires, programs, and arguments from the political
arena. Without any pressure from the ideological Left, present-day
reformism became even less distinguished from a conservative, probusiness stance than was progressivism.

Another factor affecting the political thrust of economic demands is in large measure a consequence of an individualistic
and anticollectivist ethos, of which bipartisan anticommunism is a
present-day outgrowth. We have made sharp distinctions between
public and private, between what is a legitimate issue for governmental action and what is an unjustified intrusion on personal
freedom. This ideological bias results in an inhibition against
looking toward politics for redress of many social grievances. It
is difficult to politicize conflicts that have been defined by society
as private, requiring private resolutions. This attenuation of the
political sphere combines with the cold war animosities previously
mentioned to moderate redistributive impulses at the start. They
are part of the formative ideological environment, and, as such,
they affect the way in which citizens view the legitimacy and
efficacy of public solutions to problems of inequality and want.
But these conceptual obstacles to politically instigated income

redistribution are reinforced by other factors that flow from the social structure itself.

It is easily demonstrated that supposedly nonclass divisions (regional, religious) and nonclass issues (crime, pollution) are either minor in comparison to or encompassed within class distinctions. Nevertheless, the Madisonian notion persists that our role as a member of an economic class is only one of numerous group commitments that we must respect. Regional, religious, commercial, and racial divisions create their own loyalties and antagonisms. A society so fragmented into diverse, overlapping, and crosscutting groups has as its counterpart an individual whose political interests and passions must also be spread rather thin. James Madison, fearing a majority faction of debtors and propertyless organizing to redistribute wealth, supported the prophylactic nature of this social and political arrangement.

> Either the existence of the same passion or interest in a majority at the same time must be prevented, or the majority, having such coexistent passion, or interest, must be rendered, by their numbers and local situation, unable to concert and carry into effect schemes of oppression [i.e., redistribution].[6]

The practical political consequence of a fragmented society is that problems of a structural nature are camouflaged behind divisions and conflicts that appear more immediate and important. As we perceive our general problems more narrowly, we unconsciously change the focus and target of our economic demands. Hartz states: "What [conservative strategy] did was to smash the 'mob' into a million bits, so that its fierce acquisitive passion, instead of being expended against property, would be expended against itself in the quest for property."[7] Redistributive policies, when consciously pursued as such, necessitate a broad perspective. As our perspective shortens, we look for closer causes of our personal problems; structural criticism and class consciousness thereby give way to intraclass friction and parochial animosities.

The persistence of issues and divisions that blur and even break down class ties has additional consequences with respect to the degree of political conflict engendered by economic demands. If redistributive desires have to compete in the public's consciousness with other problems and concerns, then egalitarian policies must become as palatable as possible in order to gain majority support from an increasingly disinterested public. In addition, since issues as they are presently defined cut across group lines, antagonists in one battle may be allies in the next. Thus, if one seeks more economic advantage than an opponent would maximally want to give away, one threatens one's position and strength on other non-economic conflicts that one hopes to wage in the future. All this is by way of saying that we formulate economic demands within a web of conceptual and strategic constraints that impel deference, caution, and moderation, even to the point of political impotence.

Given these constraints, most economic demands on the part of lower- and middle-income groups conform to the pluralist model. Issues must be framed in terms that allow for give and take, for compromise. This seemingly innocuous condition, central to plural-ist democracy, eliminates from consideration redistributive policies whose primary justification rests on a moral rejection of inequality and its consequences. As Theodore Lowi states, "there is some-thing about [our political system] that prevents us from raising the question of justice at all, no matter what definition of justice is used."[8] Moral concepts and arguments become instrumental rather than basic to our policy debates in government. Notions of freedom, equality, and justice, when they do arise, are used as weapons with which to buttress one's bargaining position, not as a substantive comment on the righteousness of the stratification system. Indeed, amoral politics provides no means by which to challenge inequality as such save in the personal desire to better one's economic situation relative to that of one's neighbor.

Given the fragmented, fratricidal nature of U.S. society, this is precisely the thrust of economic demands. Groups suffering under or threatened with economic hardship seek to bolster their market position vis-à-vis competitors rather than to align themselves with these equally victimized groups for the purpose of attacking the structural causes of their common plight. They are unmindful of or unconcerned with the coalition that could arise because they conceive of these potential allies, if they directly consider them at all, in terms of an adversary relationship. Out of this situation come demands of limited impact on the extent of inequality but of great strategic importance on its future strength.

Some proposals for the alleviation of the sting of inequality center on the creation of a governmental agency responsive to a narrow pressure group, an enclave of public authority promoting and protecting the interests of its client. Groups thereby hope to go beyond direct legislative pressures with its continual battles and insecurity. However, the attempt to set up governmental privies of private power, opportunity, and material gain ignores the generalized causes of hardship and, in fact, creates obstacles to conceiving demands in such terms. In this way, a fragmented demand structure complements a fragmented social structure. Though writers like Grant McConnell and Lowi have called into question the political wisdom and democratic virtues of such techniques, others like Charles Lindblom commend them as an appropriate and beneficial outgrowth of pluralist democracy: "Even partisanship and narrowness . . . will sometimes be assets to rational decision-making."[9] For Lindblom, as for James Madison, "rational decision-making" means consensual, nonstructural, nonredistributive political processes. In terms of long-range strategic considerations, interest-group/bureaucratic-agency ties inhibit class consciousness by reinforcing narrow perspectives. In addition, these ties are system supportive as a form of co-optation and social control. The institutionalization of a group's political power is mistaken for the reality of economic improvement—repressive tolerance, bureaucratic style. This type of demand is quite common not only with respect to the promoting of bureaucratic footholds but, in a more general way, with improving the bargaining position of groups, narrowly defined, versus other groups, also narrowly defined; "the creation of countervailing-power situations has become a major—perhaps the major—domestic function of the state. Much of the legislation passed by Congress in the years since 1933 may be fully understood only from this point of view."[10]

Economic demands that reach the political arena are not solely or even primarily concerned with establishing bureaucratic agencies to act as spokesmen for private interests. The political system must respond to an array of requests from economic groups seeking various types of special treatment. Given the factors controlling the demand-formation process, it is not surprising, then, that the policy requests coming from disadvantaged groups are totally devoid of redistributive content and structural implications. The political consequences of economic want are demands for incremental reform.

Incrementalism in the United States reflects a pattern of demands and decisions without conscious structural and theoretical intent. Political proposals having economic impacts depend upon limited comparisons between current policies and marginally different alternatives. Rarely are issues raised that bring into question the whole range of values (benefits and burdens) and alternatives. Policy choices are built upon a basic and unstated accord with previous arrangements. This accord stems from a fragmented demand structure that seeks to maximize certain values without reference to other values adversely affected by policy proposals. For example, higher minimum wages may result in more unemployment; or investment credits leading to more jobs lead, in turn, to an increasingly inequitable tax structure. Demands are never coordinated in order to challenge the decision-making process of value balancing. Rather, the individual, taking his cue from what he perceives to be the accepted model of political action, formulates his demands to conform to this proven pattern. Thus, incrementalism as practiced in our political system is not merely a reflection of the type of economic demands with which political institutions must cope; given the probability that values percolate down the social system much more effectively than they drift upward, it is more likely that the incrementalism of the decision-making process molds the political desires of the citizen. This relationship cannot help but be system supportive.

An incrementalist policymaking pattern, a fragmented social context, and a very narrowly defined political sphere combine to foster and reinforce consensus politics. For the most part, class conflict over redistributive political demands are deflected at the initial point of entry—the citizen's political awareness. Without a perspective that would give structural and critical dimensions to personal needs and problems, an individual can either adhere to the dominant ideological explanation of inequality and resign himself to a lowly and deprived state, or he can modify this perspective along very calculative, short-range, and limited paths. The economic claims that would consequently be offered pose no threat to the existence of inequality because the attitudinal, psychological, and tactical context underlying these demands does not constitute a challenge to the legitimacy of stratification as such. In fact, they reveal an acceptance of the basic outlines of stratification and a willingness to work within the political system for personal rather than structural amelioration. Thus, it has been argued that "the subordinate value system represents something of a bulwark to political class consciousness, insofar as it entails adaptive rather than oppositional responses to the status quo."[11]

If the forms that economic demands take do not put into jeopardy the reality of inequality, they may affect the extent of inequality. This outcome would not be improbable, especially if demands as initially construed and offered were supported with the passion and pressure needed to insure their final passage. The impact of many separate expressions of disadvantage, however fragmented and limited, may result in a net lessening of the range of stratification in the United States; marginal shifts in the rules of stratification, consciously pursued over time, can result in substantial change in distributive arrangements. At the very least, these demands can be the catalyst for an escalating political battle between defenders and opponents of economic privilege. However, this scenario presupposes a strategic single-mindedness of purpose that proponents of redistribution have rarely displayed. The important point here, to be examined in more depth in the next section, is that political strategies are as accommodative to the stratification system as are the economic demands that they are designed to promote.

Those egalitarian tendencies that manage to sift through the constraints of the demand formation process are confronted with an equally restrictive set of ideological and institutional factors that limit the public appeals and political strategies employed by deprived and underprivileged groups. A type of cumulative biasing process is at work. Inhibitions against the proposing of redistributive demands are supplemented by psychological and political conditions insuring their eventual revision or withdrawal. Why some economic claims, once made, appear untenable in the context of give-and-take politics is a result of this biasing process as it relates to the realm of effective and allowable political strategies.

Policy Formation

Americans, both leaders and the electorate, have been loath to acquire political support based on outright class appeals. While the liberal rhetoric of defending "the little man" is pervasive, the radical tactic of organizing the working man on a class basis has always seemed un-American. Part of this reaction is due to the belief that there is a consensus of interests out of which will evolve a solution beneficial to all groups in society. Perhaps more importantly, a long-range appeal to class self-interest is a corollary to proposals for outright economic redistribution. A fierce anticommunism moderates both the choice of strategies and the content of demands and does not give to either the force needed to truly threaten the stratification system. This historical adversion to class appeals has been augmented by relatively recent changes in the nature of liberalism and the preferences of its spokesmen. The Democratic party, the champion of the underclasses (but only relative to the Republican party), has shifted its base to become more suburban and elitist. Jack Newfield has noted that, "beginning with Stevenson's two presidential campaigns, the Democrats began the slow process of disengaging from the needs and hopes of the white lower middle class."[12] They ignored the economic problems and class conditions that were still important to many people. This trend has continued to the point at which George McGovern's 1972 campaign, while appearing radical to conservative and upper middle class voters, seemed almost irrelevant to the lower middle class.

Associated with this bias against class-based political strategies is a decline in the prevalence of moral discourse and appeals to justice. The rejection of an ethical stance that is an end in itself stems from a fear that the strategic commitment that this stance may entail will turn politics into an all-or-nothing battle. But conflict between competing definitions of economic justice (or stratification's justifiability) is an integral part of ideological diversity and structural criticism. When we amoralize political debate, we remove the raison d'être of a critical perspective—the contrasting of present conditions with an idealistic and ethically desirable alternative. Politics stripped of moral appeals leads to strategies grounded in a narrow self-interest. David Reisman's account of changes in popular attitudes toward politics recognizes this point. While the inner-directed man of the past tended to be a "moralizer," the other-directed man of today is an "inside-dopester," viewing politics cynically and from a distance.[13] Consensus politics can easily accommodate itself to such an outlook; structural criticism cannot.

This amoral objectivity moderating political conflict conforms quite well with other ideological biases. It is not accidental that pragmatism found a very receptive audience in our society and political system. The problem-solving approach isolates rather than interrelates social analysis. Strategic appeals are directed at narrowly defined interests rather than structurally situated classes. If redistributive policies are proposed, they are defended by reference to the immediate problem, not by reference to broader questions of justice. Norman Thomas's criticism of the New Deal's pragmatic experimentation states the case clearly; Roosevelt was exhibiting "a kind of American progressivism which calls itself practical because it has no general principles."[14] Our emphasis on pragmatic, nonideological responses to concrete individual problems stems from an optimism that the whole will take care of itself. In truth, the system is protected as a result of the ideological context within which piecemeal, pragmatic solutions are sought. Political pragmatism mirrors an unconscious ideology: the general principles of consensus politics. But the ideology goes unchallenged because, given the strong emphasis placed on pragmatic approaches, its impact on policy formation is often unacknowledged. This constitutes another bias against strategies in support of structural change.

An additional consequence of this pragmatic emphasis is the depoliticizing of certain social issues. The reliance on technical expertise in garnering political support is necessitated by the problem-solving perspective. The claim is that "the problems which are pressing for the society are of a high complexity, do not have clear solutions, and political methods do not appear the most fruitful means of treatment."[15] Thus, if citizens are ever called upon to judge on a certain controversy, they are forced to decide on the basis of conflicting technical information, not on the basis of subjective self-interest or ethical principles. Strategies that have drifted from these personal moorings are unable to gain a firm footing in appeals to scientific accuracy. The growing emphasis on management and administration depoliticizes the citizen's role by conceptually divorcing his personal situation from his political problem. The black-and-white distinctions underlying most redistributive demands cannot be easily seen through the gray glasses of technical deliberation.

The institutional context of consensus politics also exhibits a firm bias against strategies associated with structural pressures and redistributive demands. Edward Shils states what are the established institutional expectations regarding political strategies:

> Pluralist politics is marked also by the moderation of political involve-
> ment. A lukewarm "politicization" is a feature of pluralist politics.
> . . . Pluralist politics . . . also prohibits emotional intensity, especially
> emotional excitement continuing over long stretches of time or running
> on without intermission.[16]

Anticipation of the growth of a mobilized, politicized mob under-pins fears of mass participation. However, in the process of prevent-ing imagined revolutionary threats, the United States has tolerated, condoned, and even fostered an incredibly high level of political apathy. A style of politics that locks the average citizen out of the decision-making process stems from "an ideology which is grounded upon a profound distrust of the majority of ordinary men and women."[17] The elitism implicit in consensus politics is justified as the primary means of inhibiting the formation of redistributive demands, moderating those that do get presented, and insuring the maintenance of accommodative processes, all toward reducing threats to the political and economic systems. This fits in rather well with the redefinition of political issues; "what once were ideological disputes have now become mere technical administra-tive difficulties suited to the problem-solving skills of managerial elites."[18] Given the fact that redistributive demands are by their very nature threats to the status quo, the existence of massive non-participation and elite decision making protects current structural arrangements. Strategies aimed at mobilizing underclasses to bring about basic change are successful within an atmosphere of angry resentment, not one of disillusioned apathy.

Even for those who do participate—in elections, for instance—the passive role of the voter and the lack of accountability of the elected combine to minimize the utility of that arena of politics. The fragmented nature of the demand structure mitigates against relying on party victory as the means of achieving one's goals. In-stead, between election periods the operating mechanism to pro-mote policy objectives is conflict among organized interest groups within governmental institutions. The reliance upon the pressure-group system rather than the party system has three consequences detrimental to redistributive demands. First, the former forum is highly oligarchical; in E. E. Schattschneider's words, "The flaw in the pluralist heaven is that the heavenly chorus sings with a strong upper-class accent. Probably about 90 percent of the people cannot get into the pressure system."[19] Based upon class bias alone, there seems to be little chance of redistributive policies emanating from pressure-group politics. Second, the leader of an interest group often grows so distant from his disadvantaged followers that he consciously or unconsciously ignores their interests. In an effort to protect his own quasi-elite position, or perhaps out of a well-intended desire to maintain his influence with the powers that be, the leader is unable or unwilling to act upon the economic discontent of the membership. The interest group's hierarchical structure mutes rather than amplifies criticisms of the system and demands for basic change. Finally, the pressure-group process of decision making lessens publicity, thereby further reducing mass awareness and involvement. Questions of a political character that can lead to periodic battles and uneasy truces are kept out of the public's eye, relegated to regulatory agencies or congressional subcommittees. As conflict is made private, the range of values (the viable alternatives) inherent in a specific problem is narrowed. For the most part, the decision makers have made their peace with the dominant groups operating in a policy area and have come to a conclusion from among various policy approaches and objectives. The public is kept out of this process, often to the point of being left ignorant of the decisions that are finally reached. Without popular input, public policies will reflect both the ongoing biases in the policymaking process and the established balance of power among contending interest groups. Public policy, therefore, will merely perpetuate the distributive status quo.

Within committees and agencies, the decision-making procedures follow a well-recognized pattern of bargaining and compromise. This give-and-take has been labeled the very definition of democracy: "democracy is not only or even primarily a means through which different groups can attain their ends or seek the good; it is the good society itself in operation."[20] Viewing the system as a specific mechanism of conflict resolution ignores the biased ideological and institutional context within which demands are formulated, strategies are selected, and potential conflicts either gain attention or remain latent. Only by overlooking these aspects of the political process can we assume the democratic fairness of group negotiation. But even with respect to the use of bargaining and compromise, objections can be raised. Here, too, bias against structural criticism and redistributive demands are found.

If, as has been argued, *veto groups* populate and police the policymaking process, then powerful interests can easily defend their positions of privilege in the face of challenges from disadvantaged groups. Compromise with these privileged interests can only occur at the expense of reaffirming their entrenched position and the benefits that accrue. Once the threatening aspects of a demand are eliminated (i.e., its redistributive intent is deflected), agreement becomes possible—but the resulting policy is structurally conservative (that is, system supportive). The commitment of the government to compromise as an end in itself strengthens the conservative implications of the group negotiation process. The political system finds it very difficult to make coercive decisions even if agreed to by a majority of citizens (or representatives). We confuse majority rule with majority tyranny. The use of legitimate (democratic) authority is rejected in favor of nonconflictual bargaining relationships between potential combatants. However, the nature of redistributive policy involves the requirement that government give special treatment for the benefit of a group or groups against the resistance of those interests that stand to lose. Consequently, the bias against political procedures allowing for winners and losers, majority and minority, results in the freezing of allocative arrangements and the preservation of structural continuity.

The political process has been construed so as to guarantee the inadmissibility of redistributive demands; elites and nonelites have joined, intentionally and unconsciously, to make inequality a nonissue. This comment recapitulates the analysis of the factors that enable the system to avoid considering the topic of relative shares. Consensus politics is supported by the strength and viability of this invisible counterpart to the decision-making process:

> nondecision-making is a means by which demands for change in the existing allocation of benefits and privileges in the community can be suffocated before they are even voiced; or kept covert; or killed before they gain access to the relevant decision-making arena; or, failing all

these things, maimed or destroyed in the decision-implementing stage of the policy process.[21]

The effectiveness of nondecision making does not depend upon the presence of overt elite manipulation or a devil theory of history. Consensus politics is maintained through the specific behavioral patterns, political norms, and power relationships of our society, often in the face of well-intentioned but politically naive challenges. Admittedly, this political structure is not free from pointed and well-planned attacks. However, the presence of such a successful attack is itself dependent upon, and thus is an unlikely product of, the ideological context and institutional arrangements. The structure nurtures itself, as demands and strategies lead to programs that reinforce inequality while, ironically, responding to the initial desire for change.

The type of conflict resolution that our political system permits can be expected to go no further than the demands and strategies that it allows. The structural bias against economic redistribution and political mobilization succeeds in restricting the range of feasible policy choices. Few of these choices can alleviate actual social ills, though each is a response to a political want. Policies respond to wants by "satisficing"[22]—satisfying only partially and sufficing only temporarily—and since this is usually enough to minimize conflict and maintain the appearance of progress, our political process need do no more. Even radicals are aware of the ability of pluralist democracy to avoid structural change while meeting specific economic desires. Note this comment by Andre Gorz:

> Certainly, capitalism is incapable of fundamentally resolving the essential problems which its development has brought about. But capitalism can resolve these in its own way, by means of concessions and superficial repairs aimed at making the system socially tolerable.[23]

And these concessions also result in a low level of intensity with respect to political strategies. If demands are met to some extent, the political frustration that breeds redistributive conflict cannot fester.

This is not to say that personal needs are being fulfilled simply because policies respond to political demands. Indeed, the linchpin in the demands-strategies-policies cycle is the system's ability to isolate actual need from expressed political want. Unable to connect their specific plight to the issue of inequality in general and unable to imagine how egalitarian arrangements would benefit them, disadvantaged groups are forced to rely on system-supportive formulae for relieving economic need: narrow and nonclass perspectives, privatized governmental power, increased expenditures for superficial programs, and security against "threats from below." The desires and attitudes reflected in these political prescriptions do not speak to the issue of inequality. The rhetoric of political action advises us only that demands are satisficed, conflicts are resolved, wants are responded to, and change is held to a minimum. Regarding the real needs and interests of those near the bottom of the stratification ladder, no promises are made, and none are kept. Consensus politics may eliminate the system-destabilizing impact of political frustration, but feelings of hopelessness and powerlessness indicate that frustration has now turned inward. The resulting attitudes of apathy, resignation, submission, and acceptance strengthen consensus politics still further.

Specific political demands may be met in a number of ways. Some of the alternatives that are eventually considered by policy-makers may even have redistributive ramifications. Among these are transfer payment programs involving cash allotments given directly to the beneficiary. Such programs go against the ideological grain of most middle-class Americans; the values of individualism, ambition, and competition emphasized in the culture of capitalist society are undermined by governmental support programs of this type. In a more general way, policies that allow for direct transfer payments result in a pattern of benefits and burdens quite unlike the pattern of power within society. And if this dissimilarity is recognized, then power holders will push for alternate policies allocating benefits more in line with the prevalent structures of power. As long as the stratification system itself is not open to challenge, nonstructural and nonredistributive alternatives will reflect and therefore perpetuate economic and political stratification. Howard P. Tuckman has termed this relationship between public policy and economic gain "the internalization of wealth." As Tuckman puts it, no sooner is a new program proposed than a new method is found by which the wealthy may benefit. Provide a medicare program and watch doctors' profits grow; build new schools and observe the increasing prosperity of large contractors; create a federal housing program and develop a new class of wealthy property owners.[24]

Policies of this sort can satisfice only because economic demands do not stem from or are not likely hitched to a thoroughgoing critique of inequality. Instead, they are usually couched in terms that allow for various means of and degrees of fulfillment. The lack of any structural awareness results in policies conforming to structural requirements.

Cases in Consensus Politics

Ideological context, institutional biases, and power relationships combine to form the general political/economic/social structure. As might be anticipated, when we focus on specific areas of conflict, the structures that are revealed conform to the precepts and processes of the overarching framework of consensus politics. Its perpetuation depends upon its maintenance and stability within arenas of stress, not only during situations of calm and cooperation. The strength of this style of politics is indicated by its ability to keep the political peace under conditions that would otherwise have led to divisive and perhaps ideological clashes. The following comments on party conflict and labor-management relations demonstrate the practical application of consensus politics in areas most vulnerable to the redistributive impulses that economic stratification foments.

Party Politics

The party arena has always been a focus of social and political conflict in the industrialized West. It is often during election campaigns that the tensions of a society come to a head: privatized issues become politicized by parties seeking to profit electorally from social conflict; since party conflict is the largest political game around, elections encourage parties to mobilize and involve the masses, thus threatening the elitist tendencies of entrenched power; the organizing efforts of parties depend upon and help to encourage high levels of emotional involvement that make the citizen open to appeals and arguments that he would dismiss under calmer circumstances. Often, analogy is made to the struggles of war, and this is not an absurd comparison. The potential for overwhelming victory, crushing defeat, and basic changes in power relationships is present here more than in the accommodative styles of congressional, bureaucratic, and interest group politics. In a nation of great economic disparities, the party system seems a likely avenue for promoting redistributive policies. But the operation of consensus politics maintains stability and protects the structural status quo by blunting the ideological potential of party conflict.

In other capitalist democracies, especially those with strong Labor, Socialist, or Communist parties, political campaigns often air egalitarian views and discuss redistributive policies. This involves a challenge—though sometimes perhaps only implicit, partial, and symbolic—to the current patterns of economic stratification. There is consequently a parallel need on the part of status quo forces to defend and justify inequitable allocative arrangements. Whatever the actual electoral outcome, the fact is that ideological diversity, structural alternatives, and even moral debate enter the political arena. Issues and perspectives are brought up in these countries that, if raised during our party contests, would be tantamount to political suicide. And workable policy positions are supported by reference to general and diverse theoretical frameworks. Pragmatic problem solving does not become a cover approach for unconscious ideological unity.

Our parties and electoral processes are a far cry from the style of conflict just described. In most elections we have little choice regarding the range of viable alternatives offered. The "Tweedledum and Tweedle-dee" syndrome cannot be fully recognized for what it is if the electorate has been trained to accept slight variations in political outlook as major differences in basic philosophies. To a citizenry working within a Lockean paradigm, Edward Kennedy and Barry Goldwater appear on opposite poles of the political spectrum. What is readily apparent to an observer with a comparative perspective is that the Democratic and Republican parties operate under similar ideological assumptions, in response to similar power holders, utilizing similar organizational arrangements. Their actions—the appeals that they make, the candidates that they offer, and the policies that they promote—help to mold the public's opinions and behavior with the ultimate result of insulating the party system from redistributive pressures and protecting the political system from structural attacks.

The Democrats and Republicans are examples of electoral as opposed to programmatic parties. Their efforts are directed toward the short-run goal of gaining power, not necessarily toward the more elusive aim of changing society. Single-member districts and a two-party system strengthen this bent; winner-take-all elections—with the executive, committee chairmanships, contracts, and patronage hanging in the balance—discourage minor-party campaigns by making coalition government highly unlikely. On the contrary, intraparty coalitions and campaigns appealing to numerous and diverse interests are decidedly more common. This power (rather than policy) emphasis of our election process leads to unconscious patterns of thought and behavior, all in line with the dictates of consensus politics.

First, successful coalitions between divergent groups contribute to and reinforce narrow, nonclass perspectives. Piecemeal demands are balanced and moderated in order to achieve electoral victory. The multitude of groups and issues are not forged by party leaders into an alliance with a common campaign promoting shared structural objectives. Groups remain isolated and narrowly defined, and therefore each party can realistically attempt to form a pragmatic (nonideological) majority coalition by appealing to all. Without an obvious class enemy, class consciousness and ideological perspectives are inhibited. Consequently, so is the desire for redistributive change.

Second, emphasis on immediate electoral success and the subsequent need for intraparty coalitions lead to the politics of the middle. The argument is familiar and deceptively practical. Public opinion, seen as a bell-shaped curve on most issues, treats any sort of extremism harshly. Find the golden mean before your opponent does, and the voter will reward you with victory. The dominance of this view of campaign strategy results in the vague, indeterminate, even two-faced oratory so typical of our election politics. But more importantly, it forces a moderation in economic demands that eliminates any realistic redistributive impulse. Institutional arrangements of give and take predominate; economic redistribution is extremism. Demands that threaten income groups go against the need for a broad-based moderate and successful economic coalition (funds as well as votes must come from non-working class groups). In addition, economic demands face the multitude of noneconomic issues with which parties and candidates must contend. At the very least, the cross-pressures of numerous overlapping interests and issues, coupled with conventional wisdom's definition of campaign strategy, prevent a concerted emphasis on inequality as *the* central social problem. The formulae for effective political strategies in consensus politics preclude one-issue candidates, however critical that issue may appear to be.

Third, admittedly there are some class loyalties determining voter preferences. The Democrats receive their major electoral support from the lower middle and lower classes and labor unions. However, this loyalty is not a reflection of class interests in the same way that a labor party represents the interests of labor. The aim, let us not forget, is to gain political power, and as long as Democrats can count on working class votes without treading on the interests of the wealthy and powerful, there is no motivation to promote redistributive policies. The liberal rhetoric of the Democratic party has become a substitute for substantive recommendations and structural challenges; it is thus a functional attempt to gain electoral victory with the minimum of ideological friction within the party and within society. And if the rhetoric sometimes is not enough to satisfice, it does not matter. After all, in consensus politics, where else can the workingman go?

The final consequence of electoral parties is strongly suggested in the preceding analysis. Political parties are elitist, and political campaigns are manipulative. The increasing emphasis on public relations in insuring the election of a candidate attests to this latter claim. While some manipulation is conscious and planned, some is unconscious and regretted. Both types are outgrowths of an elitist mentality pervading voter and leader roles. If the electoral success of an individual candidate is seen as the major goal and thus is thrust ahead of a commitment to that candidate's constituency and his program, then he personally becomes elevated above supporters and principles. Elitism is legitimized in the eyes of both leaders and voters because we elect a personality rather than a representative of certain policy positions.

Compounding these psychological supports of elitism is an organizational separation between party leaders and party identifiers. A highly hierarchical structure with little chance for building rank-and-file input between elections encourages a sense of distance between representatives and those represented. Indeed, this distance receives justification in the notion of buffer institutions (i.e., groups) insulating and protecting elected officials from the demands and pressures of the masses. Values and interests diverge, giving vent to the feelings of frustration so typical of the average voter.

But despite these feelings, despite the unresponsiveness of the Democratic party to the economic pressures experienced by the working class, party loyalties remain. Party voters still respond to the periodic appeals of an office-seeking clique, but they remain unorganized, unmobilized, inactive, and therefore ignored between elections. This limited and temporary nature of party loyalty is a reflection of the types of demands made upon the party and upon the political processes generally. Because few long-range structural objectives are seriously entertained, there is little need to maintain a mass-based, grass-roots, permanently active organization to push and politic between elections. Once the campaign is won (or lost), the potentially powerful electorate has served its primary function, the filling of elective offices. The party's supporters are not consulted any further in their role as party supporter. Instead, the narrow band of party spokesmen presume to speak for the followers until the next surge of organizational and electoral fervor. The manipulative and elitist character of party politics, stemming from the nonideological, pragmatic nature of our political parties, shores up consensus politics by defusing the potential for structural change inherent in election campaigns.

We cannot underestimate the impact that party organization has on muting electoral threats to consensus politics. Many critics of our political system have pointed toward the fragmentation of power in the party as a major obstacle to political, social, and economic change in our country. The debate over party responsibility (by which is meant both ideological unity and central discipline) is revealing, but it seems to be one step removed from the realities of U.S. politics. The weakness of party authority, the diverse positions of party spokesmen, and the subsequent independence of elected officials are quite in line with other aspects of consensus politics previously mentioned—fragmented demand structures, emphasis on electoral victory rather than long-range political change, and policies based on bargaining instead of authoritative decision making. The party system shapes and is also shaped by the operation of consensus politics; critical evaluations and political activity must be focused on this more general level.

Whatever the causative factors, the lack of party responsibility is a crucial aspect of our political system. Its consequences affect the viability of redistributive electoral strategies in very detrimental ways. The notion of voting cues provides a case in point. With the plethora of candidates, issues, and offices involved in any election campaign, the individual voter cannot be expected to make separate determinations on each contest. Party labels provide voting cues, simplifying the numerous options and making the ultimate choices rational in light of an individual's own desires and problems. That is, a party claims to support certain groups and interests, and those groups give their electoral support and hold the party generally accountable for the protection of the groups' interests. But this thread of reasoning and the validity of party labels as voting cues break down in our party system. The lack of a coherent party position and the organizational inability to deliver on policy promises impel the voter to look for other guidelines. Often, elected officials are chosen because of the personal characteristics they seem to exemplify; thus, campaigns are increasingly becoming personality contests, with the individual candidates produced and directed by public relations firms. This voting appeal, supplemented by other common cues (ethnic background, regional loyalty), undercuts and ignores whatever ideological and policy-oriented potential that party conflict has. Class orientations are less important to the voter because the party-class relationship is loose. Therefore, in terms of voter perceptions, the lack of party unity undermines class appeals and forces the voter to rely on cues having little connection to redistributive demands.

Organizationally, the lack of party responsibility prevents the coordination of forces needed to push through structural or redistributive programs. The outright opposition to change on the part of status quo groups is magnified by the institutional bias of consensus politics. The political obstacles to attacks on inequality necessitate determined, persistent, and coordinated activity. Only unified effort can bring policy promises to fruition in the face of these obstacles. But party leadership will not gain this unity if it cannot draw upon common ideological motivations. The upshot is that individual representatives must either conform to the formulae for political action within government, or they must seek change on their own, as individuals. The futility of this situation for a well-intentioned official is obvious. Elected on the basis of a host of extraneous, minor, and sometimes mistaken reasons, he finds that this reasoning process itself tends to inhibit orderly policy-making and coordinated governmental action. Redistributive strategies cannot succeed without the discipline and practical focus on the issues that responsible parties bring.

Futility is not solely the prerogative of the sincere, elected representative. The public sees that the connection between their vote and governmental policy is at best coincidental. And, more critically, the lack of responsible parties clouds the issue of blame, for no one accepts failure, while everyone claims to deserve credit. Under these circumstances, feelings of powerlessness, hopelessness, and withdrawal are understandable—and frequent. Structured apathy of this sort is just one aspect of structured nonparticipation that closes electoral politics off from those groups most likely to demand and press for redistributive policies. The low level of citizen involvement in our electoral processes is justified by system apologists in terms of the anticipated consequences that mass participation would have. To be sure, among these consequences would be increased class conflict and the potential for structural changes. Nonparticipation protects the system from these "threats." The price we pay in terms of the democratic ideals of citizenship is supposedly minimized in light of an updated, descriptive definition of democracy. The lack of mass involvement in election politics, stemming in part from the lack of responsible parties, maintains the stability of consensus politics even as it restricts the meaning of democratic politics.

The ongoing disintegration of the party system, a result of many of the factors mentioned, gives rise to compensating trends. The beginning of this section described the possibilities of political decision making through party conflict. In the absence of this type of party conflict, there is increasing reliance on another focus of demands and pressures—the pressure-group system. As has been previously indicated, this arena offers even less chance for redistributive policies and structural change than the party system.

The biases that surround conflict between organized, narrow interests moderate demands and blunt disruptive strategies. But more importantly, the pressure-group system is seen as the legitimate alternative to the frustrating and ineffective party system. Failure in the latter field of battle means dependence on the former. The structure supplies this choice, but the related biases against redistributive policies and strategies in both systems leave the individual citizen at a loss on how to formulate and fight for his economic demands. Most groups remain in the boundaries of consensus politics, working through the biasing structures of both political arenas. Those few who cannot be satisficed via either of these alternatives have by definition gone outside the sphere of consensus politics and can thus be viewed as legitimate targets of political repression.

Labor-Management Relations

We might tend to think that in comparison to electoral contests, conflict arising out of union-management differences is potentially a more fertile ground for redistributive demands and class-based strategies. It would seem that the clear nature of the "economic enemy" should bring out a sharper awareness of class divisions than possible in the arena of party politics. Indeed, in some respects this is the case. "The United States has had the bloodiest and most violent labor history of any industrialized nation in the world."[25] But this militancy has been directed toward system-supportive paths. Just as a set of structural constraints affects the thoughts and behavior of people as voters, so does a parallel set influence people's beliefs and actions in the sphere of labor relations. While the restraining impact of modern trade unionism has been felt by other industrialized nations, it is probably most evident in our own country. Despite the militancy, violence, and bitterness of labor history in the United States, the labor movement still operates within the narrow bounds of consensus politics.

Descriptions of trade unionism in the United States usually take the European labor movement as a point of reference. The absence of a Socialist-oriented party that is ideologically (though perhaps not actually) devoted to egalitarianism and working-class interests is only the most notable symptom of divergent orientations. "The American worker's lack of class consciousness is most often singled out as the characteristic that distinguishes him from his foreign counterparts."[26] Many view this mind set as a sign of trade union maturity, as an indication that trade unions have chosen to spend less time crusading for political/economic utopias and more time involving themselves in the practical goal of bettering their members' lives. However, the lessened awareness of class in industrial relations is not the result of conscious and autonomous decisions by workers. Rather, the ideology and institutions shaping the working class in the United States conspire to limit labor's economic demands and thwart its economic power. The result is that the types of union-management contracts agreed upon do not seek to redistribute corporate wealth or work-place authority. The clashes that do arise, however intense the posturing by the combatants, are over nonstructural differences, thereby leading to system-supporting resolutions. This segment of social life conforms very closely to the patterns, norms, and expectations of consensus politics.

Chief among the ideological supports for consensus politics in U.S. trade unionism is the desire for an interdependent, symbiotic relationship between labor and management. The corporatist ideal held by the early American Federation of Labor spokesmen is the exact antithesis of class conflict. Its aim of achieving "industrial stability, order and social harmony"[27] goes completely against the notion that within capitalist society there is an unbridgeable clash of interests between workers and the corporate elite. Instead, the direction trade unions have taken is toward making unions a partner, albeit perhaps a junior partner, in the political economy and the entire productive function. Thus, the labor movement seeks to strengthen rather than overturn existing economic institutions, to integrate the role of unions within these institutions. William Appleman Williams has argued that, despite ideological rhetoric, even the "radical" Congress of Industrial Organizations (CIO) sought corporatism, a conservative form of syndicalism that would insure labor's place in the economic status quo.[28] In this way we can view the growing acceptance of unionism as the result of a growing realization of its accommodative nature; it is an alternate to, not the manifestation of, a Socialist and class-oriented ideology.

One of the consequences of this general attitude that pervades U.S. trade unionism is the clouding over of issues of power and responsibility—thus the claim that Adam Smith's "invisible hand" still holds sway in economic decision making. If both labor and management are part of the same productive function, then both are subject to the operation of immutable economic laws. Supply and demand, not power and exploitation, determine wages, prices, products, and profits: "the domination of man by man no longer appears an injustice but a biological or legal necessity. The power of the employer over the worker has the force of economic necessity and its human substance is entirely suppressed."[29]

Corporatist ideology also has the effect of creating alliances that impede the development of class consciousness. Daniel Bell has pointed to the fact that "a trade-union, operating in a given market environment, necessarily becomes an ally of 'its' industry."[30] Attitudes of "my company first" or "my industry first" are the result of and in turn reinforce the narrow perspectives of trade unions. Unlike the "One Big Union" approach of the Industrial Workers of the World (IWW), the labor movement is divided into functionally competing units. Improvement for one segment is not coordinated ideologically and organizationally with the impact such changes have on other sectors, and, indeed, often this seeming progress for part of the working class is made at the expense of other workers. Besides undercutting the leveling impact of some labor-management agreements, this institutional arrangement, having its roots in the corporatist ideology of labor leaders, divides workers conceptually from each other and foments a form of internecine warfare that prevents class consciousness.

Another aspect of the ideological context that has conservative impacts is the consumerist orientation of our society. This affects the types of demands made by workers and their leaders and also provides the criteria with which to judge the success of union efforts. The emphasis has always been placed on the "bread and butter" aspects of unionism. Thus, George Meany's quote, "Ideology is baloney," signifies the unconscious acceptance of the dominant ideology through the labor movement's support of "pragmatic" trade unionism.

In addition, our mass society has increasingly weakened and restricted that nexus of working-class values and personal relationships out of which social movements can emerge, a development that is also occurring in other industrialized countries but to a lesser degree.

Capitalist development during the post–World War II period has transformed the character of everyday life for the working masses of the
Western nations . . . [by] the replacement of all the traditional forms
of proletarian culture and everyday life—which gave working class
communities their coherence and provided the underpinnings for the
traditional forms of proletarian class-consciousness—with a new, manipulated consumer culture.[31]

The social potential for redistributive strategies has been reduced
and undermined as a result of the filtering down of upper-middle-
class values on to the not-so-middle-class worker.

One additional aspect of our social ideology as it pertains to
labor-management relations is the belief that politics and economics are or ought to be separate. Government action in the
many clashes between unions and companies is limited to a referee
role. The sanctity and integrity of the collective-bargaining process
in the face of potential political interference are values held by
workers and managers alike. The European contrast model indicates the relatively narrow sphere encompassed by our form of
trade unionism given these ideological inclinations:

we can distinguish a trend toward the development of two different
types of unions: those in which the main emphasis of union work is
on the bargaining process and those which tend to exert their main
impact at the level of legislation and administration [the continental
model]. . . . The first group is primarily concerned with the arrangements that affect the union member directly at the work place—not
only wages, but also work loads, working conditions, seniority rights,
his right to a particular job, and so on. The second type places heavier
emphasis on the factors that determine the general economic and social
conditions of the country, leaving the determination of a good deal of
the detail of industrial relations as it arises in the work place to non-
union organizations.[32]

Thus, the bulk of union power in this country is devoted to in-
fluencing the minor and peripheral aspects of worker well-being.
The major decisions are left to political and economic elites,
beyond the ken of the collective-bargaining process. This attitude
blunts the power of organized labor not only by creating self-
imposed limits on the influence that unions can have on major

economic decisions. There is also a bias against using political pressure in order to place government on labor's side in the bargaining process. That management has never been reluctant to accept governmental support (e.g., troops) is proven by any reading of labor history. In effect, unions foreclose the use of one of their major resources, numerical superiority, when they reject spreading the conflict into the political forum. Ideological restrictions, among them the artificial and biased distinctions between public and private and between polity and economy, go a long way toward making redistributive strategies unworkable.

Institutional factors add another protective layer surrounding consensus politics. The organizational hierarchy of trade unionism, as it has grown in complexity, has become less a promoter of the interests of workers and more a mechanism for their integration and control. Unions have been transformed into elite-run big businesses, handling huge pension funds and huge memberships with the same manipulative techniques. In order to protect and strengthen their position in the union and with other groups in society, union leaders have sought to suppress militancy and initiative from the rank and file. An army of experts (lawyers, accountants, economists, etc.), with little or no contact with working-class life, seems to function as professional obfuscators, insuring that important matters (the true consequences of a collective bargaining agreement, the explanations of union investment policy, etc.) are beyond the comprehension of most workers. Aided by these experts, union leaders are further insulated from workshop problems and grow increasingly sensitive to the needs and expectations of their supposed economic adversaries. In addition to these purely social aspects, the union hierarchy functions as an arm of the government. It is legally responsible for enforcing the contractual agreement by which labor is sold for a pre-arranged price. For the workers to assert themselves against this prior arrangement—through wildcat strikes, for example—threatens not only the company's but also the union's leaders. Given this state of affairs, it is no wonder that many of the rank-and-file union members feel as alienated from their union spokesmen as they do from their plant managers. This situation, the result of the structured elitism of trade unionism, conforms to the elitism of the political system generally. There is no doubt that it has conservative and inhibiting consequences on labor's ability to effect redistributive change through union activity.

The fragmentation of society into competing groups and the division in the union hierarchy between leaders and members has its counterpart in a similar institutionally fostered fragmentation of the working class. Racial, religious, ethnic, and, until recently, linguistic distinctions divided workers and impeded the creation of a common labor awareness. These divisions were either supplemented or replaced by differences in craft, trade, or level of skill, leading today to an economic and social hierarchy within each union as well as within trade unionism as a whole. The wage differentials that evolve out of this hierarchy of functions are forms of privatized power and class distinctions the protection of which cannot help but create hostilities and barriers between segments of the labor movement. And a divided working class insures the continuation of class inequality.

Add to these internal inhibitions against class-conscious unionism the external limitations of social and political realities. Primary among these is the low level of union organization in the United States. Only 22 percent of the work force is organized into unions, a much smaller proportion than is found in other industrialized countries. And the bulk of the work occupations is in the less-class-conscious, more difficultly organized white-collar sectors. While the limits of industrial unionism have not been reached—witness the battle over organizing farm workers—it is plain that even with further growth the movement would still include only a minority of working-class groups. More importantly, organizational and ideological solidarity would be a rhetorical rather than an actual characteristic. So, except for the marriage of convenience between organized labor and the Democratic party, unions tend to operate as separate entities within the political system. When we remember how the bias of the pressure-group system works in favor of big business, we realize the extent to which the working class has been boxed into and has boxed itself into a politically ineffectual position.

What does all this imply as to the style of labor-management conflict? As stated previously, a political system, broadly defined, has a bias not merely with respect to which policies and perspectives will emerge victorious and which will be defeated. It not only shapes the system's conclusions (winners and losers); it shapes the issues as well. The structure will not allow issues to be raised that bring forth antistructural alternatives. Thus, with respect to current trends and perspectives in the U.S. labor movement, proposals of a structural, redistributive nature are not seriously entertained. Indeed, they may not even be considered legitimate demands. Labor movements in other countries are interested in challenging and ultimately sharing management's authority position by sharing in responsibility for administrative decisions that affect both sides. In the United States, demands of this type would be rejected as socialistic. More limited challenges to the work-place authority of management (e.g., on safety, pace, conditions) are given a very low priority in the bargaining strategy of negotiators since a plea for more money is invariably substituted for these more structural concerns. The power orientation of European unions is in marked contrast to the limited, short-range perspectives of our material-benefits approach.

Of course, demands for higher monetary benefits *can* have enormous structural implications. Discussions over how the corporate pie is to be split might bring up issues of personal need, economic justice, and social priorities. Instead, these demands have arisen from a consumerist mentality; they are a reflection of corporate advertising rather than a means toward egalitarian change. More importantly, unions have allowed such demands to be tied to price rises and productivity campaigns. These ties represent the union's admission that collective bargaining arrangements cannot and will not be used to upset current distributions of corporate income and wealth. Moral rejections of inequality are out of place in the amoral bargaining relationships of industrial confrontation. Worker demands for "more" are objectified and made contingent not upon fairness but upon the success of his firm, his industry, his nation. Ultimately, the decision revolves around the means by which corporations can maintain and expand their economic position. Unions that demand higher wages while going along with and countenancing these "means" (productivity and price increases, governmental subsidies) are giving tacit approval to the perpetuation of inequality.

It is on this level that intraclass divisions are most effective at inhibiting redistributive thoughts and actions. There is, in the final analysis, a critical division of consciousness *within* each worker. Trade unionism does not enable him to see the connections among his varied social roles—as worker, as consumer, and as taxpayer.

Without a framework and an organization coordinating his thoughts in these disparate roles, he is forced to concern himself exclusively with one, then exclusively the other role. He cannot succeed in improving his relative position on this treadmill of divided consciousness.

The classic strategies of trade unionism in this country (collective bargaining and job actions) can be used either to subvert or to further worker interests. In many respects our deification of the collective bargaining process has been detrimental with respect to the most efficient use of labor's political power. "It is the preoccupation of the U.S. trade unions with collective bargaining that has tended to keep their attention away from broader social goals."[33] But even if we focus on the more limited scope and more immediate concerns of the labor movement, we should be aware of the conservative, elitist, and regulatory nature of collective bargaining and strikes. An excellent case study by William Serrin, *The Company and the Union: The "Civilized Relationship" of the General Motors Corporation and the United Automobile Workers,* makes the point that the strike is used to coerce worker compliance, not to gain corporate concessions.[34] As for collective bargaining, it is difficult to believe that, except in the presence of other critical factors, one side would peacefully reduce its share of corporate wealth without the expectation that immediate developments will bring a large return on that investment. After all, the process of bargaining occurs within a context of unequal power relationships. Indeed, bargaining is expressly designed to reveal and reflect these differences. Stratification is safely protected by this strategy of conflict.

The labor union hierarchy has succeeded in convincing its membership of the union's limited role for the worker and the worker's limited role within the union. This lowering of expectations and participation augments and is in turn encouraged by the general social outlines of consensus politics. Economic inequality and the structures that support it constitute the silent partners in labor-management agreements. In this forum of conflict, inequality remains unattacked, undefended, and therefore unacknowledged as the formative context motivating both sides. It is safe to say that unions have become part of the supportive structure of the status quo:

> major unions in both advanced and developing countries serve as an
> integrating link, helping furnish political and organizational support for

government, union, business bureaucracies. . . . [U]nions help to preserve the system and the established power and status relationships
within it.[35]

Like the Democratic party, trade unionism presumes to speak for
the disadvantaged without ever speaking against the advantaged.

The conservative consequences of U.S. trade unionism are due
to the fact that unions and union leaders have found a niche in the
social order. Thus, the social order is now beyond serious (structural) challenge. The pitched battles that we sometimes witness
might convince us that basic changes are in the offing. The rhetoric
and maneuvering, however, are not those of real combatants; the
ritualistic posturing and symbolic reassurances are aimed at persuading a constituency, the workers, that its interests are being
protected. While debate may rage over the extent to which the
workers are being improved due to union action, the relative
political peace in industrial relations indicates that a primary aim
of union leaders has been largely successfully accomplished. The
workers are persuaded of the legitimacy of the forms of conflict
operative within the framework of consensus politics.

Conclusions

While the existence of consensus politics is generally acknowledged, its legitimacy is an object of debate. And this is to be
anticipated. Consensus politics implies the tacit rejection of structural criticism and the tacit acceptance of the stratification system
on the part of most working-class people. The understanding of
this attitude, its nature, and its source, is a point of sharp disagreement between establishment apologists and radical critics
of the political system. Do lower-middle- and lower-income groups
operate within current political and economic arrangements out
of a true appreciation of their self-interest, or is their complacency
the product of manipulative socialization and institutionalized
repression? The answer depends in part on how we evaluate the
costs and benefits of the status quo.

Defenders of consensus politics claim that the majority of lower-
class people consciously support the system, and this is so because
the system "delivers the goods." The creation of a welfare state
has raised minimum standards of living for most Americans. In

addition, political procedures and social mobility have insured that economic growth is distributed to all major sectors of society. This commonly shared affluence has given all groups a stake in preserving the institutional, ideological, and political components of our economic system. Indeed, with respect to redistributive issues, the argument is made that we are in a postpolitics era. In short, class-based politics is declining, and rightfully so, due to (among other things) the fact that we are solving the problems caused by inequality in the process of our overcoming the problems of scarcity.

Critics are not quite as quick to see consensus in consensus politics. The benefits of society are not fairly distributed. Thus, support for the system, or even acquiescence in its operation, is the result of a structural co-optation of the underprivileged. Even the touted reform policies of Western democracies do not substantially improve the lot of the average worker. However, they do have the co-optive effect of securing "the dependency of larger segments of the underlying population on state welfare measures."[36] Countering the claim that we need to move away from the outdated class-based conflict of quantitative liberalism (e.g., New Deal) toward the noneconomic concerns of qualitative liberalism, Jack Newfield and Jeff Greenfield plead for a return to those issues and divisions that accurately reflect the interests of middle America.[37] The eclipse of class conflict and redistributive demands—if, in fact, they were there to be eclipsed—has been imposed unnecessarily on a political system now blinded to the tensions and pressures underneath the "consensus." And worse, middle America has blinded itself to economic explanations of its plight. False consciousness is the critical concept in radical analyses of public acquiescence.

It is in the nature of establishment explanatory frameworks to interpret apathy as acquiescence, complacency as consent. There is no hesitation on the part of apologists to point to increases in the general living standard as proof of the authenticity and legitimacy of working-class support of stratification. Such an admission would not sit well with critics of our political and economic systems, but radicals have been forced to come to terms with affluence. The theory of absolute impoverishment—that the internal contradictions in capitalism will lead the working class into increasing misery and increasing class solidarity—is no more than a museum piece. However, it does have the effect of tying the strength of false consciousness to the economic conditions of non-elites. Begrudgingly, it is becoming clear even to some radicals that material conditions for the lower strata of society have improved. There is little perceived need for a class-based mass movement or ideologically oriented political conflict: "immediate economic demands no longer suffice to express and to make concrete the radical antagonism of the working class to capitalism. . . . [They] no longer possess an urgency great enough" to result in questioning or the mounting of a challenge to the economic system.[38] For many leftists, then, consensus politics is a consequence of *perceived satisfaction*—falsely perceived perhaps, but maintained and strengthened by an economy that has shown the capacity to "deliver," even if only partially.

Thus, there is a measure of agreement between critics and defenders on a major support for the continuation of consensus politics. However much they may differ with respect to the justice of relative deprivation, they both realize that inequality can be a source of anger and resentment that can spread into the political sphere. What is preventing these emotions from breaking through the mechanisms of conflict control described in this chapter is the economic growth with which this country has been blessed. Exactly how economic growth has ameliorated conflict and how it has softened the anger and resentment mentioned above are subjects of the next chapter.

Economic Growth and the
Moderation of Class Conflict

Introduction

To recount the lessons of the previous chapter, our political and social systems are generally insulated against the potential strains of economic inequality. Though a person's economic class is perhaps the paramount factor in determining his life-style or life chances, the stratification system seems impervious to challenge from either a viable egalitarian movement or a well-publicized ideological position. This development is not merely coincidental. The mechanisms of consensus politics have successfully thwarted the creation of social or conceptual alternatives to inequality. Even the confrontational possibilities in electoral politics or labor-management relations have been defused. The pervasive impact of consensus politics is responsible here as well. Indeed, in analyzing the basic thrust of the Women's Liberation and Black Power movements of recent decades, we cannot help but be impressed by the way in which opposition to the economic game takes the form not of "change the rules" but, rather, of "deal me in." Egalitarian rhetoric notwithstanding, the tremendous social forces unleashed by these movements constitute a major threat neither to the privileged nor to the system of privilege generally. In John Kenneth Galbraith's words, "Few things are more evident in modern social history than the decline of interest in inequality as an economic issue."[1]

The lack of general opposition to economic stratification is a source of interest to political analysts on both ends of the ideological spectrum. Most conservative and liberal social scientists find working-class acceptance of inequality to be a predictable reflection of working-class support for most established political,

45

social, and economic values. Social critics, however, view public acquiescence as more of an anomaly; therefore, it necessitates a more complex explanation from them than consensus theorists require. The paradox is amplified by two central questions: why have disadvantaged groups tolerated vast differences in material standards of living; and why have they continued to participate within a political system that distorts their economic demands and misrepresents their individual interests?

Radical analyses cite the role of the formative structural context—institutional processes, power relationships, a conservative ideological environment—in repressing class consciousness and political unrest. What passes for tolerance of inequality is more probably complacency, a result of the system's ability to sap much of the resentment and cloud much of the accountability for deprivation. In addition, it is easy to overstate the actual level of class acquiescence by misinterpreting signs of anguish and bitterness. Yet, we cannot attribute all popular toleration of inequality to the manipulative features of our political economy, to structural repression, or to coerced compliance. In leaving open the possibility that feelings of deprivation and resentment may increase, we acknowledge a *voluntaristic element* in mass acquiescence.

The lack of overt antagonism between the classes is in part genuine, an authentic though unstated admission that, despite the real costs of inequality, *on balance* the economic system delivers. The frustrations experienced in the political realm are softened and can be accepted if the benefits arising out of economic activities appear as fair compensation. An extreme statement of this position was offered by Werner Sombart, writing about the United States of 1906:

> as the material condition of the wage worker has improved—and the increasing comfort of his way of life has enabled him to savor the corrupting effects of material wealth—so he has been impelled to love the economic system which has shaped his fate and to adapt his spirit to the characteristic operations of the capitalist economy. . . . All socialist utopias have come to grief on roast beef and apple pies.[2]

Even radical opponents of the stratification system, who, unlike Sombart, have no facile adoration of our nation's economy, begrudgingly admit that the low level of working-class consciousness and the depoliticization of the issue of inequality reflect popular *belief,* whether well founded or not, that improvements in one's economic condition can and will occur within the present economic, social, and political framework.[3] This optimism undergirds consensus politics. The vision of a materially better future for oneself and one's family helps to justify a conscious toleration of stratification. Such visions and optimism are fed by the economic growth that has noticeably improved the living standards of each generation of Americans. The subjective consequences are dampened resentment of one's subordinate position in the economic hierarchy, lessened class consciousness and class antagonism, and acceptance of nonredistributive conflict-resolution mechanisms regarding the allocation of material benefits and burdens. In short, the patterns of economic and political conflict described herein as consensus politics are maintained in large part through the substantial benefits obtained from economic growth.

The moderating influence of economic growth is also characterized by the popular attitudes engendered in a growth environment. The role of our frontier experience in shaping our national character has been passed on to growth, industrial expansion, and technological development. These factors set the tone of a society, encouraging a set of values, goals, and behavior patterns in conformity with current political and economic realities. Of primary importance in this regard is the recognition and acceptance of the established means by which one can attain one's economic objectives. The prescribed paths for the eventual gratification of material desires—individual economic mobility and mutual prosperity through group accommodation—are proven (if far from perfect) nonredistributive mechanisms for economic advancement. But both are dependent upon high rates of economic growth in order for them to remain viable and realistic aspirational possibilities. Their effectiveness as a means to higher living standards helps to deflect attention away from more class-oriented, political, redistributive strategies and toward those patterns of conflict associated with consensus politics. Noam Chomsky clearly summarizes this theme:

> The idea that economic growth will continue without limit has been a very effective device for controlling and limiting demands for redistribution of wealth. . . . The notion of limitless growth could be employed

to bring about consensus instead of conflict by overcoming the demands for redistribution of wealth, which would certainly be heard if
one could not look forward to gaining more of life's benefits by some
other method.[4]

Economic growth provides the disadvantaged with outlets for
directing their energies that do not require redistributive adjustments. Indeed, by working through these outlets, lower-middle-
and lower-class individuals help to legitimize the institutions of
inequality, the positions of the higher classes, and the processes of
consensus politics.

The following chapter will flesh out these introductory comments. Initially, the fact of material progress must be established;
some of the criticisms and caveats leveled against exaggerated
claims of growth will be explored. Next, I will examine the two
principal means by which economic growth bolsters support for
the system or, more likely, stems resentment of its inegalitarian
elements. This involves an analysis of the impact that economic
mobility and shared prosperity have on our consciousness of and
attitudes toward stratification. To the extent that public support
of our economic system depends upon economic growth, the
future toleration of vast material inequality and, with it, the
future stability of consensus politics are likewise dependent.

Growth: Perceptions and Reality

Growth and Material Progress

"The idea of economic growth has long been a basic part of
American thinking."[5] Our politics as well as our economic system are largely products of the material abundance with which
this land has been blessed. The ideological victory of Lockean
liberalism and the forms of political conflict it portended were
definitely "helped forward by the magnificent material setting
it [Lockeanism] found in the New World."[6] True, industrial
expansion is not unique to the United States. Nevertheless, cross-
cultural comparisons indicate a remarkable qualitative difference
between our average style of life and that of citizens in almost
every other industrialized nation.

This comparative affluence is readily translated in the minds
of most people into more self-evidently worthwhile goals.

For many Americans, the pursuit of happiness and the pursuit of money come to much the same thing. More money means more goods . . . and thus more of the material benefits of life. . . . National economic growth . . . means, it is supposed, greater well-being and a happier society.[7]

The expectation and assumption is that economic growth promotes happiness by continuously widening the scope of personal freedom. By raising living standards above subsistence levels, growth releases workers from the demands of economic necessity. A multitude of purchasable goods and services frees man (and woman) from many types of everyday drudgery. With time for leisure and options for use of that time, the anxieties and constraints imposed by survival are replaced by the choices and security of affluence.

Economic growth also promotes an uplifting of the collective spirit, a mood of confidence and pride, which permeates the social and cultural atmosphere of a nation. Our humanitarian impulses are given more room to flourish when economic life is not a permanent, brutish struggle with life-or-death stakes. We can afford to consider others. Ironically, economic growth promises to solve the problem of poverty without our having to become humanitarians, without our having to sacrifice. Increasingly, the answer to absolute deprivation in the United States is perceived to be growth, raising the minimum living standards of those most deprived to levels above the poverty line. The poverty programs of the welfare state depend upon growth, not redistribution, for success. Specific policies aimed at helping depressed areas—tax incentives for investment, job retraining, education upgrading—assume general expansion in order for these programs to bear fruit. It might even be argued that the growth of the public sector (e.g., welfare policies such as health care, mass transportation, low- and middle-income housing) can only be financed, or financed with a minimum of political pain, through the government's utilization of its share of the economic surplus, its increment of the growth over the previous year's revenue. Admittedly, some of these claims are more public relations than description.[8] Yet, the statistics regarding growth do make a strong case for the reality of economic progress and hint at its influence on class consciousness and conflict.

Caveats, Qualifiers, and Doubts

The above argument is not without its detractors. There are critics who dispute the degree, direction, and depth of our assumed affluence. One set of attacks has taken aim on the nature of our growth. Our affluence is viewed by some as imbalanced, supplying a surfeit of material goods and consumer services and a scarcity of less-measurable elements of well-being. "Development goes beyond economics, politics, and technology. It raises basic questions about the quality of life in society, the relation between goods and the good."[9] It is doubted whether certain extensions of technology, certain efforts to produce more and different products, have in fact increased the public's welfare, or even individual welfare. The imbalance between our obvious quantitative progress and our equally obvious qualitative failings undermines the meaningfulness of our growth rates and statistics on living standards. John Curtis Raines puts it this way: "While moving up in things, we have not moved up in spirit."[10]

In a book entitled *The American Business Creed,* the authors demonstrate that the business elite slants its self-evaluation of capitalism's successes by ignoring or playing down the qualitative side of economic development.

> The creed . . . concentrates on the material and the practical in its enumeration of achievements. Claims that the business system has yielded significant cultural or esthetic gains are almost completely absent. Spiritual and moral achievements are limited largely to freedom.[11]

Traditional economics reinforces this materialist ethos by emphasizing measures of national wealth and personal income levels. This "preoccupation with the production and consumption of material goods and services contributes to an increasing imbalance between the satisfaction of material and nonmaterial human needs."[12] In effect, material affluence has been a partial substitute for those needs not met within our economy. The psychological and social disamenities of advanced corporate capitalism (perhaps indicative of noncapitalist industrialism, too)—rises in mental illness and violence, the breakdown of family and community ties—are justified by some as temporary costs of a productive economy against which our increased material benefits should be weighed.

Perhaps, as these analysts would contend, this presumed trade-off of nonmaterial for material benefits is consciously made (e.g., union contracts with sizable pay increases but no mention of safer working conditions). Yet, it is undeniable that such considerations qualify our glorification of affluence by offering a set of needs that our material abundance does not satisfy. To the extent that nonmaterial factors have not improved apace with material factors, quantitative measures of growth and living standards overestimate the overall improvement in personal well-being.

A related form of imbalanced economic development is in reference to expenditures in the public and private sectors of our society. While the latter is very impressive, the so-called envy of the world, the former is often ignored. In three distinct areas of public spending, our collective interests have suffered as a result of the lack of governmental effort. Public services such as mass transportation or support for the arts pale in comparison with private expenditures for parallel services (e.g., automobiles, mass culture records, books, and television). Public policies aimed at broadening the scope of citizenship welfare rights (broad health-care coverage, publicly subsidized housing, education) are ineffective, inadequately funded, and often diverted to benefit powerful political interests. Finally, programs designed to raise the standard of living of the most underprivileged strata, to alleviate the worst consequences of economic inequality, have not prevented the formation of an almost castelike underclass. Somewhat redistributive in its idealized conception, the lauded (and feared) welfare state does not supply very much well-being to its clients; "the main beneficiaries of services are those who fill the jobs of service providers."[13] The public-private imbalance is especially stark when we examine our own efforts in light of the more effective and better funded public welfare programs in other industrialized nations. We must be suspicious of claims of affluence that rely primarily upon measures of private consumption. We should modify once more our description of economic growth insofar as public goods and services have not expanded in like proportion to expenditures for private material needs.

Another caveat to the statistics on economic growth attacks the claim of conventional wisdom that an increase in real disposable income necessarily involves a corresponding increase in living standards. Perhaps we should not be too quick to jump at the assumption that, because of economic growth, poverty and deprivation are becoming more relative and less absolute, a matter of subjective perception rather than of objective condition. Simple statements about comparative purchasing power or relative afflu-ence ignore "the historically specific support systems within which each family strives to meet its needs for food, shelter, work, health, education, transportation and recreation."[14] Christopher Jencks's observations on the styles of life and consumption pat-terns demanded of individuals in a given time and place illustrate this point.

> The goods and services that made it possible to live on $15 a week during the Depression were no longer available to a family with the same "real" income (i.e. $40 a week) in 1964. Eating habits had changed, and many cheap foods had disappeared from the stores. Most people had enough money to buy an automobile, so public transporta-tion had atrophied, and families without automobiles were much worse off than during the Depression. The labor market had also changed, and a person without a telephone could not get or keep many jobs. A home without a telephone was more cut off socially than when few people had telephones and more people "dropped by."[15]

This is especially significant for the lowest strata of society.

The cost of participating in a social system may go up faster than increases in one's income (measured in constant dollars). The available goods and services to meet unavoidable biological and social needs are not fixed; they change with changes in tech-nology and culture. Options once purchasable when real income was lower are priced or structured out of the market. One's higher salary now must be applied to a new and more costly set of alter-natives. The conclusion some have reached is that "the workers' social standard of living tends to stagnate, to worsen, even if their individual standard of living (expressed in terms of monetary purchasing power) rises."[16] A related observation concerns the hidden labor costs in achieving present levels of real income. Very often a family's life-style depends upon the availability of over-time or part-time work for the chief breadwinner and a separate job for another member of the family. Wives are entering the labor market not out of choice but out of necessity. Crude statistics on family income hide the increasing time that working-class people must allot toward maintaining their position; the fifty- to sixty-hour week has returned (if it ever left). So I conclude with a warning against simplistic analysis. At the very least, we should be aware that, irrespective of trends in real income levels, the effect of economic growth on average living standards remains an issue for separate study.

The Argument Restated

In light of these points, a straightforward connection between economic growth and consensus politics is somewhat open to debate. The previous objections, precisely because they have so little currency in people's awareness of their economic condition, serve to illuminate those values and interpretations that are screened out of the public's consciousness in shaping its attitudes toward growth. The following discussion will explore the biases of ideology and structure that maximize the moderating impact of economic growth on class conflict. This analysis is imperative since it is not merely high economic growth but also the perceptual context within which we view that growth that explain the role of affluence in deflecting redistributive demands.

Part of that perceptual context concerns the definition of concepts used in evaluating our social and economic life. Criteria such as efficiency, affluence, progress, and success are conceptualized primarily in quantitative, materialistic terms. The social structure fosters this bias because the resulting set of perceptions and expectations tends to implicitly justify the operation of the economy. Quite understandably, the system encourages the application of supportive criteria in the public's evaluation of the system. Economists and commentators overemphasize aggregate measures of growth (e.g., GNP), leading to a like-minded public obsession with productivity statistics. This is the heart of the following comment by E. F. Schumacher:

> Having established by his purely quantitative methods that the Gross National Product of a country has risen by, say, five per cent, the economist-turned-econometrician is unwilling, and generally unable, to face the question of whether this is to be taken as a good thing or a bad thing. He would lose all his certainties if he ever entertained such a question: Growth of GNP must be a good thing, irrespective of what has grown and who, if anyone, has benefitted. The idea that there could be pathological growth, unhealthy growth, disruptive growth is to him a perverse idea which must not be allowed to surface.[17]

The fact is that such quantitative definitions of growth are the most publicized and accepted. While there may be serious deterioration or stagnation with respect to other less quantifiable facets of our life (social justice, community), these failings are played down by the ideology and therefore are more than compensated for within the mass consciousness by real growth in private and tangible consumption.

There is an important auxiliary consequence in our conceptual bias toward "tangible" outputs. The social structure encourages a range of material demands that is in keeping with the strengths of the economy, with its ability to provide a relative abundance of consumable goods and services. In our society, style-of-life symbols have an immense effect on self-esteem. Advertising creates desires for these newly produced and marketed symbols, playing upon the self-images of the consumer. By persuading the public to demand those outputs that the economic system is prepared and capable of delivering, advertising diverts attention from lapses with respect to the intangible aspects of our political economy. The values of power, authority, participation, etc., are especially difficult to deal with in typical union-management negotiations and are difficult to distribute amicably within the procedural confines of consensus politics. They represent "outputs" that highlight perhaps the ultimate imbalance in capitalist development. Thus, the materialistic ethic is critical for the stability of the economy and the dampening of class consciousness.

Ideological biases also influence one's self-definition, and this has ramifications for the way in which we determine the economy's success. How an individual views himself is increasingly as a consumer, not a producer. The growing role of consumables in shaping our psychological makeup partially explains this shift.

> Our way of consumption necessarily results in the fact that we are never satisfied . . . [since] our craving for consumption has lost all connection with the real needs of man. Originally, the idea of consuming more and better things was meant to give man a happier, more satisfied life. Consumption was a means to an end, that of happiness. It now has become an aim in itself.[18]

Economic growth emphasizes man as a consumer. The hierarchy and authority lines that are ever present in the productive sphere accentuate traditional class differences and may lead to class resentment. But the consuming side of individuals clouds those distinctions. Robert Lane has speculated along these lines: "The more emphasis a society places upon consumption—through advertising, development of new products, and easy installment buying—the more will social dissatisfaction be channeled into intraclass consumption rivalry instead of interclass resentment and conflict."[19]

This consumerist orientation, directed by culture and structure along rather individualistic paths, encourages a distorted sense of self-reliance. The availability of goods and services that augment one's private life enhances the conviction that collective problems (e.g., pollution or crime) can be successfully evaded by appropriate *individual* purchases (e.g., "wilderness" vacations, suburban residence, home security systems, home insurance). Consumerism and the ideology of self-reliance that it spawns also make one indifferent to the fate of autonomous others. After all, they *could* take care of themselves—unless they are stupid or lazy.

The criticisms of economic growth examined in this section might weaken positive attitudes toward growth only if people could conceptually step back and evaluate economic results from a broader perspective (with an alternate set of values and criteria). Yet, given the ideological screens through which Americans perceive economic expansion, this is quite a difficult undertaking. The dominant point of view predisposes most Americans to minimize the importance of these criticisms and to rely on future economic growth to rectify whatever imbalances and deficiencies past economic growth has caused.

We must, therefore, restate the hypothesis with somewhat more sophistication. It is not economic growth per se, but rather the kind of economic growth we have experienced, coupled with the cultural values and social structure of the society, that makes us receptive to the appeals of consensus politics. Consider for the moment that in many societies industrial expansion had exacerbated class conflict by intensifying demands and increasing expectations. Past growth "made people more aware of their misery or at any rate of the gap between actual and potential living standards."[20] Heightened perceptions of deprivation and the politicization of economic grievances have enabled economic development to become a catalyst for a revolutionary consciousness among middle and lower classes. But not in our society. In the United States, growth promotes not anxiety but confidence in the future, and thus the patience to wait for future rewards. Peter Jenkins has discussed this point:

> Growth is favourable to the democratic habit because it makes it less necessary to insist upon instant gratification of wants or needs at the expense of others. The prospect of things getting better confirmed by a consistent experience of things having got better helps to contain relative deprivations within a more general social expectation of progress.[21]

The ideology that has shaped this response to economic growth is strengthened by the two principal mechanisms in our economy by which individuals seek economic achievement. They help to exploit the moderating side of expansion and to repress its potential for social disruption. The remainder of this chapter will be devoted to an examination of economic mobility and shared prosperity.

Mobility

The Opportunity Thesis

One of the major underlying assumptions of this study is that inequality is a source of social instability that functioning societies are more or less capable of submerging as an issue. Within our society, the ideal of equality has been not so much submerged as conceptually reshaped into a system-supportive goal. The resulting redefinition is a direct outgrowth of abundance on our way of thinking. The ideal of equality has been operationalized so as to mean the same as equality of opportunity. This has entailed an immense reduction in its critical and normative content; "equality came to mean, in a major sense, parity in competition. . . . The term 'equality' acquired for most Americans exactly the same connotations which the term 'upward mobility' has for the social scientist."[22] This terminological shift allowed people to speak of a society of equals without having to prove equality of condition. A fusing of ideal and description evolved.

> The myth of equality held that equality exists not merely as a potentiality in the nature of man but as working actuality in the operation of American society—that advantages or handicaps are not really

decisive and that every man is the architect of his own destiny.[23]

An image of a fluid class structure became our definition of classlessness.

Because this image pervaded our descriptions of society, we tended to ignore class distinctions. To point out such distinctions, to deny the belief in an open society, was almost un-American. Indeed, the "American Dream" is built upon the assumed opportunities of an open society. The opportunity to succeed, to be wealthy (for that is what "success" has come to mean), is theoretically present for everyone. The Horatio Alger rags-to-riches stories provided the model for the hero of our social mobility passion play.[24] And the happy endings of most movie and television story lines simply update the theme, reinforcing our striving for success. Movements built on sharing the wealth found it difficult to compete with the well-cultivated belief that personal success was always possible. In effect, equal opportunity became the United States's ideological egalitarianism, with the strong cultural supports that a cherished national symbol acquires.

Economic symbolism has a role to play as well; "the ideal of freedom of opportunity depends upon a free market to establish comparative value."[25] To the job market is attributed all the sanctity, givenness, and immutableness of the consumer price market. Laws of supply and demand (Adam Smith's "invisible hand") are responsible for the distribution of positions and the rewards that accrue to them. Thus, if equal opportunity is interpreted more as description than prescription, then challenges to stratification are inefficient in addition to being un-American.

The impact of the cultural embrace of the success ethic upon the collective attitudes and behavior of disadvantaged groups is not difficult to gauge:

> Class consciousness and class mobility are the fundamental concepts of class theory. They refer to the two chief dynamics of class structure. They are also antithetical: while consciousness is the indispensable condition for the formation of classes as politicized groups and hence serve an *associative* function, mobility keeps the classes demographically open to each other, thereby promoting the diffusion and fragmentation of internal ideologies—hence, mobility serves a *dissociative* function in the evolution of class phenomena.[26]

Seymour Martin Lipset has demonstrated statistically the validity of this statement using the hard data of voting studies: "perhaps the most important effect of mobility on politics which should be noted is that the bulk of the socially mobile . . . vote for the more conservative parties."[27] Actual advancement is not a necessary precondition for conservative tendencies. Often, the perception of a reasonable expectation of upward advancement (or the belief that one has in fact advanced, whatever the reality of that belief) is sufficient cause for political caution. Stated in general terms, "There is an inverse relationship between the degree of openness of classes and the intensity of class conflict."[28]

The degree of openness in a society is a function of economic growth. Stagnant societies tend to distribute positions by self-recruitment (that is, from within the same class), but a dynamic economy creates new industries and requires new skills in greater proportion than can be acquired in a static class system. "In America, the processes of an expanding economy . . . have provided a constant supply of advantageous positions to which enterprising people could advance from less favorable beginnings."[29] New leadership positions attract middle-class competitors, while their places can be offered to aspirants from still lower strata. (We should not minimize the effect that the rhetoric of opportunity and growth has in encouraging individuals toward greater occupational achievement.) Lipset and Reinhard Bendix have pointed out that "a high degree of social mobility is a concomitant of industrialization and bureaucratization;" these two developments (related directly to the extent of economic growth) are the structures through which economic expansion increases social mobility.[30] Admittedly, a major change in the primary path of upward mobility has occurred. The rise of the salaried, dependent, white-collar middle class has altered the imagery of mobility, from capitalist entrepreneur expanding a privately owned and operated company to underling climbing the bureaucratic institution ladder.[31] Nevertheless, economic growth continues to aid aspirants in the corporate hierarchy as it opened business opportunities for embryonic industrialists one hundred years ago.

This is not to claim that the class system is as fluid and opportunity as available as the dream images suggest. It is at least partially true that most mobility takes place within "a social and cultural 'buffer zone' between the middle class and the working class proper."[32] Marginal class fluctuations within this buffer zone tend to insulate each group and protect the advantages of the middle class while giving some appearance of mobility. Statistics indicate that our levels of mobility do not greatly exceed those in other industrialized nations. At the heart of the issue is not differential rates of opportunity. Rather,

> it may be necessary to account for political stability by . . . the cultural value attributed to social mobility. . . . [Because] social mobility receives positive encouragement, the existing opportunities for upward mobility probably help to sustain the acceptance of the social and political order by the lower classes.[33]

The purported existence of great opportunity in our economy legitimizes the economic order. Thus, public perceptions of opportunity are the focus of efforts by those wishing to create support for redistributive policies. But while the Left seeks to unveil the truth behind what to them is the myth of opportunity, the weight of the culture influences perceptions in the opposite direction. Pause upon the impact of publicizing modern-day, real-life Horatio Alger stories. The humble beginnings of a handful of our business leaders are proudly heralded as examples of the reality of the U.S. success dream. In England, the probability is that such a background for its elite, equally as uncommon, would be hidden in the family attic. In the same vein, the existence of the frontier as *symbol* of opportunity had more to do with relieving the mobility pressures of Eastern laborers than did its actual use as an escape route. Awareness of its existence allowed it to have the same psychological function as a safety valve.[34] Despite the presence of comparable rates of mobility in other, more class-divided nations, mobility has had a uniquely moderating effect in the United States. This is because of the unique ideological context through which we interpret and respond to mobility. For most, the ideal need not be proven for the American Dream to influence our consciousness. "People care less about equality of opportunity than about the availability of some opportunity . . . for all, however unequal this distribution may be."[35] However far from the ideal the true mobility figures are, they provide hope enough for most people in their desire for a materially better life.

Mobility and Political Attitudes in Three Cases

Different individuals might be expected to react to mobility perceptions differently. The irony is that rather diverse experiences of material success in the United States will mold quite similar attitudes regarding political and economic arrangements. For three broadly disparate types of people, the existence of economic opportunity provides a strong basis for collective support of consensus politics. First are the aspirants, the hopeful and expectant. Next, we will look at the partial success stories, those who settled for much less than the dream promised. Third, there are the economic failures, for whom opportunity and mobility promises are threats to self-respect. In what ways does social mobility modify the economic demands of these groups (dampen class consciousness) or prevent the collective expression of those demands (inhibit class conflict)?

The Aspirants. We are all touched by the Midas dreams that the success ethic spawns. Yet, rational (and politically relevant) aspiration goals are not of such fanciful dimensions. Aspiration for the workingman means raising himself occupationally into the middle class (through small business ownership, educational upgrading in night school, achieving supervisory or white-collar advancement within the company). This dream necessarily diminishes consciousness of group interests and the utility of group actions at redressing economic grievances.

> It [opportunity] breaks up solidaristic opposition to existing conditions of inequality by holding out to the ablest and most ambitious members of the disadvantaged groups the enticing prospect of rising from their lowly state into a more prosperous condition. The rules of the game remain the same: the fundamental character of the social-economic system is unaltered. All that happens is that individuals are given the chance to struggle up the social ladder, change their position on it, and step on the fingers of those beneath them.[36]

Economic groups are fragmented into competitors striving to do better than others in the group, often at the expense of these others. The debilitating effect that this attitude has on class or group consciousness is obvious. Anselm L. Strauss claims that the divisive individualism fostered by the standard U.S. success story is not in accord with the actual nature of mobility in the United States.

> Americans tend to forget, or never know that much of our mobility is collective rather than simply individual . . . movement. . . . Analytically, one ought not to regard those individual rises and falls as merely individual, because the respective units [industry, region or town, profession or occupational group] have acted collectively in behalf of their members.[37]

Nevertheless, mobility aspiration weakens class loyalties because there is no realization of the collective nature of most mobility—women and minority groups to the contrary notwithstanding.

For those who do substantially move up the career ladder, changes in life-style, attitudes, leisure activities, and residential areas result in total or near-total breaks with the past. The individual has been co-opted and within his new setting is taught (socialized) to accept the values and behavioral patterns of his new equals. The saga of the nouveau riche has its complement with new entrants at each step of the economic hierarchy. Because the individualistic mobility ethic is stronger here than in Europe, the loosening of community and class ties becomes an accepted sign of personal success. Thus, mobility has a far greater effect at weakening working-class loyalties in the United States than in other developed economies with similar mobility rates. Just as important, the skilled and ambitious who become upwardly mobile thereby are removed as potentially gifted leaders of the groups they left. Lipset and Bendix refer to this point in discussing the ability of an elite to absorb qualified newcomers without undermining its own privileged position. Obviously, this element of social stability depends upon the degree of mobility (and therefore economic growth) within the system.

> In an expanding, dynamic society, such barriers to mobility as inherited rank can be a fundamental cause of instability, since expansion calls for an increase in the number of qualified leaders. As long as the ruling group is flexible it will allow ambitious and talented individuals to rise from the lower strata; yet an ever-present tendency toward the formation of an aristocracy tends to restrict such individual mobility in any society. If the restriction is sufficiently tight, it can provoke dis-

content, which may result in efforts by members of deprived groups to achieve collective or group mobility, sometimes through a struggle to supplant the dominant group.[38]

Mobility effectively removes many of these leaders from contact and identification with the underclasses. But, as the above quotation indicates, adequate levels of co-optation (without massive and dangerous downward mobility) depend upon the existence of economic expansion to create a certain rate of growth in the absolute number of middle- and upper-level positions.

Yet, to reemphasize my concern with perceptual as opposed to purely factual descriptions, this real and objective form of co-optation is not the only type that weakens class consciousness and, thus, prevents class conflict. Individuals who feel relatively deprived but aspire to higher stations often identify with the groups they hope to someday join. The dominance of middle-class values in the working-class consciousness attests in part to the expectation that advancement has or will soon come. Such distorted self-images are the substance of claims of false consciousness. "We are in danger . . . of identifying with the dreams beyond us and so voting against the place we really are."[39] Social mobility contributes to two types of false consciousness: that of an individual who identifies with a higher class to which he *unrealistically* aspires; and that of a skidder who identifies with the class from which he has *irreversibly* fallen. It is the nature of an economy like ours, which effectively merchandises hope, that the words "unrealistically" and "irreversibly" used above are subject to intense debate. Misrepresented class position is almost a certainty in a dynamic, growth-oriented society. A careful assessment of one's true status is psychologically difficult for those who are not self-evident successes; all the more in the United States, a nation that preaches the gospel of classlessness and opportunities for all.

This co-optation of the ambitious and optimistic affects not only class consciousness but also support for redistributive demands. In Louis Hartz's words, "the dream of new and greater wealth doubled the desire to protect wealth in general."[40] In a society that prides itself on the opportunity that all individuals have to achieve riches, the lure of this promised reward is often sufficient to repel attacks on those who have previously been rewarded (the wealthy). If people are willing to accept the proba-

bility of deprivation in order to preserve the admittedly slim possibility of enormous wealth—a life-as-lottery mentality—then the
resulting distribution of rewards, while not popular, might be considered fair. Aspirants implicitly acknowledge the validity of this
line of reasoning through their political and economic biases. For
them, mobility appears to offer a more immediate and a *more
realistic* route to securing personal economic goals than class unity
and the possibilities of redistributive politics.

Partial Mobility. For those who feel partially successful in the
opportunity race, who believe they have achieved some upward
mobility in exchange for their ambition and abilities, and who
contend that the system has delivered for them, though perhaps
incompletely, support for consensus politics is more solidly
founded. This group's support is based upon gratitude and a sense
of obligation, not unlike the emotions of many immigrants who,
coming to the United States penniless and often persecuted, were
appreciative of any job they were given. Consequently, they have
been among the most supportive of the economy's mobility/
opportunity ideology. Those who have had limited success in ad-
vancing themselves have not been co-opted in the same sense as
have the aspirants. They have not been raised to a new class or
strata; the mobility they have experienced will not dramatically
break down past ties or cause them to reject past values. Their
perception of success and advancement stems from basic evolutionary changes in the job structure that have made certain forms
of mobility more possible and that simulate mobility for those in
a basically static class condition. The ability of the system to deliver in the eyes of these individuals is also a function of rates of
economic growth.

Industrialization that has proceeded beyond the initial stages
(i.e., those stages that Karl Marx thought typified capitalism)
results in transformations in the job structure conducive to the
expectations of the opportunity myth. In terms of occupational
categories, this development takes the form of more white-collar
and service jobs and less rural and assembly-line positions, the
growth of the governmental sector as a major employer, and the
differentiation of the labor force that increases the number of jobs
requiring some technical and professional skills. "Occupational
and income changes have brought a vast heterogeneity to the labor
force. . . . Advanced specialization has made for finer distinctions

of status and a multiplication of occupational worlds."[41]

One result of this development is to complicate the claims of inheritance in the face of the training that these new positions demand. "The process of specialization makes *exact* occupational inheritance increasingly unlikely."[42] Much more importantly, advanced specialization makes partial mobility more likely, and this will engender almost the same deleterious impact on class consciousness as results from the full mobility sought and experienced by aspirants. Cued to be aware of mobility, we become sensitive to it and tend to inflate the true value of even minor occupational improvement. Because the range of one's expectations is narrow and tied to one's original place on the economic hierarchy, these slight indications of personal progress have much of the psychologically gratifying effects that large advances would have. The creation of minor career ladders within a much larger hierarchy postpones frustrations and extends the mobility expectations of individuals. Opportunities for advancement increase, while at the same time the rewards for each advance become less meaningful. Morris Rosenberg summarizes the political consequences of this development:

> It has been very plausibly suggested that a large number of minute rank differences in a bureaucratic hierarchy is likely to discourage unity among workers for two reasons: first, members tend to view one another in terms of superiority-inferiority instead of equality; and second, workers on an equal level feel antagonistic and competitive toward one another on the basis of their struggle to obtain the next slightly higher position. In both cases consciousness of class unity among these people is undermined. Rather than feeling united against a common class enemy, they feel mutual distrust on the basis of their struggle against one another.[43]

The actual extent of advancement is small, but the impact on class consciousness is substantial. The attitudes and behavior of those individuals climbing this attenuated career ladder exhibit the same divisiveness as would be expected from the fully upwardly mobile. In addition, the probability of some advancement ensures that the ambitious, now rewarded, will hold a sense of obligation toward the system as it is presently constituted. After all, so the feeling goes, "If I can make it, so can you."

To some degree, partial mobility of the sort just described is simulated mobility. It is the magnifying of slight amounts of improvement that makes the positions attained seem more prestigious and higher on the authority hierarchy (but not nearly as progressive in terms of the measurable quality of income) than they really are. Our society has various means of simulating mobility, thereby inflating one's true class and station. An often cited example is the rise in title (which implies an upgrading in position) without any commensurate difference in career chances, income levels, or work responsibilities (e.g., private secretary reclassified as administrative assistant). The upgrading of manual into nonmanual occupations simulates mobility into the middle class and thus moderates loyalties to working-class groups.[44] A parallel development is the professionalization (through degree programs, professional associations, technical journals) of previously nonprofessional job categories.[45] But with this trend has also come a proletarianization of many white-collar occupations. The assembly-line operation of large offices (rows of desks, routinized work) attests to the blending of white and blue collar—the "buffer zone" discussed above.

Mobility is often built into the job itself. "Age phasing" for middle-class positions[46] and the promotional privileges of seniority for factory workers (as well as for schoolteachers) artificially induce mobility expectations. More deserving aspirants are somehow delayed as others slowly rise to the top (or what is assumed to be the top) of their respective ladders without competition from newcomers. Slight mobility, even that which is normally expected as a result of institutionalized recognition of increased experience and skill, is mobility nevertheless, with all its psychological ramifications. Also to the point, advancement through a bureaucracy rather than through business entrepreneurship creates vague and indeterminate signs and steps of progress. Uncertainty about career lines allows people to confuse dead-end positions with "grooming and seasoning" posts. Blocked mobility is often given other rewards that belie the actual prospects of the individual. When the signs of stagnation can be misinterpreted as improvement, then mobility perceptions will invariably outdistance reality.[47]

Finally, there are other forms of mobility that can substitute for or give the appearance of actual economic advancement. Basic changes in residence—farms to cities, cities to suburbs, Europe to the United States—or even geographic movement in and of itself can easily be misunderstood and inflated. The assumption that change equals progress works here as well, with consequences on the potential of class unity; "in . . . blue collar occupational groupings (where geographic mobility is not intrinsic to the job), such mobility is probably a good indicator of the weakness of class community."[48] The most frequently cited surrogate of mobility is education. The actuality of higher educational opportunity sustains the belief in increased social and economic opportunity. However, higher educational attainment does not guarantee upward mobility; more likely, the stress we place upon education tends to justify the superior position of the educated. To some extent, therefore, the belief in education acts as an intermediary obstacle, insulating class divisions while diverting lower-class strivings toward system-supportive processes. Educational success becomes not only a necessary condition for economic success but quite often a substitute for it. "Thus, many mobility studies based on a set of broad occupational categories probably underestimate the extent of psychologically and socially relevant mobility."[49] For the partial success stories, the structured simulation of mobility and opportunity (itself a result of economic growth), while not reflected in statistics, is a major source of support for the economic system and, therefore, for consensus politics.[50]

The Failures. In discussing the attitudes of the partially successful, we are also confronting the issue of the political consequences of partial failure. Gratitude is easy enough to understand, but why have these dreamers not been highly frustrated and highly animated with the meager lengths that their ambitions and strivings took them? How can a society, which emphasizes opportunity so much in legitimizing its distribution of material rewards, deal effectively with the feelings of those who have had hardly any gains from the opportunity promised them? The first reaction to this critical question is that a large number of aspirants feel, justifiably or not, that some improvement in their relative situation has or will inevitably occur. Admittedly, this is not equivalent to the rags-to-riches stories of Horatio Alger, although *that* dream dies hard for many Americans. However, more feasible and attainable goals eventually motivate our conscious behavior; one's position and life chances modify one's expectations. Not surprisingly, achievements within these reduced parameters may elicit magnified feelings of accomplishment and therefore mobility. Reference groups for skilled workers are most frequently other groups within the working class, not relatively better-off, mid-level office personnel. Continued comparisons with less affluent members of the same class result in heightened satisfaction for those at the top of the manual working-class ladder.[51] Obviously, it is more satisfying to meet traditional aspirations, to see how far one has come, than to look up at heights never to be attained. Relative deprivation is kept at moderate, stable levels due to the selective perceptions and narrowed range of comparisons that disadvantaged individuals employ.

Simulated mobility, lowered aspirations, and nonthreatening reference groups do not soften the pangs of failure for many Americans who have never known even partial achievement and mobility. Ironically, it is the emphasis on the success ethic that insures that these feelings are not transformed into anger toward and rejection of the economic promises (and mechanisms) of mobility: "the American culture tells its members: 'achieve,' 'compete,' 'be better, smarter, quicker, richer than your fellow men'; in short, 'be unequal.' "[52] This appeal for individual achievement operates in conjunction with the belief that sufficient opportunity to succeed is available within the present economic system. Consequently, when expectations are not met, individuals hold themselves responsible in accounting for lack of mobility. The anxieties, self-doubts, frustrations, and humiliation associated with failure are the distorted mirror images of those emotions (gratitude and obligation) associated with upward mobility. "The notion of equality of opportunity . . . places responsibility on the individual for social failure while attributing successes to the institutions."[53] Because the psychic and social price of failure is so high, people tend to inflate their own success and claim more self-satisfaction with their position than is actually experienced. The attempt to deceive others as to one's own real economic condition leads people to believe more in the rhetoric of opportunity and thereby to place blame for failure more squarely on their own shoulders.

To avoid the emotional traumas of failure, a whole host of excuses, rationalizations, and psychological outlets are employed. Lipset and Bendix point to two common patterns that help to soften the pains of internalized blame:

(1) transvaluational religion, which teaches that the good rather than the rich will be rewarded in an afterlife; and (2) a high degree of child-centeredness that encourages parents to seek satisfaction in high aspirations for their children when their own personal goals have not been achieved.[54]

As to the former pattern, many individuals minimize the importance of class distinctions. The belief in social equality allows the disadvantaged to take refuge in the well-refuted myths that the rich are not happy or have more ulcers and mental worries or have a less satisfying home life. The playing up of working-class satisfactions and the minimizing of benefits associated with wealth are attempts to shift value priorities, although not in so institutionalized a fashion as a transvaluational religion. The minimizing of the importance of class differences reduces frustration by claiming that the prize is not always worth the effort.

Lipset and Bendix's reference to the promise of intergenerational mobility is vital in understanding how failure is dealt with in system-supportive ways. The promise of success, indeed the whole American Dream itself, has never been denied—merely delayed and then renewed. Through one's children, hope breathes eternal for the American Dream's dreamers. Whether stressing educational attainment, artistic or sports talents, beauty (which improves one's chances of "marrying up"), or business sense, the parents' raising of a child expresses those qualities that are thought to be translatable into economic success. The impact of this form of mobility on class consciousness may be less than that of other, more directly (personally) experienced, forms; but as a mechanism for perpetuating the sense of opportunity, even after the final distribution of positions and rewards has occurred, it is effective enough.

Resignation, in one of a number of disguises, is the most common reaction to failure for those who have few realistic defenses and stratagems on which to fall back. Many, recognizing their relative economic situation, try to gain maximum psychological advantage out of their acceptance. The most typical reflection of resignation is apathy ("the race is over, the pressure is off"). Another related attitude stems from the admission of individual responsibility for one's disadvantaged position; the corollary notion to this admission is that wealth and high station are earned.

Thus, workers who accept a paternalistic relationship toward their superiors take comfort in being guided by a seemingly natural elite.[55] Identifying with upper-class life-styles and personalities is a vicarious substitute for real mobility. In addition, the economically and socially disfavored can participate in the spirit (if not the substance) of national growth and power, gaining satisfaction through identification with the perpetually victorious home team—the United States. The hope for intergenerational mobility is also a form of vicarious mobility. While these reactions may be less than adequate personal substitutes for real advancement, they are nevertheless effective politically in inhibiting resentment and moderating frustration.

An additional aspect of the resignation-acceptance response to failure, one that is the most telling of all, is the prevalence of gambling as a means of achieving upward mobility for those with no other realistic possibilities. Gambling is, of course, a method of rekindling hope in the success ethic, but it also reflects a view many people have toward their economic fate.

> We are easily inclined to think that a man gets what he deserves, that rewards are primarily products of one's talents and industry, secondarily the consequence of luck, and only in small part the function of properties of the social-cultural structure.[56]

Another's economic success, if interpreted as the result of chance happenings, is less threatening to our self-respect than if it seems to be an indication of his merit and, therefore, our relative lack of merit; "the goddess of chance, as of justice, is blind."[57] By derationalizing the processes of mobility operating within society, by minimizing the rule-governed nature of the opportunity contest, the public also depoliticizes mobility, putting the "rules" beyond the bounds of human understanding or collective control. This final psychological stratagem is perhaps indicative of all the mechanisms by which individuals deal with economic failure within the confines of consensus politics. "It is this tendency for the underclass to throw up symbolic systems which explain their life situation in secular, non-political terms which is perhaps the most important of the 'safety-valves' [maintaining stability in an inegalitarian society]."[58] For the vast majority of Americans unable to fulfill the promises of the American Dream, some combination of resignation, rekindled hope, and psychological defense explains the generally moderate nature of their reaction to their disadvantaged condition.

All this is not meant to deny that unrest exists. Ideological claims of opportunity and mobility unbounded inevitably conflict with the awareness of upper-class privileges and a partially closed class system. Expectations evoked through the culture's socialization process are never totally met, and the gap between promise and the perceived reality represents potential political tensions. As long as the gap is not too large, as long as economic growth ensures certain "adequate" levels of class fluidity or partial advancement, then the ideological supports will be effective in lessening these tensions. By enlarging perceptions of mobility, the society tries to align aspiration to achievement. Failing that, numerous factors protect the legitimacy of the economic system by diverting blame, providing personal outlets and psychological defenses to deal with failure, and, in general, promoting attitudes and behavior patterns that depoliticize failure and insulate inegalitarian distributive arrangements.

Yet, it is undeniable that the rhetoric cannot totally explain or excuse the reality; the gap is too wide to be fully bridged. For minorities, especially, the system is rigged in very transparent ways. Speeches proclaiming equal opportunity and the rewarding of merit cannot cover over the obvious ease with which people from upper-class backgrounds maintain their position or the obvious obstacles confronting disadvantaged individuals in their quest of higher station. We might therefore expect more instability in consensus politics were it not for an additional mechanism supplementing the moderating influence of mobility. Chapter 3 now turns to an analysis of this factor and of the means by which it, too, bolsters the stratification status quo.

Shared Prosperity

Shared Prosperity and Relative Deprivation

The ability of economic growth to mitigate class consciousness and thereby preserve economic inequality is not solely a consequence of the effects of growth on levels of economic opportunity and social mobility. The American Dream of economic affluence continues to dominate working-class consciousness even after expectations of *individual* mobility have been dashed.[59] Economic growth provides the disadvantaged with another alternative route toward affluence within an inegalitarian distributive system. In economist Henry C. Wallich's words, "Growth is a substitute for equality of income. So long as there is growth, there is hope, and that makes large income differentials tolerable."[60] Unlike mobility aspirations, which offer possibilities of affluence only to the extent that individuals struggle as individuals to move from their working-class or middle-class situations, the alternative path to a better material existence evolves out of a person's self-definition as part of the working or middle class (or at least a clear segment of those classes). Optimism about the future stems from the hope that, as a member of an economic grouping, one will gain in real wages and living standards as the nation grows; being part of the whole, one will be able to share in the general prosperity of the economy. Expectations of shared affluence, like expectations of individual mobility, are somewhat overstated. But conceptually and concretely, these expectations operate to minimize class consciousness and mitigate class conflict. The high standard of living enjoyed by most Americans, coupled with their belief that the nation's economy and therefore their own economic situation will improve over time, helps to deflect attention from the inequities of the stratification system, thus preventing the presentation of redistributive demands that threaten consensus politics.

There is a basic objection to measuring national well-being by reference to increases in average living standards. The "economic abundance thesis" is "based on the notion that absolute rather than relative deprivation is the primary source of labor radicalism."[61] The argument raised against this assumption needs to be explored and in some way refuted in order to continue to maintain the connection between growth and acquiescence.

While economic growth promises to meet our physical and psychic needs, it may be the case that only redistributive policies will truly suffice. Richard A. Easterlin examined data from thirty separate surveys relating happiness and income.[62] Within all societies, as individual income rose, so did measures of individual happiness. However, raising the income levels of all had little or no effect on happiness levels. For example, between 1940 and 1970, the United States experienced a 60 percent increase in real income, but, according to Easterlin's surveys, no appreciable change oc-

curred in overall levels of perceived contentment, security, satisfaction, etc. One explanation of these findings is that evaluations
of one's material well-being arise in a cultural context of expectations regarding what is the norm. Admittedly, Americans in the
1950s through 1970s generally have enjoyed higher levels of real
wages than have past generations.

> But this is no consolation at all, for their needs have been shaped in
> this society today. There is no divinely-ordained standard of adequacy
> for housing, diet, medical care, education, entertainment, etc. What
> feels adequate is inescapably dependent upon what is available to others
> in the society.[63]

The fact that deprivation is comparatively and contextually determined does not make it any less grating. The connection in the
public's mind between relative income or position and images of
worthiness (or worthlessness) is not erasable through the mechanism of shared prosperity. One can argue that, even within a context of increasing general prosperity, inequality will inevitably
foster envy, frustration, humiliation, and deprivation. It is significant that a high rate of economic growth tends to inhibit the
achievement of equality of condition—that is, it widens the absolute gap between income groups—even as it promotes prosperity
among society as a whole. Thus, relative deprivation has been increasing. The import of this line of reasoning for consensus politics
is clear: to grievances arising out of stratification, only economic
redistribution can respond.

This argument, powerful in its logic, tends more to implore than
to explain. The truth is that, within the context of a consumerist,
materialist, individualist perspective, improvements in living standards and real wages do have a moderating influence on class consciousness and class conflict. Relative deprivation may affect social and personal happiness, but the reality of material abundance
as discussed above and the ideological supports underlying our
economic system prevent the easy transformation of unhappiness
into social discontent. The perception of affluence, like the perception of mobility and opportunity, is in large part the consequence of the conceptual screen through which we interpret our
economic situation. To understand why feelings of relative deprivation have not led to redistributive economic demands, we must

examine the way in which members of the working class view their own economic circumstances relative to those of other groups in society.

The relative deprivation thesis ignores a form of mobility that is perceptually meaningful for lower- and lower-middle-class people. The accumulation of savings and possessions, even if in conjunction with a similar development by one's neighbors, is not without its benefits. "Entry into the propertied sector of the working class was . . . an important form of social mobility."[64] Clearly, the worker is using his economic situation at an earlier stage as his current reference point. This comparison implicit in "goods mobility" leads us to believe that individuals might sense an improvement in their situation over time and gain satisfaction from such progress, the Easterlin data notwithstanding. "A man who can buy his own house, or a new car, will feel that he has moved up in the world even if he has not changed his occupational position."[65]

An additional factor often overlooked by those who belabor the relative deprivation argument is the indeterminacy of most material inequality. Differences in consumption styles have to a great extent been narrowed due to overall increases in wealth:

> the emergence of mass production during the past half-century has caused such a redistribution of highly valued prestige symbols that the distinctions between social classes are much less immediately visible than they were in nineteenth-century America.[66]

Qualitative differences aside, the distribution of, say, automobiles or television sets is egalitarianizing in its impact on people's perceptions of injustice, plenty, hope, etc. In effect, the idea of "goods equality" in an affluent society—by this I do not mean to imply that such equality actually exists—is a second aspect of the classlessness myth as introduced in the discussion of social mobility. A leveling of the ownership of material possessions, consumption equality of a sort, is compensation to the working and lower middle classes for a continued lack of political and economic leveling. Karl Marx might be correct in predicting the *proletarianization* (downward occupational mobility) of the independent middle class. However, he was obviously wrong in anticipating the *pauperization* (downward consumption mobility) of the working class. And it is our self-images as consumers, not producers, that are most dominant on our consciousness. The reality of inequality and relative deprivation must be placed in this context.

A further point on the goods mobility argument concerns the distinction to be made between types of goods and services. The distribution of the latter (health, education, recreation) and some elements of the former (the quality of food, clothing, and shelter) are highly inegalitarian but also relatively invisible. Upper-class luxury items (jewelry, multiple dwellings, a yacht, numerous high-priced automobiles) lack functional relevance for most Americans. Such expenditures appear frivolous, to be envied without resentment.

The relative deprivation that does surface is deeply felt. However, its structural roots are not apparent. Jealousy, rising expectations, and demeaning comparisons are interpreted not as products of our economic system (via inequality, advertising, etc.) but as elements in human nature, the signs and pains of striving and ambition:

> average people are not able to translate their personal problems into public issues and to discuss them at that level. Their world of complaints and enthusiasms is denied the means by which to transcend the interpersonal world and place that world within the wider structures of society. [67]

The unhappiness to which relative deprivation gives rise is directed away from displeasure with the economic system and instead is transformed into frustration with oneself.

One final qualification of the relative deprivation thesis alludes to a point made earlier. The reference group we use to evaluate our own level of affluence in large measure determines how we view our economic circumstances. Thus, control over our perception of the group to which we compare ourselves is a critical factor in maintaining economic and political stability. Promoting the use of lower-class reference groups (e.g., comparing our standard of living with citizens in India) helps to heighten our perception and appreciation of goods mobility and thus encourage a false consciousness of the true range of wealth and income levels in our economy. But we need not go out of our national borders to be confronted with reference groups worse off than the average American.

The Negroes have formed a distinctive American proletariat, with the lowest incomes, the most menial and subservient tasks, and the lowest social prestige . . . of any group in American society. The existence of this large, relatively homogeneous, easily identifiable, and exploited group has meant that every white American, even the lowest paid laborer, possesses a certain social prestige which raises him, at least in his own view, above the level of a proletarian.[68]

As has been often demonstrated, the concept of relative deprivation is intimately and inseparably associated with the concept of reference group. Society can minimize the former through careful manipulation of the latter.

The relative deprivation thesis states that shared prosperity does not mitigate against redistributive politics because it does not solve the problem of invidious distinctions. This argument has merit, but, stated in its extreme form, it ignores the ideological supports and perceptual screens that have successfully defused the class issue in U.S. politics. The mass of Americans for a long time have been denied the conceptual resources necessary to understand and evaluate the social morality and personal consequences of stratification.

It became difficult for workers and farmers to define their opposition to elites, for the separateness of elite and mass was obscured rather than clarified by ideological developments. . . . [Thus] the philosophy of economic expansion had entrenched itself as the popular answer to American problems [of inequality and deprivation].[69]

Most people, products of a very effective socialization process, do not possess the ability to evaluate their personal circumstances free of the biasing influence of the dominant ideology. In fact, the ideology of shared prosperity not only minimizes the disruptive impact of relative deprivation upon our attitudes toward the stratification system. As the next section demonstrates, it also creates a highly system-supportive framework for class interaction while at the same time encouraging working-class compliance with economic arrangements.

The Ideology of Shared Prosperity

The continued strength of consensus politics hinges on the continued prosperity of the nation's economy. To the extent that this prosperity is more reality than rhetoric, there exists the possibility of labor's progressing within the boundaries of the existing social and economic structure, "thereby lessening the attraction of those political appeals propounding the inevitable deterioration of living and working conditions under capitalism."[70] Given this perspective, a good dose of political caution is quite justified. The worker who believes that he has a stake in the future is not a ready target for redistributive politics and the unknown consequences such a change may entail.

> Once the worker has won a position of basic economic security and reasonable expectations he has considerably more reason to be conservative on social issues than the middle-class executive or professional man. . . . For the workingman, everything could be jeopardized by radical change.[71]

The national goal of economic growth dampens class consciousness, while the behavior associated with gaining one's share of the growing economic pie mitigates against class conflict. The remainder of this section explores each of these two themes.

Our cultural and social obsession with economic expansion plays a major role in inhibiting the growth of class consciousness. The following discussion examines the highly conservative implications of our concern with growth. While I do not want to imply that this position has totally persuaded the disadvantaged sectors of society into acquiescing in their fate, it has had and continues to have an impact. To the extent that the following line of reasoning influences class attitudes and perceptions, it serves to diminish the ability of deprived groups to think in terms of group antagonisms and redistributive demands.

The primary assumption in the shared prosperity thesis is that economic growth is a social goal that unites all economic groups, a national project that ought to consume our collective energies and loyalties. Economic growth has historically led to economic integration and interdependence. The trends of economic rationalization (e.g., division of labor, large-scale organizations, hierarchical authority structure) lead to a blending of talents and functions for all groups in society. Each segment, so the argument goes, is part of a larger organic unity—the economic system—and must be dedicated in function and attitude toward one common goal—the preservation and growth of the economy. In operating with that objective in mind (or in being constrained from obstructing that objective), we improve not only the whole but also its parts. Like the mutually beneficial relationship between parts of an environmental system, the economic system profits from its own naturally evolved symbiotic interactions. Adam Smith's "invisible hand" guides as well as legitimizes the economy. The doubters of this American Business Creed need only look at the outcome—affluence and opportunity—to reinforce their wavering loyalty. "Both the material and the non-material achievements are explained by a rigid cause-and-effect link with the System: the achievements flow from and validate the System, and the two are inseparably bound together."[72] The normative implications are obvious. We praise the shared affluence stemming from our growing economy, thus unavoidably supporting the economic relationships that supposedly contribute to and are such an integral part of economic growth.

In accepting the collective goal of economic growth, working-class groups commit themselves to the economic givens upon which future prosperity is premised. Inequality may not be wholeheartedly embraced as part of the natural way of things, but it is a central aspect of the economic order and, as such, probably is indispensable to the overall functioning of the system. If, as is claimed, U.S. business is responsible for our growth, then to successfully attack business privileges, including, of course, the wealth that accrues to business leaders, is to somehow weaken the ability of the economy to continue its climb. Likewise, such sacred economic tenets as property rights, the free market, minimal governmental involvement, and managerial authority are accepted, if only in part, as sharing credit for past and future economic growth.

Belief in this ideological framework carries with it the perception of very conservative class interrelations as part of the economic givens. A survey among New Jersey textile workers revealed a surprising tendency to invoke the standard defenses of social stratification in explaining the inevitability and desirability of the class system. In reviewing some of the responses to their questionnaire, the authors concluded, "The members of different classes are thus seen to serve complementary needs of the society and of each other."[73] This almost feudalistic acceptance of inequality parallels a highly paternalistic notion of class roles. Dichotomous views of society, long thought to be connected to levels of class conscious-

ness (e.g., the rich versus the rest of us), also reveal a strong paternalistic streak (smart versus fools, the intelligent or educated
versus the masses).[74] Feelings of obligation and inferiority toward
the economic elite (or its corporate representatives) undermine
the growth of radical class consciousness by offering a more conservative self-definition of economic roles and responsibilities.

Partnership rather than paternalism describes the class relationship for others seeking the shared gains of economic growth. This
aspect of the American Business Creed is a central theme of corporate public relations. For example:

> How have we achieved all this [progress]? Through the American
> kind of teamwork! And what is teamwork?
> American teamwork is managers that pays [sic] reasonable wages
> and takes fair profits. . . .
> Our teamwork is labor that produces as efficiently and as much as it
> can—that realizes its standard of living ultimately depends upon how
> much America produces—that expects better wages as it helps increase
> that production. . . .
> It will continue to take teamwork, but if we work together, there's
> no limit on what we can all share together of even greater things.[75]

The "teamwork" theme stresses the common interest that both
labor and management have in the goal of growth. In the process, this appeal overtly tries to minimize class consciousness
by ignoring the reality of economic antagonisms and conflicts
of interest.

Continuing this argument, workers are said to have a stake
in and responsibility for the economy through their partial control
of a major element of economic success—productivity.

> The rise in real wages in the last few decades . . . has not been due to
> any direct influence of labor unions on wages. . . . It is the rise in the
> total product itself, however, especially the product per man . . . which
> has been the major factor in the long-run increase in real wages.[76]

Productivity and teamwork explain a beneficently functioning
economy. Politicizing the system by demanding gains over and
above productivity increases may result in specific victories but
with deleterious consequences on long-range class unity. "While
the power to strike can redistribute income in favor of the mem-

bers of particular unions, it cannot redistribute income in favor of labor in general at the expense of capital in general."[77] The claim is made that such gains as are won by that method undercut the viability and future growth of the industry, occupation, factory, region, etc. Thus, worker concern with wages is often understandably directed at improving the employer's ability to pay.

An additional consequence of the ideological perspective presented here has to do with the prevalence of the work ethic. Work at all levels of the occupational hierarchy is ennobling, performing a necessary function for the economic system. We should take pride in that function and do the best job we are capable of doing. More importantly, we should remain loyal to the larger unit upon whose success our own success rests. The work ethic evolves out of expectations of mutual progress, paralleling the success ethic's expectations of social mobility. The implicit promise is that if we do our job, we will grow with the company, region, industry, nation, etc. The extent to which this promise mitigates class consciousness is a function of the actual economic improvements that have been experienced. The recent decline in the effectiveness of the work ethic is a sign of disillusionment. Hard work seems to go unrewarded, while others succeed despite a seeming lack of worthiness. Even so, the ethic has a conservative impact on the class consciousness of segments of society.

Acceptance of the goal of economic growth tends to force an acceptance of conservative decision-making processes. Once the commitment has been made to the goal, the values of technical efficiency and rationality provide the means by which the end can be achieved. But these values depoliticize the conflict. "Politics and rationality are considered antithetical to each other. The developmental process is characterized by the replacement of politics with technology."[78] Deference to expertise becomes the order of the day. Consequently, worker involvement in the carrying out of economic growth policies is discouraged as counterproductive interference by untrained laymen; it signifies the threatened interjection of conflict in what is basically an issue of objective technique and scientific administration. However, this view, if conceded by disadvantaged groups in society, is not without an important impact on the possibilities of class conflict and redistributive policies. The engineering approach to the goal of economic growth is inherently biased in favor of consensual strategies. As Clark Kerr observes:

The experts help settle the inevitable conflicts of interest on the basis of facts and analysis, and also with an eye to preservation of the existing system, rather than on principle except for a general attachment to the concept of a reasonable and balanced society.[79]

In this regard, any structural criticism of the economy that would spawn redistributive demands is rejected; such an analysis is ideological and utopian (not objective and scientific) and thus dangerous in its potential impact. The working class, not privy to the "knowledge" of the experts and denied the conceptual tools to challenge their biases and assumptions, defers its judgment. Once again, the vision of a mutually beneficial prosperity has impaired the class consciousness of disadvantaged groups. They have been led to believe that class considerations are irrelevant to certain areas of decision making. As a result, they have, in effect, disenfranchised themselves.

Teamwork, an important aspect of the ideology of shared prosperity, is more a slogan than a statement of interclass relations. The actual substance of this relation is predicated upon the ability of economic growth to provide mutual benefit. In the absence of common interests, the ideological invocation of the teamwork theme is a screen to cover actions beneficial to an elite and harmful to most others. The following statement by David Potter compares European and U.S. perspectives on the appropriate means by which improvements in one's standard of living can be achieved. With not surprising bias, he notes the effect of economic growth in shaping the U.S. proclivity toward class cooperation. Affluence and abundance has

given a characteristic tone to American equalitarianism as distinguished from the equalitarianism of the Old World. Essentially, the difference is that Europe has always conceived of redistribution of wealth as necessitating the expropriation of some and the corresponding aggrandizement of others; but America has conceived of it primarily in terms of giving to some without taking from others. Hence, Europe cannot think of altering the relationship between the various levels of society without assuming a class struggle; but America has altered and can alter these relationships without necessarily treating one class as the victim or even, in an ultimate sense, the antagonist of another. The European mind often assumes implicitly that the volume of wealth is fixed; that most of the potential wealth has already been converted into actual wealth; that this actual wealth is already in the hands of owners; and, therefore, that the only way for one person or group to secure more is to wrest it from some other person or group, leaving that person or group with less. . . . The American mind, by contrast, often assumes implicitly that the volume of wealth is dynamic, that much potential wealth still remains to be converted; and that diverse groups—for instance, capital and labor—can take more wealth out of the environment by working together than they can take out of one another by class warfare.[80]

We may object to Potter's descriptive accuracy—the distinction is not as clear-cut nor is the process of cooperation as nonmanipulative as the above quote implies. Yet, an important point has been raised regarding the mechanism by which mutually beneficial arrangements are reached. A standard analogy is often made comparing the situation in which two individuals fiercely battle over the division of a fixed economic pie with the situation in which conflict over the division of the pie (the issue of relative shares) is subsumed by cooperation in enlarging the pie (economic growth), thereby ensuring a larger absolute piece for each. This conceptualization of the above comparison in Potter's statement forms the gist of most arguments favoring the moderation of redistributive demands. The potentiality of shared prosperity via economic growth makes class conflict counterproductive. "A politics of compromise has flourished in this atmosphere as one person's gain has not been another's loss."[81] In the next section, I want to examine this theme from the point of view of game theory to see what light such a perspective can shed on the stability of the stratification system and the lack of redistributive politics.

Game Theory as a Demonstration of the Theory of Shared Prosperity

The dichotomy in perspectives that formed the basis of Potter's quotation is explained in game theory as the difference between two types of game situations. In two-person, constant-sum (also called zero-sum) games, the sum of the payoffs going to both players is always the same, and what is at stake is the share or proportion of the total that each side will receive. Conflict of interest is inevitable, cooperation is useless. Antagonism is built into the game. An example follows:

Player 2

		a	b
Player 1	A	−1, +1	+1, −1
	B	+1, −1	−1, +1

Each player chooses a strategy—Player 1, a row, and Player 2, a column—and the cell that is selected from the conjunction of these strategies determines the rewards or penalties for that round. The first number in the cell represents the payoff for Player 1, the second for Player 2. Obviously, in this game, indeed in all zero-sum games, when one player progresses, the other by definition regresses. Potter's perception of European class politics takes this form. Classical Marxian analysis also believed that the interests of the classes (players) were diametrically opposed.

Therein lies the problem for radical theorists. They have been forced to admit that productivity increases have allowed advances in real wages. Economic growth has enabled capitalism to avoid the potentially explosive antagonisms inherent in constant-sum games. The ability of the system to legitimately promise gains for everyone "is precisely the aspect of capitalist economics emphasized by those who wish to direct attention away from the 'class struggle.' "[82] The social and economic flexibility possible in an expanding economy reflects a *partial* coincidence of class interests. The two-person, positive-sum (nonzero-sum) game is therefore more appropriate as a descriptive tool.

The positive-sum game can be structured to become conducive to a search for collective strategies (a form of behavior that is precluded in constant-sum games). Maximizing one's own return often involves an awareness of the other player's interests. Thus, the strategies of bargaining, negotiation, and compromise, so prevalent in the political system, are integral aspects of games of this variety, making them useful lenses through which we may analyze class interaction. The following example demonstrates the point:

Player 2

		a	b
Player 1	A	−1, −1	+3, 0
	B	0, +3	+2, +2

Player 1 will prefer outcome A,b, while Player 2 desires B,a. If each aims for his most advantageous outcome, the result, A,a, would leave both worse off. However, the players can reach an agreement to accept B,b, maximizing their total payoff and insuring a fair reward for each. The process of reaching a satisfactory agreement is abetted greatly if certain conditions are absent and others are present. For instance, while a purely cooperative spirit between the participants is not a necessary element of this game, it is undoubtedly true that intense feelings of envy and spite are irrational, inappropriate, and counterproductive attitudes. Game players must somehow curb their rivalist mentality in order to profit from the game's cooperative structure. Also, assuming the ability to communicate with an opponent, the possibility of making binding agreements lessens problems of distrust and greatly facilitates the recognition of complementary interests and the search for accommodative strategies. Sociologically speaking, tension is reduced by the existence of both a common interest in a mutually beneficial outcome and a set of conditions conducive to strategies of cooperation.

It is possible to solidify this relationship (and to make the game more realistic in terms of the analogy I am developing) by introducing a third perhaps hypothetical player against whom the original players align in order to increase their total payoff. If nature—the physical environment in which the economic system operates—is viewed as the third party, then a coalition of labor and management (or capital) versus nature for the purpose of maximizing material growth would cloud still further the perception of distinctive antagonistic economic interests. For theorists seeking to explain the low level of class conflict in an environment of high economic growth, the accommodative strategies associated with two-person, positive-sum games offer a touchstone from which an explanation can evolve.

Such an explanation also must take into account the inaccuracies and omissions found in the theory of shared prosperity, deficiencies that game theory is quite adept at reflecting. What we need to understand are the mechanisms of game play in a less idealized context. Inequality, among other factors, ought somehow to be incorporated in the game in order to determine the extent to which the theory of shared prosperity is merely a justificatory ideology or an idea with descriptive merit.

What first must be examined is the game's schedule of payoffs. Those used in the previous example are not indicative of the actual gamelike situation between labor and management. Look at the following as an illustration of a rather different two-person, non-zero-sum game.[83]

Player 2

		a	b
	A	1, 2	3, 1
Player 1	B	0, –200	2, –300

The usual assumption behind most games is that the power to follow a rationally chosen course of action eliminates the factor of coercion. The above example, however, demonstrates that bargaining leverage and, therefore, power considerations, are a function of payoff possibilities. While Player 2 would prefer outcome A,a, the threat of Player 1 selecting strategy B forces Player 2 to comply with his opponent's demand that A,b be agreed upon. The potential of such a threat will lead to an exploitive rather than a fair division of the spoils; feelings of injustice and resentment could potentially arise as if a zero-sum game were being played.

In terms of real-life examples of similar types of interaction, labor's demand for a fairer distribution of the total product may lead management to institute counter strategies (factory lockouts, strike breakers, capital investment directed to other regions or nations) that harm the workers much more than management. Redistributive demands handled in this manner deteriorate the union's position, encouraging labor strategies in keeping with consensus politics and economic inequality. In point of fact, the labor movement has gained in strength as it started to gain respectability and "play the game." The best *possible* labor strategy, the path of compromise and bargaining within the context of economic inequality, still may not be a pleasant option. Yet, the institutionalization of conflict, often singled out as an indication of consensus politics, might best be interpreted as *the begrudging acceptance by labor of the game's skewed schedule of payoff possibilities.* For other more disadvantaged segments of the economy, business's bargaining leverage is even greater, and thus the relative rewards are even more imbalanced. At this point, the psychological distinction between zero-sum and nonzero-sum games is highly blurred. The basic form of a positive-sum game can in this way hide elements of coercion and exploitation, belying the oft-stated accommodative nature of the game.

The concept of bargaining leverage is critical in understanding how the rewards of the game and of prosperity (economic growth) are shared. This factor is not simply a reflection of payoff possibilities; other elements of the game situation enter the picture. Witness this example.

		Player 2	
		a	b
Player 1	A	-2, -2	4, 1
	B	1, 4	3, 3

If each player aims for his most advantageous personal outcome, they both will end up with the worst collective result, A,a. The anticipated compromise solution, B,b, seems to be the most rational and fair choice if communication and negotiation are normal procedures of the game. However, imagine that Player 1 is quite able to afford payoffs of -2, while Player 2 is equally unable to tolerate that outcome for any extended period of time. In economic terms, Player 1 is wealthy, while his opponent is poor. This set of circumstances (discussed under "utility theory" in the parlance of game theorists) allows Player 1 to continually choose strategy A, forcing Player 2 to select strategy b or face the "financial" consequences. In short, the context of inequality allows the economic elite to maintain its strategy, even at a temporary loss, in order to force the working class to comply with a less desired outcome. The issue at hand is not so much the maximization of one's rewards as it is the long-run conflict over power, dominance, and submission.

Other elements of the economic game help to clarify the actual role that differential power plays in determining the "sharing" in our shared prosperity. The vast interdependence of the economy has effectively removed games with nature (farming, fishing, extraction industries) as viable *personal* options. For all intents and purposes, one must play within the economic system for, as the saying goes, "it's the only game in town." Once one has decided to play, the possibility of side payments represents a means by which seemingly redistributive results can be transformed into nonredistributive ones. Unions that conclude favorable wage agreements with management rarely protest the corporation's raising of prices. Finally, games in which one player does not know the actual payoffs give major advantages to the other player. A union may hesitate about being too militant in its demands upon being told that the company will fold (or cut back on personnel) if those demands are not moderate. Business, knowing the true size of the economic pie, can underestimate its ability to pay, thereby giving the appearance that some union goals are unattainable. The power of information is one of a number of factors putting into question the inherent justice of the positive-sum game.

How, then, can the theory of shared prosperity maintain its validity? The reason is that these games and their real-life counterparts do represent means by which opposing groups in society seek to benefit from economic growth, if not in equivalent amounts, then in proportion to their relative leverage in the game situation. Once the rules and context have been formulated and accepted, play proceeds according to plan; the outlines of the game fairly well determine the long-run behavior of the players. Yet, the style of play (accommodative) is as much a tribute to the *perception* of the game as it is to the game's true nature. If the structure of rewards becomes skewed even further toward economic elites, and if the gains from playing the game do not compensate for the felt injustice that may be brewing below the surface, then nonaccommodative behavior will become the norm rather than the exception. The game will approach the zero-sum ideal type in terms of the psychological attitudes it engenders. What prevents this escalation of antagonism is the fact that economic growth has provided a large enough payoff among deprived groups to justify the continuation of the game.

It is important to realize that the rewards, in game theory and in real life, are individualistic and quantitative. Our consumerist cultural biases allow the game analogy—and the processes of economic growth—to function as I have described. Anthony Giddens makes the same point in summarizing this section:

union-management clashes involving [issues of economic distribution] are in principle reconcilable in a way in which those over control [of the workplace] are not. For while at any given point in time there is only a fixed amount on the income "cake" to be divided between wages and profits, over an extended period the size of the "cake" can be increased, and hence wage increases can be exchanged against productivity agreements, etc. In the long-term, such a process can only operate . . . if there is a continuous rise in real incomes; but this is exactly what has been achieved by the capitalist economies in the twentieth century.[84]

Economic growth evokes a spirit of shared prosperity and promotes a set of procedures that institutionalize conflict within the bounds of current distributive arrangements.

Conclusions

Most people recognize the central role that economic growth plays in molding our spirit as a nation and our outlook on its future. "Every optimist speaking about the future of American society, heralding its potential if not its actual accomplishments, assumes some version of *national progress.*"[85] The merchandising of hope, as with most products on sale today, is directed toward filling basic structural needs along with personal desires. A 1975 *New York Times* survey sought to measure "confidence, expectations and aspirations" during a major economic downturn. The results revealed that the lessening of previously high levels of optimism had a marked impact on the acceptance of traditional ideological supports for the economic structure.

The survey . . . showed that a growing segment of the public had doubts about the doctrines it grew up with—that things will get better, and that, if they work hard, they will get the things in life they want: new home, a better job or other things deemed necessary for a completely fulfilled life.[86]

The maintenance of belief in these and similar system-supportive "doctrines" rests on the continuation of economic growth. This is the pivotal feature in our nation's makeup.

But is all this history? It may be argued that we can no longer

take for granted our ability to sustain the growth rates that consensus politics requires for stability. This self-doubt reflects an
expanding sentiment in the society, but it is still a minority position. A report published by the Committee for Economic Development pointedly summarizes the dominant attitude among those
endeavoring to perpetuate current arrangements: "Factors which
promote growth should be encouraged. Policies and activities that
can be identified as retarding growth should be opposed."[87]
The tone of security that we sense behind this statement harkens
back to an earlier era in U.S. political, economic, and social life.
New research on science and on society, in the domestic sphere
and internationally, has undermined that security for many Americans. Now as never before, a cloud hangs over the economic future
of the United States. While confident spokesmen may propound
the inevitability of permanent prosperity, an increasing number of
social and physical scientists, interest groups, critics, and economic
and political leaders, equally secure in their evidence, envision a
different fate for our nation: "Ahead lies the . . . formidable problem of a world in which growth may encounter ecological barriers
on a worldwide scale, bringing the need for new political and
economic arrangements for which we have no precedent."[88]

The conflict is thus joined. The issue then becomes which side
has the weight of evidence. But that analysis oversimplifies the
matter. In a debate so crucial to the social and political future of
the United States, we should be made aware that a mere weighing
of evidence is insufficient. The risks are too great, the consequences
too immense, for us to ignore the *possible* in a quest for the
probable. The following two chapters will examine the limits-to-
growth controversy. Their aim will be to see if there is enough
merit in the no-growth or slow-growth predictions to warrant an
examination of the potential impact that such a *plausible* development might have on the future of our political system. To err on
the side of optimism (continued growth) rather than caution
threatens to do a disservice to future generations who would have
welcomed our thoughtful handling of their world.

The Limits-to-Growth Debate:
The Physical Environment

Introduction

Limits to growth—the concept is as current as today's headlines but has a tradition of relevance that goes back to the droughts, floods, epidemics, and wars of primitive societies. The notion of limits to growth has flourished and faded in every era. Ours is no exception. The image has been reformulated and updated by numerous writers, the most widely quoted of which are the authors of *The Limits to Growth*. They state their position succinctly: "If the present growth trends in world population, industrialization, pollution, food production, and resource depletion continue unchanged, the limits to growth on this planet will be reached sometime within the next one hundred years."[1] This conclusion, seemingly sanctified by computer printouts, is not without its detractors. The cry of "wolf!" has been heard many times before. Yet, this flippant and oft-stated retort to the limits-to-growth position does not confront the issue on its merits and therefore does not effectively dispel the modern-day Malthusians. After all, in the fairy tale the wolf did eventually arrive. So the intellectual confrontation must take place anew in each era to see whether this time, unlike the past, the warnings and fears are justified.

Chapters 4 and 5 review the various aspects of the limits-to-growth debate. After sketching the outlines of the controversy, this chapter explores the evidence regarding the two most frequently cited threats to future industrial expansion. These are the limits to our supply of necessary raw materials, especially energy resources, and limits to our (and the environment's) tolerance of industrial effluents. In effect, trends with respect to some of the physical inputs (natural resources) and physical outputs (pollution) of our economic engine are causes of concern. Chapter 5 focuses on other major elements of the limits position that bear examination. Developments in the human environment take the form of an evolving complex of economic, social-psychological, and political-managerial problems that also may have a negative impact on long-term growth rates. Thus, in five specific areas the battle has been joined.

My organization of the material into five distinct areas of study should not obscure the interrelatedness of the topics addressed. A full analysis can be achieved only by examining each aspect of the debate in its relationship to the others and by appraising their collective influence on economic growth. Dennis Pirages alludes to the connections among these separate concerns: "Political conflict is conditioned by *both* physical and social environments. The physical environment . . . places constraints on economic and, indirectly, political possibilities. . . . Physical environmental conditions establish parameters within which social developments take place."[2] The physical context structures our social development by biasing our options and eliminating certain alternatives. In a similar manner, the human environment—economic, political, and social decisions and behavior—will influence developments in the physical environment. Funding of energy technologies is a case in point. In short, the fate of our nation's economy cannot be adequately discerned without systematically integrating the diverse elements of the debate. The conclusion of Chapter 5 will take up that task.

The Outlines of the Controversy

Extremist Rhetoric

First we must define the primary elements of the controversy. But this is a difficult task given the ever-changing nature of the subject matter. The issues get recast with each book, each teach-in, each television special. The strategies employed by the debaters further cloud the topic. While scientific accuracy becomes the stated objective of the combatants, in reality many proponents and opponents of the limits-to-growth thesis stereotype their opposition, present stacked alternatives, then portray their own position in terms of clichés and aphorisms. Doomsday paranoia battles growth mania, blind faith balances out blind fear, leaving the public both anxious and unenlightened. There is some inner need on the part of those scholars most involved in the controversy to establish or refute every point of the thesis and to do this with a degree of self-assuredness not in keeping with the evidence or the topic. The appeal to pessimism based upon the by now shopworn phrase of environmental protectionists, "if current trends continue," is as subject to doubt as is the professional optimist's claims of inevitable salvation through technology. Few seriously feel that this nation can and should blithely ignore current environmental, social, and economic crises; "full speed ahead" is the slogan of the lemming. Yet, on the other side, zero economic growth (ZEG) is an equally narrow slogan, equally without vision or realism. The preliminary goal of clarifying the issues is thus obstructed by the extremism and overkill of the debaters' rhetoric.

And yet, there is method in the madness of this style of confrontation. Extremism provides some tactical advantages in spite of its factual inaccuracies. Environmentalists are wary of the low social and political impact of less strident or sensationalistic presentations. The supporters of increased economic growth receive the public's attention every single day. Politicians, corporations, advertising firms, and our public ideology continually extol the material success of our economy. The costs of such growth are rarely mentioned or are grossly underestimated, while the more tangible benefits invariably get more than their share of publicity. In this context, extremist rhetoric can instill the social awareness and create the political clout needed in the battle for a moderate but effective policy response from government. This has been a common approach in the formation of other political movements.

There are, however, disadvantages to this style of political confrontation that may outweigh its tactical benefits. It stifles rational deliberation, offering policymakers no guide to the subtlety and complexity of the issues. Doomsday predictions of the future are counterproductive in other respects, too. They tend to overwhelm many listeners, undermining people's ability and determination to deal with specific and curable problems. Excessively gloomy forecasts also deflect our attention toward long-term obstacles and away from more immediate opportunities. Environmentalists deemphasize the potential positive impact of subjective factors such as human ingenuity, cooperation, social and psychological flexibility, thereby foreclosing possibilities for improvement. On the other hand, their opponents tend to take the adequacy and beneficence of these variables for granted. Finally, ecological hyperbole plants the seeds of disillusionment if "bad science" by some analysts weakens public faith in the many valid and well-substantiated points of the general hypothesis.

> The common justification [of the doomsday rhetoric] is to say that it is necessary to exaggerate to get people stirred, to get things done. But people are easily anesthetized by repetitions and there is a danger that, in spite of its achievements so far, the environmental movement could still find itself falling flat on its face when it is most needed, simply because it has pitched its tale too strongly.[3]

Thus, even in terms of its political utility, extremist rhetoric is suspect. We have to go beyond the popularly held half-truths, to cut past the rhetoric and approach the central issues in the limits-to-growth debate.

Crisis Perceptions and the Need for a "Futures" Awareness

One way to grapple with the issues presented in the controversy is to explore the conception of "crisis." Although the word "crisis" is much abused, in this context it is far from meaningless. The perception of a crisis situation in the human environment might be well-founded on evidence, but at heart it is a subjective evaluation, very much dependent on one's time perspective. Most people cannot think very much beyond the problems immediately facing them. Their identification with generations-to-come is weak. There is, therefore, a limit to the degree of "anticipatory decision making" they can be expected to make. Crises telescope our time framework by bringing the risks and options of the future closer to the present. Crises shock us out of the parochialism of routine existence.

In noncrisis circumstances, we have a highly short-term perception of the future, demonstrated by our understanding of growth, sacrifice, and investment. In general terms, economic growth involves sacrificing present consumption by diverting resources toward investment in order to increase future consumption. Thus, investment in new power plants, automobile assembly factories, roads and the like are expenditures for growth. Yet, benefits from such sacrifices are not long in coming; our investments promise relatively quick dividends, and these dividends usually imply an advance in living standards, not merely the maintenance of current life-styles. A radically different view of investment requires a longer time perspective. Following this new line of reasoning, we would continue to sacrifice present consumption—now defined in terms of decades or even generations—by *investing in the preservation of our existing stock of resources* in order to guarantee minimal levels of future consumption. Yet, since we consistently discount the long-run future, we are unable to pursue the type of sacrifice that is inherent in such a conservational understanding of investment.

The crux of this dilemma concerns differences not in time perceptions but rather in perceptions of a crisis regarding future levels of consumption. Examining the historical record, most observers can anticipate that future generations will be materially better off than we currently are; thus, long-range sacrifice involves an inegalitarian redistribution of wealth (and well-being) from the poorer present to the richer future. Yet, intergenerational redistribution of wealth can be justified as egalitarian if we envision a drastically reduced living standard for the citizens of the twenty-first century. As I have implied, the objective of our investments may be not only to increase future consumption levels but also to insure that future economic decline can be averted. This is what the time framework is all about—the plausibility of the limits-to-growth argument and the realization of the crises that surround that argument.

Progrowth advocates see little unique in our present predicament. The calls for intergenerational redistribution as discussed above rest on very uncertain grounds, and, given past trends, the likelihood is that the future will be better, not worse, than the present. What environmentalists see as immediate threats to society, growth advocates perceive as vague and very distant constraints on permanent industrial expansion. It would be foolish to turn our car to the left now because a passenger suspects that there might be a bend in the road three miles hence. Yet, we can use the same analogy to make the opposite point. It would be wise to slow down now in response to our rider's warnings, especially given: (1) the high and increasing speed of the vehicle (rate of growth and pace of change); (2) doubts regarding our ability to handle any necessary shift in direction (complexity, interdependence, limited knowledge); (3) the wobbliness of the car as it currently moves (environmental, social, economic, and international problems); and (4) the high risks associated with a lack of caution (disaster). It is still possible for people to recognize the possibility of a crisis even though there is little immediate and personal contact with the crisis events. We need not wait to see the mushroom clouds before we comprehend the dangers of nuclear warfare.

A "futures" awareness and the realization of a crisis situation will occur when people seriously perceive a connection between the short-run concern over the quality of their lives and the long-range interest in the survival of their society and species.[4] We are involved in a series of events any one of which can be viewed as a crisis point for any number of individuals. Without at least some elements of a crisis mentality, we would not be disposed toward the positive actions that crises encourage. In such a case, we would be heading farther and faster down the road, fearing the hypothetical turn instead of watching and perhaps preparing for it.

Narrowing the Idea of Limits to Growth

The preceding examination of crisis perceptions has served to clarify some of the issues arising out of the limits debate. Further understanding can be achieved by interpreting the crisis of growth as a matter of definition. This interpretation is not self-evident at first glance. Certain limits-to-growth spokesmen are quick to condemn *growth* as such. Garrett Hardin's formula brings things down to basics: Population X Prosperity = Pollution. Others have refused to label our ecological problems as an avoidable by-product of the growth process; rather, the assumption is that increased growth will invariably worsen the physical and social environment. Many have accurately countered this stance by noting that zero economic growth (ZEG) or the so-called stationary state is no solution because it does not assure us of ecological balance, the real goal of the growth critics. The general attack upon growth per se is part of the extremist rhetoric and strategic maneuvering that were discussed previously.

The posturing of pro- and antigrowth forces hides the real question we must face, a question that is at the same time more complex and more personal than we may have anticipated. Does *our* current mode of growth maximize the potential of our economy, our society, and our environment, or are we in fact systematically minimizing that potential now and for the future? The limits-to-growth debate should be viewed as a search for the answer to that question, as the following quote makes clear:

> The cutting edge of the environmental movement today is . . . a demand for change. People are opposing what we have called "growth" and "development" because that is the only way for them to express their concern at this stage. It is a holding action, yes; but in reality it is a demand for new goals and new directions.[5]

What is at stake are directions and goals, not, as some might imply, the existence of the economic, productive side of life: "the issue of growth versus no-growth is a sterile debate that distracts attention from the more important concerns of 'what kind of growth?' "[6]

The focus of the controversy, the object of so much ridicule and defense, is economic growth as defined and sought in the United States. Being the most prosperous nation on the earth, we exemplify both the promises and fears of growth. In truth, our reputation does not fully accord with the facts, at least as to recent history. Other nations, notably Japan and the Soviet Union, come closer to the paradigm case than we do. In many respects, they are more willing than the United States to sacrifice their mineral, ecological, and human resources to promote industrial development. However, our reputation is deserved enough. When critics decry growth, they are not denying the desirability of growth in social amenities (e.g., feeling of community, social justice, health care); they are not ignoring the broad range of economic arrangements that allow for material prosperity at various levels of environmental impact. Limits-to-growth proponents see the U.S. model as synonymous with the dominant productive mode of industrial society. It is growth in this sense, in perhaps the only sense we have come to understand, that requires limitations. Likewise, defenders of growth are implicitly using that same model, or else they would be demanding the institutional and ideological transformations long advocated by the other side. Growth has proceeded in this country as a result of a combination of factors and forces that for all intents and purposes prevent any major reversals of form. So it is quite realistic to initially define growth in terms of the U.S. example, knowing that alternative definitions do exist but that their present (immediate) economic, political, social, and ideological applicability to the United States is highly questionable. Within the confines of our political economy, the separate ideas of *limits to growth* and *a radically different definition of growth* are equivalent. Economic growth as exemplified by U.S. industrial expansion will be the focus of study for these chapters, the lens through which we can evaluate the many facets of the limits-to-growth hypothesis.

Central Themes of Chapters 4 and 5

Three major factors weave through the following analysis. Together they constitute the primary themes of the controversy. The first stresses the impact of technology on the strength and direction of economic growth. Besides examining the promised potential of technology, broadly defined to include economic, behavioral-scientific, and political-managerial skills, I discuss limitations on its successful application, including the conceptual biases (e.g., the technological as opposed to the ecological perspective) that reduce the full utilization of technology in solving the dilemmas surrounding growth. The second overarching element, the political variable, also has been defined broadly. It encompasses the attitudes and activities of a multitude of groups, institutions, individuals, and nations in the exercise of political, economic, or social power. Politics can be viewed as both a resource and an obstacle. Thus, we can note the possible contribution of public policy toward maintaining current growth rates and also the probable negative impact it may have, given the constraints of ideology, institutional procedures, power relationships, and the various circumstances surrounding the policymaking process. The final theme, the role of time, provides the drama to this issue. If we afford ourselves the luxury of endless deliberation, we will have discovered that events have overtaken us. The quickening pace of change—geometric or exponential growth—allows us little opportunity to pause. Time forever threatens to turn problems into crises, to transform remediable harm and danger into irreversible damage and disaster. It therefore creates extreme pressure on our technological, political, and psychological capacities to cope with new and hazardous circumstances. The working out of these three themes in our society will help to create the context for political change. The direction we take as a nation in confronting the threats to growth will by and large be the consequence of the intermeshing of these elements.

Natural Resources

The Problems of Dependence and Scarcity

The most easily conceptualized element of the limits-to-growth argument is the depletion of natural resources, especially those involved in energy production. The 1970s have made us aware of the increasing use (and waste) of nonrenewable raw materials. Even hard-nosed, progrowth economists admit that there inevitably are limits to resources in our finite world. Yet, that truism skirts the important question of what those limits are at a given time, with a given technology under given demand pressures, and within a given political context. The issue is basic, for natural resources are the food that our economy needs to sustain our life-style. This is no more true than in our appetite for energy. The signs of our affluence, the consumerist dreams of our future, are somehow plugged into our energy-intensive economy—clothes dryers, color televisions, second and third cars, and the single-family dwelling.

> An abundance of energy has become synonymous with a high standard of living and a healthy national economy. Indeed, a correlation between the gross national product and total U.S. energy consumption is often cited as evidence that continued economic growth depends on ever greater supplies of energy.[7]

The correlation has remained strong because, until recently, energy costs have risen more slowly than labor costs, thereby encouraging technological developments that substitute machines for workers. However, in gearing our economic growth to energy production and resource consumption, we have become more vulnerable as a nation to one of the physical constraints of our environment—the finite supply of raw materials.

Recent events underscore our vulnerability. Cutbacks, dislocations, and general hardship followed the 1973 Arab oil boycott. The absence of self-sufficiency in this vital area of our economy had a debilitating social impact on our national confidence and marked the start of a seemingly long-term drag on growth.

Higher prices for the necessary imports of oil and natural gas and the resulting huge trade deficits reconfirmed what one observer had pointed out a year before the boycott: "The Energy 'Joyride' Is Over."[8] Additional verification was provided by the harsh winter of 1977. Natural gas cutbacks and massive worker layoffs revealed that imbalances in our distribution system can lead to the same harmful consequences as actual resource shortages. Our energy economy operates without a large energy cushion, and thus we are quite unable to deal with temporary unexpected events.

Our dependence on foreign suppliers for natural gas and low-sulphur oil (the most environmentally sound fossil fuels) as well as for many other crucial raw materials is a primary source of such unexpected events. Economic growth requires security of supplies and of prices. However, the vagaries of international relations, potential cartelization and price increases on specific resources, and the political weakness or unfriendliness of the governments of raw-material-supplying nations work against needed economic stability. Such artificially induced shortages can also be attributed to the market power of multinational corporations over the availability of raw materials, especially fuel. In either case, we will suffer from the uncertainties of resource supplies. Assuming the adequacy of global reserves, we still must address ourselves to the separate issue of domestic sufficiency.

Technological and Economic Responses

The general fears of resource depletion discussed above have not dampened the optimism of many analysts. Scientists of assorted disciplines, but most notably economists, readily see solutions that would avert and postpone, until the indefinite future, limits to growth based upon this problem. Indeed, the mechanisms to initiate these solutions are for the most part automatic. They are: (1) the desires for profit that inevitably encourage certain economic actions and discourage others; and (2) the cues supplied by the price system that change the direction of profit-seeking activity. Scarcity in the face of increasing demand can best be handled by raising the cost of the item, thereby distributing it to those who desire it enough to pay the higher price. More importantly, other actions are then promoted that would help further to alleviate the problem.

> In the real world, rising prices act as an economic signal to conserve
> scarce resources, providing incentives to use cheaper materials in their
> place, stimulating research efforts on new ways to save on resource
> inputs and making renewed exploration attempts more profitable.[9]

Thus, the flow chart of economic adaptation to resource scarcity
is quite simple. Price increases prompt development of technological mechanisms to reduce costs. Technological feasibility plus
economic profitability of new scarcity-avoiding processes will
result in either increased supply or reduced demand for the resource. Inevitable technological advance, private market incentives,
and the allocative function of the price system insure that the impact of resource scarcity will be temporary adjustment and long-
term sufficiency. The following optimistic projection is the consequence of the above analysis:

> I am confident that for millennia to come we can continue to develop
> the mineral supplies needed to maintain a high standard of living for
> those who now enjoy it and to raise it for the impoverished peoples
> of our country and world. . . . Our experience justifies the belief that
> these processes [of resource expansion] have dimensions beyond our
> knowledge and even beyond our imagination at any given time.[10]

Yet, in light of the well-publicized concern expressed by many
over the threat of resource depletion, such an optimistic forecast
and the economic analysis that supports it ought to be seriously
examined. Specifically, what is the effectiveness of the scarcity-
alleviating activities that are encouraged by higher resource costs?
Conservation is the most immediate response to higher prices. It
implies not only doing with less of the metal, fuel, etc., but also
making fewer do the work of more. We are all too familiar with
the calls for energy conservation directed toward consumers:
home thermostats set at sixty to sixty-five degrees, gas-efficient
automobiles, turning off unnecessary lights. Industrial conservation efforts are equally important. The usable-energy-to-waste-heat
ratio of most electric generating power plants is forty to sixty. For
the average automobile, the ratio is ten to ninety. Such inefficiencies are indicative of the waste existing in our economy and
the opportunity for effective conservation efforts. Stretching the
usefulness of natural resources is common practice. Less tin is

needed in the tin-plating process; equal levels of structural support are achieved with less steel. There probably is enough flexibility in living patterns and productive processes to reap sizable cutbacks in the use of scarce raw materials without significant reductions in living standards.

There is some doubt regarding the extent to which short-term, voluntary, and individual conservation steps, taken in response to the continual pressure of high energy prices, can lead to more basic changes in living patterns and consumer demands. Can there be a transformation to an environmentally sound life-style without recourse to collective—that is, political—actions? According to a recent study, Sweden uses 60 percent less energy than the United States in producing one dollar's worth of GNP. Standards of living are comparable, but conscientious use of public policy (subsidies, taxes) has brought about a different, more energy-efficient mixture of goods and services in Sweden. Americans have more appliances, cars, and television sets and eat more red meat—all indices of a very energy-intensive economy. Swedes, on the other hand, have more second homes, better public transportation, health and education systems, and more efficient energy utilization rates for productive processes and consumer durables (e.g., resource extraction and refinement processes, the paper industry, electric power generators, gas mileage of cars, home insulation). The authors of the study confirm the point made in the preceding paragraph: "The most important variable affecting energy use and energy efficiency is the relative price of energy with respect to other resources."[11]

However, the study also emphasized "the institutional and social factors" that direct the economic and technological responses to higher energy costs. Higher prices alone will lead to individual conservation (or, if you will, increases in individual energy efficiency), but only collective action can promote the life-style changes and conservation-conscious culture that would maintain living standards in the face of increased resource scarcity. In order to encourage the most economical use of energy in the society as a whole, we must recognize the political along with the technological elements of conservation. But our economy and ideology are geared to high levels of resource consumption. Imparting a conservationist mentality onto our "cowboy economy" will be deeply resisted, as President Jimmy Carter has discovered. The conservational aspects of his energy proposals have received the roughest treatment. Thus, we are limited in the technological adjustments to scarcity that we can expect given the social and economic constraints on political change.

Conservation is only one of three types of activities encouraged by higher resource prices. Another is the quest for additional sources of the scarce material. This takes three forms—exploiting known but previously uneconomical ore deposits, searching for new reserves, and recycling the resource by reprocessing it from various waste products. Economists make much of the effect of price increases on the application and effectiveness of each of these approaches. Low-grade ore would be an economically viable reserve if a price rise covered increased extraction and processing costs. Likewise, even though more sophisticated equipment is being used to search for new ore deposits, with proportionately less success (more exploratory wells drilled for each productive find), demand and price trends still make these efforts fruitful. Research has been directed toward better discovery methods, improved mining and metallurgical processes, and, in general, increased cost-effectiveness of resource production. Historically, in our country resource depletion has not been an inhibition on economic growth. "Techniques for exploration for and extraction of metals seem to have kept ahead of scarcity."[12] The promises of future advances cannot easily be discounted given the degree of past successes. Yet, however much the economists and technicians underscore their achievements, it would do well to restate a major truism of the limits-to-growth thesis: While price increases and new technology can transform unavailable (offshore oil) and unprofitable (low-yield deposits) mineral concentrations into useful reserves, they cannot increase the deposits themselves.

To those interested more in maintaining the world's stock of resources rather than in promoting a growth flow of goods and services, the natural response to resource depletion would be recycling. The fact is that, with the exception of fossil fuels, which are burned, most raw materials are not used up or destroyed. Rather, they are transformed into a new form and transported to a new place. The economics of recycling concerns the effort we wish to expend to reconcentrate the resource. Many industrial users of raw materials are attracted by the savings that recycling offers. An especially significant incentive is the increase in profit to be achieved by reducing energy costs; it takes forty times more energy to process one pound of aluminum from buried ore than from recycled material. Again, economic feasibility is the necessary signal for an expansion of the recycling industry. The usefulness of the scrap iron and steel gathering rust in the nation's junkyards is another case in point. In the event of scarcity-induced price increases of foreign and domestic ores, recycling offers a readily available alternative supply of needed iron and steel. The example of viewing junkyards as potential reserves of raw materials highlights an ironic element of the overall environmental problem. Pollution can sometimes be defined as "a resource out of place."[13] For instance, commercial and residential wastes can be reprocessed to help generate electricity, produce synthetic gas, provide fertilizer for agriculture, and/or become a source of metals, glass, paper pulp, etc. As refuse and sewage treatment costs rise and the prices paid for these alternative uses increase, this form of recycling will become more common. Yet, despite these examples, recycling has severe limitations on its ability to solve the scarcity problem. Its utility varies from resource to resource, and it cannot deal with increasing demand except in a secondary way. Most importantly, it does not *directly* address itself to our most pressing concern— energy supply.

The third means of avoiding resource scarcity is through the substitution of a more plentiful material for a less abundant and therefore more expensive one. Substitution technology does not merely buy time; it seeks to solve, for the short-term future at least, the problem of depletion and rising demand. Economists justifiably ridicule the fear of some that one day we will use up a critical resource, and the wheels of industry will thereupon grind to a halt:

> materials do not "run out" for all applications at once. They do run out for the marginal use, and the marginal use is precisely the one for which a satisfactory substitute can be found as the cost of the original material goes up.[14]

Plentiful aluminum can replace copper wiring as copper becomes too costly. Still further down the technological road, even more available silicates (refined from common sand) are being tested for use in electronic circuitry. The preservation of a given resource stock for its own sake—that is, above and beyond the incentives for hoarding provided by the price system—may be more wasteful than rational in light of this technological response to scarcity. The growth of the petrochemical industry is in large part the consequence of the growing substitution of oil-based synthetics (fabrics, plastics, etc.) for goods based on metals or animal and plant products. Other such developments can reasonably be expected to continue. We should not quickly dismiss these anticipated fruits of technology, for to do so ignores historical precedent and overlooks our most precious and unlimited raw material—human ingenuity.

> Resources don't exist until we invent them. . . . What we call a resource is something that each generation learns to extract and to use. . . . Some people worry needlessly about using too many of our resources and robbing the future. I think that if the future is not capable of inventing, then the human odyssey is over.[15]

This observation, from a committed environmentalist, is meant to minimize expectations of social and economic collapse stemming from this concern. It is not intended, however, to deny any and all economic consequences of resource depletion.

The Special Case of Energy

A special case—indeed the most important case—of substitution technology has to do with energy. With enough of it, we can mine the seas, desalinate water, and purify our effluents—cheaply and painlessly. But without enough energy, we face an enormous problem of economic and psychological restructuring. Energy is the linchpin of our life-style. The insecurity of relying on foreign supplies forces the United States to look inward, to find domestic sources of fossil fuel. If, as projected, world oil production will peak around the year 2000, we will be under intense pressure to develop alternatives as quickly as possible. Indeed, increases in oil and natural gas prices are even now having a disproportionate influence on a host of related industries—the so-called ripple effect. In our energy-oriented economy, the prices of so many goods and services are tied to the cost of this basic commodity. Obviously, our present as well as future economic well-being relies on a resolution to this most central of problems.

The factor of time places our efforts in sharp relief. Because of a fast doubling time in energy use (e.g., electricity demand doubles every seven years), time delays in formulating and implementing responses threaten to make our technologies obsolete as soon as they are initiated. We need to buy time via conservation, new sources, and more efficient conversion ratios until we can develop the energy resources of the future—fusion and solar power (in its many forms). However confident one may be about our technological ability to develop these alternatives (and I personally am quite confident), few claim that either energy source can become a major contributing factor for at least fifty to one hundred years. Thus, the possibility of a generation or two of great sacrifice is very real. We all must recognize that the hardships of the short-term future (the next fifty to one hundred years) might be severe enough to bring on a permanent political reaction to what is perhaps only a temporary physical condition. The issues then become: (1) the technological and political prospects of domestic substitutes for foreign oil and gas; and (2) the variables that will determine the severity of the coming economic dislocations brought on by the need for stopgap measures.

Three alternatives present themselves, each one with serious flaws that will limit its effectiveness as an energy source for the immediate future. The first is our oil shale reserves in the mountain states. A great deal of research has gone into creating an economically feasible method of extracting the tarlike petroleum product, but two problems remain, probably on a permanent basis. First, for most probable extraction methods, producing one barrel of oil requires the processing of one and one-half tons of rock and the use of large quantities of water. The localized reclamation costs of utilizing this resource, if added onto the investment capital (as it would have to be if huge tracts of land were to become possible vast wastelands), would make the price of the fuel prohibitive unless other sources became equally inflated. The second and related reason is that local constituencies from shale-oil states, seeing what resource development did to Appalachia, may band together and resist environmentally unsound extraction techniques. At the very least, resistance would delay commercial plans, raise reclamation and side-payment costs, and block the availability of some shale-oil deposits for political reasons.[16] The second alternative energy source, surface-mined coal reserves found in many Western states, is prone to exactly the same objections as is the exploitation of shale-oil deposits. These objections notwithstanding, the above mentioned resources might very well be utilized. Nevertheless, there will be a social cost that might make the whole project unprofitable to the nation but lucrative for the extracting corporation.

This dichotomy between national and corporate interests is no more apparent than in the present conflict over our third temporary energy resource, nuclear (fission) power using breeder reactor technology. By being able to create its own fuel from previously unfissionable uranium isotopes, the fast breeder reactor appears to solve the resources problem in much the same mystical way as alchemists sought to overcome the gold shortage, and with the same mesmerizing attractiveness. It is true that this method of producing energy is not cost efficient in comparison with present generating plants using fossil fuels. This will probably change, however, as technologies are developed to improve heat-to-energy ratios, to reduce downtime of nuclear power plants, etc. Yet, four strong objections to "going nuclear" remain:

1. the possibility of sabotage by criminal or terrorist organizations (including the actual theft of fissionable material for the construction of atomic weapons);
2. increases in background radiation in areas near or for workers in the nuclear facility;
3. accidents of many different kinds, some of which have already occurred;
4. problems associated with the disposal of radioactive wastes of the power and fuel generation process (including the decommissioning of "hot" nuclear plants after forty to fifty years).

Each of these objections represents serious, highly complex and perhaps unmanageable risks. As to probabilities, even a *supporter* of the breeder reactor is forced to admit that "There will, no doubt, be accidents with radioactive materials; there may even be occasional major accidents, perhaps even disasters."[17] To fully handle the four objections listed above (some of which are beyond our technological and social capacities presently) would require a major increase in capitalization and operating costs. If the nuclear power industry could buy adequate safety for its plants, the impact on energy prices would drastically reduce the economic viability of such a power generation process. Government support (e.g., taking responsibility for waste removal and storage) has improved the corporate profitability of the venture by merely passing on costs to society as a whole. Perhaps, as some would say, it all depends on how much safety the consumer is willing to purchase or the taxpayer is willing to subsidize. This choice ignores the fact that we will have to pay for inadequate safety eventually; given the dangers posed by nuclear technology, the cost may be many times the benefits achieved if we minimize or ignore the above objections.

The Political Variable

Our three short-term energy sources are not truly adequate to the task. We can expect some level of hardship over an extended period of time due to fossil fuel scarcity and rising energy prices. And whatever the hope of the future, the development of fusion and solar power is too distant to diminish the psychological and political impact of long-term economic dislocations. This is not to claim that the limit-to-growth position is accurate. I have discussed only in passing the political dimension to the problem of resource scarcity. I want to conclude this section by reviewing the political variable—its ability to soften or accentuate the anticipated dislocations, to direct technology down certain paths while foreclosing the pursuit of other options, and to lengthen or shorten the lead time for the development of a safe, clean, and economical energy source.

Economists and other technicians generally believe that the adjustments the economy will be forced to make can occur gradually, allowing us adequate time to evaluate our present policies and plan for the future. The price system is the most effective mechanism for preventing collapse. Resource scarcity, as reflected in higher prices, encourages attitudes and behavioral patterns (discussed in this section) that insure the next generation of its share of raw materials. In this way, the claims of the future can be weighed against the demands of the present. However, the price mechanism is at best an imperfect defender of the future's interests. We have a highly self-centered time orientation, a "now" mentality, which seriously overemphasizes current consumption and production. Our private desire for the good life, whether or not we can afford it, prompts us to downplay the consequences of actions as they will affect us five to ten years hence. Therefore, we really should not be expected to sacrifice consumption dreams for generations yet unborn. The corporate sector is no less guilty of chronological myopia. It may be economically wise to exploit a resource for immediate and certain profits and then to reinvest those profits in other ventures. Appalachian coal is a tragic case in point. The clash between private and public interests is not fully rectified by the price system.

In addition, the sensitivity and elasticity of prices are open to question. Can prices respond soon enough, or is there an inevitable and costly time lag that leads to spasmodic dislocations rather than gradual adjustments? Unaided, the price system may falter in performing the prophylactic function that growth advocates envision for it. Observers such as economist Henry C. Wallich have proposed a set of public policies that will "strengthen the price system for its job of conserving resources. It would contribute to internalizing the resource-depletion cost of growth."[18] Numerous governmental programs can be designed to promote recycling, tax wasteful technologies, protect selected ore deposits against present use, or in other ways counteract the effects of our tendency to stress present demands above probable future needs. Prudent politicians and administrators, after weighing the costs and benefits of these suggestions, might very well initiate policies along these lines. Yet, prudence is not the forte of our crisis-prone policymaking process. We have promoted the discovery of new sources at the expense of other options—recycling, conservation, etc. We are now even more dependent on fossil fuels, more unable to ease into a non-energy-intensive mode of living. As this section has attempted to demonstrate, price increases will encourage various social and technological responses to resource scarcity, but this says little about the degree of scarcity, the size of the price increase, and the magnitude of the sacrifices that all those responses entail. We should not assume that politics will succeed in reducing the pains of adjustment, especially given the fact that public policy, attuned to a growth economy, helped to shape the current dilemma.

In fact, politics, through its selection of alternative policy approaches, will most probably allocate rather than reduce these adjustment pains. Political solutions to resource scarcity may demand *unequal* sacrifices, reflecting the unequal distribution of political power. For example, governmental efforts to raise raw material prices directly, in hopes of encouraging society-wide conservation, continues apparently voluntaristic decisions regarding consumption patterns. The ideals of consumer sovereignty and managerial prerogative (as to investment and product design) are preserved. Yet, this legally noncoercive approach ignores the coerciveness of the marketplace: the cost of fuel for heating forces some families to endure home temperatures of fifty to fifty-five degrees, while more affluent individuals have little economic impetus to change their energy usage habits. Pricing policies are inherently unfair because they require the lower classes to sacrifice more than the wealthy (in terms of marginal utility) in order for the nation to conserve resources. An alternative tack might seek to prohibit certain types of goods and services rather than merely make such purchases more costly. Among the vast array of electronic gadgetry, we can find some items that are clearly wasteful even though such waste is affordable by a segment of the population. To ban these and similar goods and services would address the notion of efficient resource utilization in a more direct way. But more importantly, it limits the privileges of wealth and thus allocates social sacrifice quite differently. In its balance between different policy alternatives, the political system will determine which groups bear the brunt of the negative economic consequences we can expect from resource scarcity problems.

Another possible role for government is to promote investment in resource-related ventures. The economy is being encouraged to do three things in response to scarcity: conserve, increase sources, and develop substitutes. These efforts are contradictory in the sense that success in one area (substitution, for instance) will have a negative impact on the economic viability of the others (recycling, new discovery techniques, conservation). It is evident that a corporation will be very hesitant to make a large financial commitment in a promising technology if the possibility exists that parallel developments elsewhere will prevent it from turning a profit. In order to maintain a broad attack on the scarcity problem, the federal government will be required to guarantee investment and create a climate of security within which corporations may pursue their research and development free from financial risk. Without this governmental help (and assuming that the government does not shoulder the task itself), the lead time for technological developments will be greatly lengthened; consequently, the dislocations to be endured will be longer and more severe. The need for financial support is most clear in the technology surrounding fusion power. The government is forced to support the bulk of the research in this area because the vast expense of such research (especially with respect to capital expenditures) makes investment prohibitive for the private economic sector. Obviously, without such help we would have little hope for this long-term energy source.

Our final political variable is the most difficult one to anticipate. What are the international implications of resource scarcity on our economic prospects? What factors are relevant to our global economic position vis-à-vis the energy crisis? In terms of our economic strength, compared to other capitalist industrialized nations, we would be in a far better position to withstand the pressures of the energy crunch. We have alternative domestic energy sources, while other nations are much more dependent upon foreign supplies. This is true not only with respect to fossil fuels but also concerning basic raw materials generally.

Yet, in three respects we would be hurt by a general tightening of the resource market. First, while domestic substitutes can be found, foreign reserves are presently cheaper and purer. To extract and refine our own would entail increased financial and social costs. In effect, we have exported the social costs of resource acquisition. Intense political battles and price inflation would result from being forced to become more self-sufficient. The second and related point concerns our own special dependence on a resource-intensive economic system:

> The American economy, by virtue of its having become accustomed to more spendthrift ways than any other country in the world, may be in for a more extensive and uncomfortable revision of its life style than those whose per capita consumption of oil and minerals has been more modest.[19]

We will suffer less than others in absolute terms, but the economic hardships we do experience may be more severe relative to past levels of adequacy or expectations of future affluence. Finally, we should consider the interdependence of the financial structure of the developed world. National economic catastrophe cannot be easily localized within national boundaries since the interrelationship among the Western economies has made every nation more vulnerable. The bankruptcy of any debtor country (not altogether unlikely if oil prices continue their climb) would expose the international monetary system to severe financial strains.

Political responses to these concerns could take many different forms. Perhaps the most dramatic scenario is resource imperialism—insuring the availability of adequate and economical supplies of resources via military means. Even without so extreme an eventuality, it is still true that the actions of other nations and our foreign-policy reaction to the evolving international situation will be influential factors on the limits-to-growth issue.

On balance, what does the factor of resource scarcity contribute to the debate? To what extent does it validate the limits-to-growth position? It goes without saying that the unknowns in our analysis (especially regarding the crucial factors of technology, time, and politics) allow for various possible projections, but I believe that some cutback in our growth rate, some economic belt tightening, is the most plausible conclusion that can be reached. Economists hope that price increases on raw materials can avoid this outcome, but they are ignoring an economic truism: "in the absence of other events, a rise in the prices of depleting resources acts to reduce living standards through a rise in the cost of living."[20] We can also expect higher taxes (decreased disposable income) or inflationary deficit spending since federal money will have to be funneled to methods of alleviating the dislocations of scarcity (e.g., subsidies for investment in research on substitute energy sources). Finally, investment funds will be increasingly devoted not to consumer-oriented enterprises but to goods and services related to our resource problems—more money for reclamation of the land, for discovery, extraction, and refinement technology research, for recapitalization to transform the United States into a less energy-intensive society, and for energy as a more expensive factor in the productive process. It is also reasonable to assume, based on past precedent, that governmental action will intensify the negative impacts of resource scarcity for many people in the United States, if not for the nation as a whole. We are facing choices regarding the nature and depth of the adjustments that we must make. Perhaps most significantly, we also are facing a gnawing insecurity about our future and our ability to cope with it.

Environmental Decay

Stating the Argument

Sharing the headlines with the energy crisis is the increase in pollution. The expansion of the industrial sector of our economy is the source of many contaminants of the air, water, and food. Admittedly, the connection between growth and pollution is not so unicausal—an undeveloped society can suffer from water-borne diseases, and an affluent society can direct its growth toward improving the quality of its environment. However, the connection between level of industrialization and environmental deterioration has some historical credence, giving plausibility to the warning of danger ahead *if current trends continue.* Extrapolation of trends that forecast environmental disaster place the burden of proof upon those who seek to deny the causal relationship between growth and pollution.

Yet, not so long ago pollution was an excellent example of a nonissue, and not without good reason. The environment has a natural capacity to cleanse and regenerate itself, to break down wastes and dissipate them harmlessly, to incorporate man's activities into an ongoing ecological balance. The air and water are renewable resources (as is the soil, with a longer time cycle) and can theoretically be used without ever being used up. Cybernetic, self-regulatory mechanisms minimize the effect of our intrusions onto the environment by encouraging corrective responses. "The system is stabilized by its dynamic self-compensating properties."[21] This comforting analysis is not totally true, however—not for all types of pollutants, nor for all levels of pollution, nor for all areas of the nation and world. Our reliance on the regenerative capacity of the environment can lead to overreliance, for the cybernetic mechanisms are not infinitely effective: "In general, self-maintaining systems are self-adjusting only within limits. Once outside these limits, pathological possibilities exist."[22] Effluents in high concentrations or of a type that cannot be safely absorbed by the environment threaten to bring us to these limits all too quickly. We will be forced to endure an obvious deterioration in the quality of our lives and/or be forced to tolerate reduced growth rates in order to reverse the worsening pollution situation.

The most serious pathological possibility concerns hazards to our health. A proponent of economic growth arrived at the following analysis of the health effects of air quality.

> A comparison of the death rates in American cities in 1960 has shown that with a 10 percent decrease in pollution and particles in the air we reduce the death rate as a whole by more than one half of a percent. Decreasing the amount of sulfur in the air has a similar effect. On this view, a 50 percent reduction of air pollution would increase the life expectancy at birth in the United States by between three and five years.[23]

Yet, while this sounds quite ominous in itself, many environmentalists sense even broader health dangers. An overconcern with immediate economic rewards at the expense of ecological values will lead to behavior that reduces the carrying capacity of an area by, for instance, ruining the fertility of the soil or destroying the available freshwater sources. Different forms of pollution pose different threats, some of them easily remediable and some of them not nearly so. In the absence of action to reverse pollution trends, the situation will worsen (very quickly with respect to certain areas and certain types of contaminants). Our desire for basic environmental amenities will eventually force us to come to grips with pollution in more effective and perhaps in more growth-inhibiting ways. That awareness may come in response to visions of imminent ecological catastrophe or as part of a gradually evolving choice between the quality of our environment and the quantity of our material possessions. People who support limits to growth see the choice clearly enough given present levels of pollution. What they fear is that the longer we postpone the decision to limit growth and the longer we choose to pollute, the more damage will be done to the earth's carrying capacity and the steeper will be the price we must pay to avoid an ecological catastrophe and to reconstruct the ecological balance.

The Counterargument

Many analysts, employing a traditional economic approach, deny the connection between growth and pollution. Rather, they view pollution as an inevitable consequence of an imperfection in the price system that allows an individual or company to treat the environment as a free good or service, passing the real cost of environmental deterioration onto the rest of society:

There are not enough clearly defined property rights in the environment . . . ; [people] cannot easily extract a payment from anybody who wants to use [an environmental resource] up by polluting it. Hence the costs of pollution are not usually borne by those that are responsible for the pollution and are borne, instead, by the victims.[24]

The market mechanism has not been adjusted to charge for the loss of air and water quality. In the past, because these resources were renewable and man's influence on the available supply was infinitesimal, we could treat them as virtually unlimited. However, current users of water (e.g., industrial polluters) severely restrict the ability of others to use it according to their own needs (swimming downstream of the factory). While still renewable, it is now limited in any one place at any one point in time.

The solution is simple: place a price on the resource by taxing pollution.[25] This approach or others like it would help to lower effluents in two ways. First, this tax would encourage the development and application of pollution-reducing productive processes. Technology, spurred on by economic incentive, would be put to work finding ways of reducing contaminants in order to reduce the tax costs. Second, in the event that technological innovations were not forthcoming or proved to be too costly, the pollution tax would be paid and passed on to the consumer via higher prices. Thus, effluents would decrease as a result of lessened consumer demand:

The consequences would be that the price of their [the polluters'] products would have to be increased, less of them would be consumed at those high prices, and the aggregate extent of operation of these industries would be contracted, leading to some diminution of pollution by that route.[26]

An added consequence is that charging for the use of an environmental resource highlights the inevitable trade-off that occurs between growth and pollution. It is probably true that in every industrialized society some price (in terms of environmental damage) must be paid to maintain a given style of life. Likewise, to purchase a higher level of air quality entails sacrifices elsewhere. Put in this light, the extreme demands of some ecologists would necessitate a degree of sacrifice that many of us are presently not willing to undergo; "our objective is not pure air or water but rather some optimal state of pollution . . . that will yield the maximum possible amount of human satisfaction."[27] We cannot ignore the notion of marginal utility, however much we desire a totally clean environment. It would be foolish to treat auto emissions so that they are purer than the atmosphere they enter. But while the case for optimal pollution levels is indisputable on its face, it ignores the basic question: What costs and risks are we presently incurring (or can anticipate in the future given current trends) as a result of effluents in our air, water, and food? Without evidence on this score, we can hardly be expected to take collective positions regarding adequate levels of pollution and tolerable reductions in growth rates.

If the issue is therefore how to make a clear choice as to growth versus pollution trade-offs, the problem that we face now becomes evaluating the pollution threat. This is difficult to do because of the complexities associated with monitoring the effects of contaminants. The search for appropriate standards is perhaps the major initial task for technology in the pollution field. "The problem in dealing with suspected or real poison is to find a realistic 'no effect' level below which nothing happens, and a 'frank effect' level above which poisoning takes place."[28] Between is the range of insidious damage, the long-term harm resulting from chronic but low exposure. Much of the argument and confusion surrounding the pollution issue centers on delineating and examining this intermediary range. As we might expect, disagreement abounds on the environment-health relationship.[29] This being the case, the risks of further pollution remain unclear. Consequently, decisions about the growth-pollution trade-off will follow historic inclinations and power pressures rather than vague and disputed evidence. Our tendency here, as with resources, is to emphasize present consumption while minimizing future dangers. We have become tolerant of pollution, unmindful of its hidden costs. But just because our consciousness has become desensitized to the dangerous effluents around us, it does not mean that our bodies have also become desensitized. "The widespread belief that we can *adapt* or *get used* to anything constitutes one of the main difficulties in evaluating the impact of pollution . . . and in studying the mechanisms of its effects."[30] By systematically downplaying the costs of pollution, by favoring the growth side of the trade-off, we are paving the way for a more drastic reversal of economic growth rates once the actual nature of the ecological problem becomes known.

Yet, in many areas we have overestimated the dangers posed by pollution. Too much stock has been placed in the extreme charges of some environmentalists, and this has prevented an adequate assessment of the costs of pollution. Many scientists back up the economists' notion of optimal pollution levels by noting that not every human intrusion onto natural processes is somehow harmful to the system, dangerous to our health, and destined to get worse. In analyzing the strength of the case, we must attempt to sift out those problems that are so gradual in developing and/or so easy to reverse that they primarily serve to underscore the seriousness of more basic environmental threats.

I have mentioned the issue of waste disposal previously, citing it as a potential resource that, with proper economic incentives, would become an asset rather than a hazardous liability. Thermal pollution can be viewed similarly. Shellfish production has increased in estuaries warmed by industrial waste water (sanitized so as not to include chemical, metallic, or radioactive substances). This is not to say that such uses are inevitable for all places and under all conditions, or that these pollutants will not cause localized damage if no controls are imposed; however, it seems probable that the normal operation of the economic system will encourage the utilization of some wastes. This is the logic behind recycling. We would be confronted with a much larger garbage disposal problem if economics did not dictate that some by-products (wood chips from lumber mills) and some discarded materials (the lead in car batteries) be viewed as resources rather than wastes.

Other assumed dangers can be discounted even more certainly, at least for now. Take the relationship between worldwide economic activity, especially the burning of fossil fuels, and temperature changes. First, the evidence is mixed, with some scientists predicting warming trends, others anticipating cooling effects. Second, unlike the life-threatening dangers of chemical poisoning, the temperature changes (and their consequent impact on the human environment) will be gradual, easy to monitor, and in the realm of a growing inconvenience.[31] Indeed, given the normal cyclical temperature patterns that have existed for thousands of years, man's impact will remain small and perhaps even beneficial. Whatever the actual situation may be, a deep concern with this "problem" is a case of misspent energy.

Another area of overconcern is with such headline-catching topics as eutrophication of water, oil spills, and traditional forms of urban air pollution. It is true that local situations may require extreme policies in preventing damage to fresh water supplies. But it is equally true that we have often overreacted. Phosphate detergents have absolutely no impact on the oxygen deficiency of salt water, nitrogen levels being the controlling factor. Opposition to the principle of ocean dumping of sanitized municipal wastes is also based on ignorance of some environmental facts of life. "Properly used, the ocean offers man a practically unlimited resource for waste assimilation at a reasonable cost."[32] Even more to the point is the response we have to oil spills, leaks, etc. Our interest in preserving fish, birds, plants, and coastal beauty is perfectly justified, but we should not inflate the actual impact of accidents like the Torrey Canyon oil tanker breaking up off the coast of England in 1967. Four years later, no trace (visual or environmental) of the accident could be discovered. Indeed, bacteria help to decompose most types of oil into plant nutrients. Easily pursued remedies (offshore pumping stations) not only minimize the threat to the coastal ecosystem posed by oil spills; they can also be a positive benefit to the economy (utilizing larger and more cost-efficient tankers, reducing the need for elaborate dock facilities, etc.).

What has been ignored by environmental extremists is the regenerative capacity of the environment, its ability to recycle renewable resources, to break down some pollutants into harmless substances and to disperse others to harmless concentration levels. No doubt this capacity can be overstated. In the past, high concentrations of certain pollutants (carbon monoxide, sulphur dioxide, particulants, and some airborne metals such as lead), along with climatic conditions that worsened the situation by prolonging these high concentrations (e.g., temperature inversion), were more than the self-purging mechanisms of the atmosphere could handle. However, reversing this trend has not been difficult, let alone traumatic. Air quality in most U.S. cities has noticeably improved with respect to combustion-related pollutants, probably because of the use of low-polluting fuels and the addition of antipollution devices. Other improvements can be obtained by situating polluting industries in comparatively clean locations, thereby allowing the national cleansing power of the ecosystem to have maximum effect. All in all, public policies encouraging antipollution technology, pursued through profit-seeking market activity and utilizing the regenerative capacity of the environment, promise to achieve levels of optimal pollution for many effluents. However, the real menace to our health and to economic growth is more insidious than the above examples, as the following section demonstrates.

Three Cases

I have chosen to discuss three distinct pollution problems, not because they constitute the only real threats to our health and well-being, but because they are the most illustrative of the nature of environmental deterioration and the forces that prevent easy reversibility. The first is the environmental damage stemming from agricultural activity. The recent improvements in agricultural yields and especially the envious productivity of the U.S. farm are the result of a basically free-market system (agribusiness notwithstanding) and modern agricultural technology. The intensive and extensive use of irrigation, fertilizer, pesticides, herbicides, and single-crop farming (for cost-efficient, capital-intensive mechanization) has contributed to the productive success of the industry. Yet, given the competitive nature of the business, farmers must accept as much of the new technology as they can afford. The technological-economic imperative is that the immediate benefits of the new innovations of agriculture outweigh any long-term risks and dangers. "The circumstances that most farmers find themselves in allow them little choice as to whether they will use the latest technology that is made available. They still operate in their own best, short-term interests."[33] The economic situation insures that the future will be sacrificed for the present. The fear of financial insolvency is sufficient to prevent individual farmers from weighing the individual benefits of technology against the potential environmental risks. Personal survival is paramount. Within this context of structural incentives and restraints, we can begin to appreciate the pollution problem that modern agriculture presents.

What are the potential environmental risks that modern agriculture is forced to incur? One has to do with the use of chemical fertilizer. It is undoubtedly the best short-term investment a farmer can make. Even with high applications and rising fertilizer prices, the marginal increase in yields covers private costs. But there are public costs to consider, too—costs that are both *increased* and *hidden* by the *private* productivity of synthetic fertilizer. On this score, two facts stand out. First, the higher the application of cheap nitrogen-based fertilizer, the more, proportionally, that cannot be absorbed by the plants. Runoff from rains pours nitrites into streams, reservoirs, and groundwater reserves, raising this pollutant to dangerous levels in some cases. Second, nitrogen fertilizer obstructs and reduces the natural fertility of the soil (by destroying the soil's nitrogen-fixing bacteria), thus requiring ever more reliance on chemical fertilizers and therefore making inevitable still more runoff. Significantly, the use of pesticides tells a similar story. DDT is an effective, economical, and comparatively safe means of ridding farms of destructive insects. Its responsibility for increasing yields (and, in some Third World countries, of dramatically reducing the incidence of insect-borne diseases) is unchallenged. But, as environmentalists have repeatedly demonstrated, the pests build up a resistance to the previous dosage— more accurately, resistant strains of the insect multiply and dominate the colony—and the biological predators that helped to control the pests' numbers are eradicated. Thus, to achieve similar results, ever higher applications or more poisonous variants of the pesticide must be used. The polluting effects of chemicals such as DDT must be viewed in light of their ability to change the environment and thereby to encourage further pollution in the future.

This is the meaning of the concept "technological fix." "Like an addictive drug, fertilizer nitrogen and synthetic pesticides literally create increased demand as they are used; the buyer becomes hooked."[34] Technological developments, once accepted, cannot be reversed "cold turkey" without nearly prohibitive political consequences and/or economic costs (e.g., reduced growth and recapitalization expenditures). We thus require additional technological fixes merely to maintain our economic "high." This ironic cycle—the dangers of technology leading to an increased dependence on technology to have it save us from the dangers it has created—is what makes this type of pollution process so threatening.

In a sense, other aspects of agricultural pollution are related examples of this same point. One-crop farming, overcropping, and other aspects of poor husbandry have depleted the soil of many vital nutrients, requiring chemical fertilizer to compensate. They also simplify the environmental system of the farm, preventing natural balances from holding down insects and weeds. This prompts the use of pesticides and herbicides, again in increasing amounts. Finally, they lead to the erosion of the topsoil, while technology tries to compensate through the application of still more chemicals. As to the claim that the current environmental impacts of agricultural practices are not great, we ought to focus on the *process* of worsening environmental damage, not simply on the extent of damage at a point in time. The forces behind the problem are what make this type of pollution so significant.

Farmers, and with them society in general, are caught in a bind. Instituting good agricultural practices will lower yields, prevent the most cost-efficient use of farm machinery, and probably result in the financial ruin of many. (A further consequence would be the international furor that would be raised by overpopulated and underfed Third World nations.) The fact is that we operate our farms as if they were a short-term resource-extraction investment because we allow our farmers no other viable alternative. The various kinds of pollution that result from such an orientation interfere in very basic ways with the natural regenerative, cybernetic capacity of the ecosystem. When we decide to halt the pollution progression and to resurrect some of the ecological balances we had previously been so effective in destroying, the cost may be high. We have an environmental debt to repay. Just as the addict must go through a painful period of withdrawal before he can rebuild his life, we may have to face reduced agricultural productivity in order to avoid further dependence upon the technological fix.

The threat (and in some places the reality) of water pollution (fresh water scarcity) is a second important and illustrative example of environmental deterioration. "More than any other factor, the availability of water determines the ultimate population capacity of a geographical province."[35] The need for water for industrial, agricultural, recreational, and residential purposes has grown greatly in some areas of the country, outpacing the ability of the environment to replenish this renewable resource. In addition to overuse per se, there are three related pollution problems that reveal the centrality of this concern. One has to do with the impact of various types of runoff practices that increase the saline content of fresh water sources. This is a notably difficult situation to monitor as to individual responsibility, and, therefore, it is especially difficult to control via traditional economic incentives. The immensity of this problem is demonstrated best by recent trends: "As a result of man's activities, since 1914 the total salt content of the Ohio River has increased by about 50 percent and that of the Colorado by nearly 100 percent."[36] By the year 2000, current projections indicate that salt concentrations will approach the upper limits recommended for human consumption.

A second way in which supplies of fresh water are contaminated stems from excessive pumping of groundwater. The mixture of salt water with fresh in underground rock formations results from the lessened pressure of the latter upon the former after pumping. Also, because of excessive pumping, we have been forced to go lower and lower in our efforts to increase supply; in effect, we mine for water as if it were a nonrenewable mineral deposit and extract a poorer quality resource. "We have, by our heavy withdrawal of groundwater, contributed to . . . the lowering of water tables, salt water intrusion into fresh groundwater, and depletion of groundwater at rates faster than it can be naturally replenished."[37] Thus, in some parts of the country (principally the West and Southwest), we face an absolute limit to growth. We are approaching it rapidly, the possibility of substitutions or new sources is slight, and the buildup of another environmental debt (replenishing an intolerably low water table) is a very real prospect. The dynamic forces maintaining this process are in large part those associated with modern agricultural procedures (and the economic incentives that rationalize these procedures).

Finally, as discussed in the previous section, demands for more resources and increased reliance on domestic sources will require the use (pollution) of more fresh water. Within the context of the growth ethic, we will have little choice but to pay for these resources with society's consumption of poorer quality and/or higher priced water. There are also the political imperatives for growth that encourage residential and industrial expansion before adequate public support facilities (water sources, sewerage treatment capacity) are provided. Given the acceptance of the growth ethic, there will be bitter resistance to water utilization policies that threaten future economic expansion. And yet, we must expect a radical break with past attitudes and behavior if we are to solve this pollution problem:

This country has reached a point in its history when water will have to be conserved and managed like other economic goods. Large investments will be required if mounting demands are to be met, and much more systematic schemes of management for whole river systems will have to be devised and applied.[38]

When we recognize that water resource management will amount to controls on growth, we can appreciate the role that this pollution problem will play in the limits debate.

The final area of environmental deterioration on which I will focus concerns the group of modern pollutants that cannot be broken down or transformed by the self-cleansing and self-regulating mechanisms of the ecosystem. These nonbiodegradable chemicals are proliferating in amount and variety from the manufacture of plastics, other synthetics, agricultural sprays, food additives, etc., as by-products in the production of other goods and in nuclear power generation. They pose an unknown cumulative danger to the air, water, animals, plants, soil, food, and eventually to our own health and well-being. Modern contaminants make the task of determining the costs of pollution all but impossible. For instance, while low levels of a chemical may cause no ill effects (short- or long-term), two chemicals at low levels may react with each other in some way to *magnify* their separate carcinogenic, mutagenic, pathogenic, or teratogenic properties. This process, known as synergism, is especially difficult to monitor when new variables (chemicals) are continually entering the environmental equation.

Other aspects of chemical pollution are equally serious and equally fraught with problems of measurement. Chemicals and many types of metal pollutants interact not only with each other but also with the environment. They are combined, concentrated, and/or changed in largely unknown ways. This creates a built-in time lag between a given quantity of effluent and a related level of health danger. Because of the ongoing nature of these environmental processes, contaminant levels of certain chemicals (e.g., DDT) will rise naturally in spite of actions to reduce the original source. By the time public policy responds to the health danger, a chain of environmental events will have been set in motion that will inevitably worsen the situation. Such time delays tend to be little understood, and thus our present perceptions of the risks of pollution are similarly uncertain. Time delays, sometimes of as much as thirty years, also occur between exposure to a pollutant (asbestos fibers) and the observation of adverse reactions (asbestos-related diseases). Compounding this measuring problem is the fact that chemical pollutants often increase one's susceptibility to common illnesses rather than cause their own clear and pollution-specific maladies. All this is by way of indicating the obstacles to an adequate assessment of the aggregate health hazards of our chemical society. Our ignorance then becomes the greatest danger of all: "when we add misunderstood chemicals to our ambiance, we put ourselves in the position of not knowing what symptoms to expect, in addition to the usual problems of cause and cure."[39]

The information on pollutants is confusing and contradictory (often depending upon who is funding the research). However, our ignorance of this matter has not evoked a caution commensurate with the risks involved. For the most part, the onus of proof remains on the public to demonstrate danger, not with the company to prove safety. As to technological assessment and environmental impact analysis—a critical evaluation of the impact of technological innovations before they are operationalized—we have achieved some success, notably in the SST controversy. However, the testing of every new chemical for complete safety before it is marketed or discharged as waste is extremely costly; it entails investment in testing, increases time delays, and tends to discourage chemical technology. This would have an immediate impact on profit and growth rates and would be strongly opposed. We can realistically expect that the nature of this problem will worsen for some time to come, resulting in very conscious increases in health-related aspects of quality of life.

This final point on the worsening nature of the pollution problem bears repeating. To ignore the hazards of pollution in order to maximize short-run material wealth is not to ignore the standard-of-living consequences of elevated pollution levels. We will pay in quality what we gain in quantity. Eventually, the price will be so great that major sacrifices will be required to reconstruct a balance between our environment and our style of life.

The Political Variable

An analysis of the probable response of our society to environmental deterioration must include an awareness of the politics of policymaking. This is an inseparable element of the pollution prognosis. The decision of choosing between preserving environmental quality and promoting economic growth is obviously and unavoidably political. That is, factors of power and self-interest will enter into the process, competing with (and perhaps dominating) impartial analysis, the weight of scientific evidence, and the public interest. My strong suspicion is that, given the current milieu regarding growth and the context within which such decisions are made, there will be a gap between what economists say *could be done* and what in fact *will be done*. This is the crux of E. J. Mishan's observation:

> In debating the foreseeable future, it is not the potential ideal that economists believe they could realize, not the brave words of government officials or corporate executives, that are agenda, but the political likelihood of significant reductions being made over the next two decades in each of the familiar forms of pollution.[40]

Our politically determined policy response will also reflect developments in other areas. In a continuing energy emergency, for example, we may be forced to return to more economical and available types of fossil fuels (high-sulphur oil, coal), with negative impacts on air quality. The argument that we must give up an increment of environmental amenity in order to attain a higher living standard (the trade-off between pollution and growth) will remain persuasive within a supportive political context and a pro-growth atmosphere. In short, our optimism should be tempered. What can realistically be expected from efforts to control pollution?

Barry Commoner has argued that there is a strong connection between the profitability of an industry and the application of a mode of technology that uses up environmental resources: "a high rate of profit is associated with practices that are particularly stressful toward the environment and that when these practices are restricted, profits decline."[41] Technology has been directed toward increasing this process because, from an economic standpoint, any substitution of a free for a costly good will be a savings. Commoner estimates that since 1946 the technological factor—that is, the increment of added pollution per unit produced due to new productive processes—accounts for up to 95 percent of the aggregate output of contaminants in some industries.[42] We have been producing basic necessities at comparable per capita rates but with a more wasteful and hazardous technology (e.g., synthetics versus wool and cotton, detergent versus soap, fertilizer versus more land—harvested acreage has decreased—synthetic herbicides and pesticides versus more natural biological methods, truck versus rail haulage).

The profitability of this new technology (aided in large part by its ability to pass on production costs to society in the form of pollution) and the political muscle of the interests that benefit prevent the government from imposing the economists' social costs approach. Its political difficulty was starkly revealed when auto manufacturers said they would be unable to reduce emission standards for 1978 engines as required by law. Given the clout of the industry, standards have been lifted. Local efforts to impose antipollution regulations often fare just as poorly. Marginal factories that threaten to close down because of the costs of the stricter standards are allowed to maintain operation, while the local residents pick up the tab in the form of water or air impurity, hazardous work environments, noise pollution, etc.

The recent organization of an environmental movement has prompted the passage of much legislation despite the reduced-growth costs of antipollution policies. Yet, the degree of progress is very uneven, as we might expect. Eliminating pollution is relatively easy for those industries in which the faulted technology is peripheral to the society's economic structure (detergents). However, for some of this nation's major industries the issue is one of survival (chemical, agricultural, and auto industries). The likelihood of effective legislative action thus hinges on the relative political power of the combatants. Unwelcomed environmental trends may insure that this balance will change, that the environmentalists will greatly strengthen their political position, and that the government, spurred by a *quickly worsening pollution crisis,* will succeed in initiating a policy response dealing with environmental deterioration. In such a case, a new question may be asked: Who will pay the bill? Even on this point, politics, pollution, and growth interact.

What is often ignored by people seeking a political solution to the problem is that a clean environment, like many other socially valued objectives, is distributed unequally according to the political power and social position of various interests. Though pollution is viewed as a *social* cost, it tends to be selectively concentrated and localized. We perceive the problem in its particularized and isolated senses. Water scarcity is not a paramount concern to New Englanders, nor are auto emissions a threat to rural America. The health hazards experienced by farm workers (picking in recently sprayed fields) or miners (suffering from "black lung" disease) allow us all the luxury of lower food and fuel prices. Gerald Garvey notes that this situation is not coincidental:

> Externalities are not mere random distortions in the market allocation of "goods" and "bads." Often externalities systematically transfer costs and benefits from one special public to another, or from society at large to specific privileged or victimized groups. Thus spill-over costs frequently fall not on those responsible—these often being the most resourceful or wealthy, and best able to defend themselves—but on those least able to bear or avoid the burden.[43]

It is clearly possible to submerge the fundamental nature of the pollution problem by shifting social costs from a more powerful group (region, industry, occupation) to a less powerful one. Such *political resolutions* leave the target group qualitatively worse off, while the rest of society benefits through increased growth rates or reduced environmental costs.

The conclusion to be reached is a rather discouraging one for growth advocates. We are even less inclined to face up to limits of growth stemming from environmental decay than we are prepared to deal with the issue of resource scarcity. The elitist strain in the environmental movement will serve to deflect political energies away from the more serious sources of ecological breakdown, delaying our confrontation with those critical pollution problems that are structured into our economic system. This delay in our policy response will maximize the antigrowth impacts of governmental action since environmental reclamation has proven to be increasingly expensive the more the situation is allowed to worsen. The political variable—that is, the role of differential power—will likely *reduce the effectiveness* of efforts to shift the social costs of pollution onto industry. Finally, we can expect that the taxpayer and consumer will be forced to pay excessively for any increment of clean air and water that is achieved, thus placing a major drag on the growth of real income.

It is not that economic and technological responses cannot cope with the dual limits of resource scarcity and environmental decay. But coping with these situations is not the same as handling them in stride. The "solutions" that the nation finally selects will demand a price in terms of our standard of living and future economic growth. This, however, is not the only set of problems that bolster the limits-to-growth position. Trends in our physical environment parallel trends in the human environment. The next chapter will focus on additional support for the argument that economic growth will be greatly reduced in the United States of the future.

The Limits-to-Growth Debate:
The Human Environment

Introduction

Most of the evidence marshaled thus far in support of the forecast of limits to growth has stressed developments in the relationship between the physical environment and our economy. These developments, as it has been argued in Chapter 4, would inhibit growth by increasing the cost of feeding our economic engine— higher prices of raw materials brought on by real or induced scarcity—and by increasing the cost of alleviating society of the physical disamenities of economic activity—the rising price of pollution control and abatement (or of ignoring the problem of environmental deterioration). It is easy to see how such physical factors may restrain growth rates. What has been insufficiently analyzed and therefore inadequately understood is the effect of human (nonphysical) factors on our ability to sustain economic growth. Specifically, domestic and international economic developments apart from those already mentioned call into question our expectation of future economic expansion. Likewise, worsening social and psychological stress potentially could weaken our collective capacity to maintain growth, even given favorable outcomes regarding resources and pollution. Finally, we cannot dismiss the crises confronting our political system and what this portends for economic growth. This chapter explores these three dimensions of the human environment and their contribution to the growth controversy. It then summarizes the conclusions to be drawn from the analysis of Chapters 4 and 5.

Economic Developments

Vulnerability and the Contradictions of Growth

This section examines some evolving economic contradictions that have direct bearing on the contention that the United States will face a no-growth or slow-growth future. The first trend concerns the increased vulnerability of the economic system to a major business downturn as a result of the mechanisms being used to maintain present growth rates. The argument can be made that capitalism generally, and our own growth-oriented version of capitalism in particular, is fraught with operational inconsistencies, conflicting tendencies, and inherent inefficiencies—contradictions in the jargon of Marxist analysis.

> A contradiction of capitalism results when the very process of capitalist development produces simultaneously the conditions needed to transform it fundamentally; that is, when the successes of capitalist development create situations which are fundamentally antagonistic to capitalism itself.[1]

Two contradictions are especially illuminating in revealing the basic weaknesses of our form of economic development.

The first concerns the claim that, even within advanced corporate capitalism, competitive forces in the economy compel the system to extend its productive capacity. As capitalist development continues, as companies grow and industries multiply,

> There is an ever-expanding volume of profits seeking opportunities for reinvestment. Every time profits are created, they must be reinvested. And reinvestment means precisely creating more output, reducing costs (thus freeing resources for employment elsewhere), and expanding profits. Then the cycle is repeated. This expanding volume of profits therefore impels the firm to look for new markets, search for new products to be produced, and create more output to sell.[2]

Maintaining the profitability of new investments is usually no cause for alarm in a growing economy. However, recent efforts to handle the *escalating* expansionary thrust of capitalist production have not and cannot depend totally upon the guarantees that growth normally provides. What is significant is that current policies designed to bolster profit rates for investment capital offer short-run success but engender long-range risks. Two types of policy responses will suffice to clarify this important point.

The economic need to continue current rates of growth and to avoid stagnation and regression forces more and more costs and functions upon the government.

> The state underwrites business losses sustained during economic crisis.
> . . . Direct lending, indirect lending via intermediaries, and loan insurance and guarantees socialize business risk and create huge government liabilities that can be guaranteed only by further private capital accumulation and growth—and hence more loans, subsidies and guarantees.[3]

In effect, the state has become the insurer of growth. To the extent that the government is forced to make up the difference between naturally generated growth (i.e., productivity) and the growth rate required to maintain investment and profit levels, the economy is involved in a contradiction. If that gap is small, no major danger is on the horizon. However, *immense* government subsidies would necessarily involve inflationary deficit spending, with excellent prospects that welfare state programs would be cut back. The deep and visible involvement of the government in the economy would weaken the legitimacy of the state's role as a neutral arbiter or partner and may lead to the politicization of the economy (and perhaps of the issue of relative shares). Investment and profit levels that are artificially inflated through major political intervention and stimulation are signs of inherent danger in the economy. Real economic growth had enabled the system to avoid confronting this contradiction. But it is symptomatic of a weakened economic position that governmental intervention has increased enormously. The temporary remedy of Keynesian deficit spending has become a small part of the permanent repertoire of policy supports shoring up our lagging growth rates.

Another means by which capitalism stimulates growth concerns the important question of consumer demand. Improvements in our living standards are not merely *consequences* of our economic system. The demand for a better material existence and the economic wherewithal with which to back up that demand are vital parts of its successful functioning:

A continuing general improvement of condition is an imperative of a
viable capitalist system. . . . Such a system is dependent upon rising
levels of mass consumption which increasingly transform the so-called
luxury goods into mass produced and consumed commodities; . . . the
"luxury market" must be steadily transformed into a mass market,
through advertising, through the broadening of installment-buying plans
and personal consumption.[4]

Advertising is a necessary institution in an economy of threatened
overproduction; it is part of the material ideology that helps to
foster consumer demand. In John Kenneth Galbraith's words,
"Production only fills a void that it has itself created."[5]

Credit buying is an outgrowth of the intense consumer desires
promoted by advertising, but the expansion of credit spending is
a dangerous trend. The need to encourage maximum levels of consumer spending in order to maintain returns on investment capital
has led to a mortgaging of the future. Personal consumption debt
has been increasing faster than after-tax income—with no sign of a
slowdown. This stimulation of the economy, made necessary because the growth rate does not by itself sustain adequate consumer
purchasing power, buys prosperity as a speculator buys stocks on
a margin. Consumer debt makes prosperity tenuous since any sign
of regression threatens to have a snowballing effect. Our style of
personal consumption can be "devalued" by credit card companies demanding that a debtor pay on the principal, just as a
bank may force the liquidation of stocks bought on the margin—
both done in order to protect the creditors' funds. Slight fluctuations in growth rates can thus have marked repercussions on mass
buying power; the massive extension of the credit market allows
us little cushion to fall back upon; few options except for more
borrowing for those who are already overextended.

An economy that is touted to require only fine tuning is at the
same time more vulnerable to imperfections in the tuning mechanism. To the extent that productivity-based growth rates are being
heightened by a plethora of governmental supports in order to
absorb investment capital, to the extent that the level of consumer
demand is being artificially stimulated by easy credit policies in
order to absorb surplus productive capacity, the economy reflects
"softness" and vulnerability.

A second contradiction flows from the above analysis but views the same general problem from a totally reversed perspective. Instead of focusing on the ability of the economy to find a market for its goods and services, it questions the capacity of the economy to meet the ever-increasing economic demands of the consumer. The efforts to promote these demands through advertising, media images of the ideal U.S. family, the availability of credit, etc. run the risk of heightening frustrations and resentment, especially so given the related likelihood of demand-push inflation working to diminish real wages. In promising affluence and opportunity, our system "is constantly arousing expectations which it lacks the current means to fulfill and is betting on its ability to procure the necessary means by the very act of stimulating people to demand them and go after them."[6]

The issue goes even deeper than this. Our perceptions of the system's (and our own personal) success center upon the degree and form of economic growth we have experienced in the past. A new set of perceptions with new criteria of success and failure cannot be easily substituted for our present values and biases. The impact of growth reaches far beyond the hardware of goods, services, and GNP to encompass a way of thinking about living, about each other, and about ourselves—a state of being and becoming. As a result of past rates of economic growth, the mechanisms the system utilizes to foster continued development, and our psychological commitment to a growth ethos, we have burned the bridges behind us. Changes in growth rates will become more glaring, more difficult to understand and assimilate, more traumatic, more threatening to status quo politics. In short, we are more susceptible to the dominolike collapse that limits to growth might entail.

Symptoms of Economic Decline

We are currently in an economic decline relative to other developed nations. Various economies are superior to ours in measures of industrial productivity.[7] Our competitive edge, based on a prodigious lead in technological development, has dissipated in a number of areas as U.S. technical advances have been copied, improved, and applied by our rivals. Our share of the world market for basic items (e.g., steel) has declined. Add to this the investment-attracting advantages of lower labor costs found in most other developed and developing nations. For these and related reasons, the U.S. economy has been growing at a slower rate than most of the industrialized world, although its enormous economic base and therefore greater absolute growth mask this unpleasant reality. The balance-of-trade deficits we have been experiencing and the concomitant devaluation of the dollar are two visible and shocking indications of our weakened international position.[8] We can anticipate that as more nations overtake us in per capita GNP (some already have) a feeling of economic stagnation will set in, simulating in part the psychological effects of no-growth.

But such a simulated crisis tells only a small part of the story. We need to look at various problems associated with our current economic malaise and how they may affect long-term growth trends. Two problems occupy our attention in this section. The first concerns a major sign of economic troubles ahead—a noticeable decline in industrial profits.[9] An important consequence of this development concerns the connection between levels of public spending and the strength of the industrial sector. In some states (e.g., New York, Massachusetts) an economic retrenchment threatens to induce severe cutbacks in a host of programs (or higher taxes on already overtaxed citizens). In an era in which demands upon the government have never been greater, the prospect of reduced outputs is of major political as well as economic significance.

The primary consequence of reduced domestic industrial profits relates to the investment decisions of U.S.-based multinational corporations. The shift of capital from the United States to foreign business opportunities represents both a cause and a result of domestic economic decline. This nation's largest companies can prosper independently of the economic fate of their home base. This is easily demonstrated by the differential impact the oil crisis has on the U.S. economy and on the profits of major oil producers. However, obstacles arise in our efforts to shape these investment policies to the needs of the national economy. Multinationals are not effectively controlled by the political system. Not only do they exercise inordinate political power and thus can obstruct policies designed to restrict their freedom of action; in addition, their transnational character enables them to evade laws by which our economy could reap some spillover benefits from their corporate success. As our largest firms turn increasingly outward in search of higher profits, the domestic economy, dependent upon marginal investments by secondary companies, will be drained of a part of its reproductive power.

A second symptom of economic decline, as well as the best indication of the failure of economics and business administration (the business technologies) to manage the economy, is our permanent battle with inflation. Inflation is the hidden tax of our economy, reducing our gains in real income (spending power) even as increases in absolute dollars masquerade as prosperity. While we have always had this condition, recently it has become qualitatively worse. The fear is that unusually high price increases are now endemic to the system, the result of forces that are not easily reversed.

Different reasons are given for the new inflation, each one reflecting an ongoing trend that does not bode well for our economic health. A partial explanation addresses the changing structure of corporate capitalism. Major segments of the economic system are now dominated by oligopolistic or monopolistic market arrangements that immunize certain industries from the stabilizing and deflationary pressures of free-market competition. This condition exists with respect to the price of goods and services, the cost of labor (strong union monopolies predominate), and the interest charged for capital (internal financing of investment). Companies in these industries can avoid the inducements and penalties of fiscal and monetary policies. They are therefore free to charge higher prices and thereby get a leg up on the inflation ladder. The redistributive effects of this form of market power should be obvious. Inflation has been bearable, probably even beneficial for some, as income and wealth have shifted—from occupations, industries, and situations in the sphere of competitive capitalism that are more vulnerable to negative impacts of inflation to those individuals who can protect their investments and insure themselves a better market position. Consequently, inflation has created certain vested interests who realize that demands for a curb on inflationary policies can be financially threatening.[10]

In this context it is important to note that an inflationary mentality makes it politically difficult to curb further increases. An *anticipatory spiral* is in force; each industry or occupation seeks a hedge against expected future inflation by demanding *future* prices and wages *now*. At any one point in time, many people would object to not being in on the last round of increases. Short of wage and price controls (which have their own set of technical problems), the standard approaches to reducing inflation cannot and have not halted the spiral.

There is the strong possibility that inflation "is rooted in the rapid rise in demand for goods and services in all advanced industrialized nations and in the new demand from nonindustrial, supplier nations that their raw materials return to them a bigger piece of the economic action."[11] Increases in demand come not only from the developed West (including Japan) catching up to our materialistic attainments but also from a new (fifteen to twenty years) group of middle-class nations flexing their consumerist muscles: Brazil, Mexico, South Korea, Taiwan, Nigeria, Venezuela, Poland, East Germany, and the oil-rich Middle East countries. Increased demand is especially apparent regarding one very precious resource— food. Population growth, changing diet patterns, U.S. financed purchases of farm products by Third World countries, and the limits of the Green revolution will combine to apply permanent pressure on our grain supplies, with a resulting steady rise in prices. Similarly, as more nations have industrialized and can afford to utilize the raw materials of a growing economy, and as previously developed countries become even more productive and wealthy, competition and therefore prices for the limited supplies of critical resources will increase. The issue here is not whether there will be enough food or raw materials. Rather, it is whether these items will occupy an enlarging part of the family's and the economy's budgets, thereby reducing other purchases, living standards, and productivity.

If we just focus on this country, we realize that a demand-push inflation is the result of too successfully selling the American Dream. We are willing, even eager, to spend our way into debt in order to purchase the affluence that supposedly we can already afford. Indeed, inflation feeds on itself, discouraging thriftiness, economizing debt, and thereby promoting more demand. Furthermore, for a large portion of our population, the nature of our economic wants have changed in ways that prevent easy adjustments in supply. In the past, hopes for a car, a color television set, or a dinette set could be fulfilled for most Americans. However, recent demands are more positional, requiring not merely absolute but relative increases in one's standard of living.[12] But we cannot all have the finest education or medical services, eat at the best restaurants, and keep a live-in maid. The result is that prices for services have generally soared as people are less willing to take on certain service positions. The amenities of middle-class life depend to some extent on lower-class toleration of subservience. Inflation is a sign that the difference in attitudes between low and middle is not what it once was.

Another future cause of inflation, and one that has ramifications far beyond the price index, is the increasing control of mineral reserve markets by cartels (perhaps aided and abetted by multinational corporations). The Organization of Petroleum Exporting Countries (OPEC) is undoubtedly the most prominent example. This may presage the growth of other resource-based economic alliances attempting to set and maintain higher prices for their raw materials. Third World governments, pressured by or actually controlled by anti-U.S. leftist elements, desiring to get out of debt to the industrialized West and resenting the neocolonial exploitation of their land and people, will view massive price increases as an excellent vehicle for both profit and revenge. The competition for raw materials has never been more intense. "The shift from traditional buyers' market to global sellers' market for a lengthening list of commodities [especially raw materials] is bringing a host of far-reaching changes, many of which are still only remotely sensed."[13] This is not to say that cartelization is inevitable or, given issues of sovereignty, national security, and divergent economic needs, that it is even maintainable. At the very least, however, we should expect individual governments to make effective use of their newfound bargaining leverage, with a consequent negative impact for us on price stability, real income, standard of living, and economic growth.

This point needs more elaboration because it encompasses the major international component of the limits-to-growth position. The claim has been advanced that the U.S. economy has prospered at the expense of other nations. Willingly or unwittingly, they have become adjuncts to our own economy via their subservience to the objectives of foreign investors. The response usually given, that exports and imports are relatively insignificant in comparison with our domestic economy, has been challenged by Richard J. Barnet and Ronald Müller. Looking past aggregate data to indicators previously ignored, the authors point out that our dependence on foreign transactions is much greater than is generally recognized. "If all these factors are considered, some thirty per cent of total United States corporate profits can be directly or indirectly attributed to overseas operations."[14] Thus, there is some well-placed concern as to whether international developments will restrict our lucrative activities overseas. As mentioned above, having lost the lead in productivity to other industrialized nations, we are less likely to achieve the types of competitive advantages we obtained in our heyday. European countries have sufficient investment resources to maintain (regain) control over their economies. Also, it would be foolish to believe that the underdeveloped nations will ever revert to the more pliable, client-state relationships that typified an earlier era. Their demands and expectations have taken a quantum leap, as the following observation from *Business Week* reaffirms. "What the Third World is really after is a widespread redistribution of income among nations: taking wealth from the rich industrialized countries and giving it to the poor underdeveloped countries."[15] If, as some contend, our affluence has been built in part upon neoimperialist exploitation of the rest of the world, then this rise in national and economic assertiveness—the end of imperialism—is another cause of national economic decline, another trend supporting the limits-to-growth hypothesis.[16]

Conclusions

Taken in total, the ability of economic leaders to prolong the growth of the business sector is certainly questionable. A case in point is stagflation, a unique economic condition that continues to baffle analysts. As forecasts of future upturns consistently prove groundless, we have more reason than ever to doubt the expertise of the experts. Perhaps our complex and interdependent economy is in a transition period, developing the conceptual and managerial tools to meet coming threats to growth (resource scarcity, pollution, energy crisis). But we also can anticipate that the demands and pressures placed upon the economic system will increase and intensify, creating the insecurity of a permanent transition period. The decline of certain social bases of support—subjective resources such as belief in the work ethic or trust in corporate activity—cannot help but exacerbate the conditions obstructing recovery and renewed growth.

In assessing whether we can manage our economy and defuse the problems mentioned above, we must take into account the question of time. Specifically, will all of these crises converge with disastrous suddenness, or, the alternate scenario, will issues develop selectively and gradually, to be handled incrementally, within the confines of present economic arrangements? Our technical skills in business management and macroeconomics are best nurtured and utilized in an atmosphere free of panic decision making. Unfortunately, the former outcome seems more probable. The policies mentioned in the beginning of this section are intended to counteract the dangers of excess investment capital and excess productive capacity. As a by-product, they have increased the interdependence of an already highly complex political economy. This, in turn, has maximized the likelihood of a simultaneous, dominolike collapse of various economic subsystems.

The political variable in this analysis lends further support to the overall thesis. In previous sections I have argued that we should not so readily expect public policy to remedy the shortcomings of other social subsystems. It is my conviction that the governmental response will worsen the economic situation. Inflationary trends have been given enormous impetus by deficit spending, a condition that promises to continue at elevated levels for the foreseeable future. The political dynamics of the budgetary process prevent any other outcome. Demands for services and for expenditures to relieve unemployment are coupled with a rebellion against more taxes; the recent referendum in California cutting the property tax testifies to this last point. In addition, the immediate political gains to be achieved by well-timed tax reductions or by expansions in the money supply—to coincide with election-year politics—is an admission that political action is based on short-run interests. Recovery cannot occur in fits and starts; the insecurity that instability engenders is not conducive to investment and growth.

Microeconomic recovery and growth policies—that is, those policies that operate through specific programs rather than through aggregate budgetary and monetary decisions—also reveal the distorting influences of the political system. The trickle-down approach still predominates as the means of raising growth rates. This is to be expected; public policy reflects (responds to) political power, and therefore, those groups most influential are able to channel policy outputs toward their benefit. Yet, the validity of this method is increasingly open to question, especially given the rise of multinationals. The amount that in fact trickles down to *our* economy is declining as other (foreign) opportunities avail themselves. To the extent that there is a distinction between the welfare of the top business elite and the welfare of the people as a whole, a large amount of economic-turned-political power will be marshaled to further the interests of the former at the expense of the latter.

Long-range prospects are of course difficult to determine. The confluence of trends presented in Chapters 4 and 5 may or may not lead business leaders to initiate compensating adjustments after the individual problems have been revealed. Yet, not all segments of the economy are equally adept at making adjustments or equally in control of their economic destiny; "the new-found affluence of the working classes is very vulnerable to economic dislocations in the twin forms of inflation and unemployment."[17] Other groups, and indeed the welfare state itself, may be similarly vulnerable. Thus, even for those who doubt the likelihood of a general economic collapse, there should be recognition of the probability that certain areas of the economy will face serious hardship. Limits to growth, even selectively experienced, can also have major implications for the future of consensus politics.

Social and Psychological Stress

Sources of Social Distress

The current debate transcends the simple issue of the possibility of further economic growth. It is equally relevant to examine the social-psychological costs that are associated with a growth society. These qualitative disamenities (or socio-psychological pathologies) are consequences of the operation of U.S. society as it seeks and achieves material progress. These costs, too, should be placed on the balance against which we evaluate the desirability of growth. To the extent that social and personal distress—and trends portend their worsening in the future—call into question the continuing benefits of current economic goals, this factor has a major contribution to make in the ongoing growth controversy.

The socio-psychological dimension is crucial as well due to its connection to other factors in the total picture. The social manifestations of the costs of growth are reflected in a number of ways: the decline of the work ethic, the weakening of social cohesion, and limited social adjustment to change—to name three examples. These signs have quite obvious negative consequences on the ability of national institutions to meet the physical challenges to growth. Societal developments set the context for attempts to fashion a policy response to pollution or resource scarcity. The diminishing of our social-psychological resources, of the vital social supports for collective action, complicates political computations, reduces the effectiveness of our decision-making procedures, results in the failure of proposals and policies, further deteriorates political and economic systems, and continues the weakening of the public's faith in the nation's institutions.

The social-psychological concerns presented in this section are more than mere complicators of the policymaking dilemma. Implicit in these concerns are a host of problems that require separate political (and financial) attention. Thus, the social and psychological costs of growth not only set the stage but provide a portion of the plot for the economic and political dramas enfolding today. We must address ourselves to these costs as surely as we must face the energy crisis, because each threatens to undermine our commitment to economic growth.

Future Shock by Alvin Toffler represents perhaps the most widely cited attempt to illuminate the signs and causes of socially induced psychological stress.[18] Toffler described many aspects of current society (or trends that could be expected to predominate in the future) that have placed inordinate strain upon the emotional resources of the average citizen. Primary among the sources of stress is the quickening pace of change in a person's social and personal world. Imagine our being placed, permanently and irreversibly, into an environment sharply different from our own. The attitudes, values, and behavioral cues that made sense of the previous culture would be irrelevant in this setting; indeed, the surroundings themselves are in a constant state of change, thus preventing us from taking security in a set of new values, new cues, new definitions of rationality.

The transience in our lives is compounded by the diversity of choices we confront and the plethora of information available upon which we can base a decision. Yet, the multitude of personal options does not represent increased freedom, nor is our amassing of facts a reflection of increased knowledge. Information overload, as Bruno Bettelheim implies, leaves us no better off regarding how we should proceed: "[It] is not a question of the amount of information but whether it can be used constructively, whether it is understandable as a whole. . . . We must fight against the delusion that the more information we have, the better we are."[19] How, then, do we explain feelings of ignorance in the face of the knowledge explosion? I believe it is a matter of ideological incongruity. The information does not fit neatly into the conceptual categories of the past: the facts do not conform. The search for a more rational explanatory framework for the problems of the modern age is triggered by the realization that anomalies make past frameworks unacceptable. The sense of information overload is the sense that our world view is getting more inconsistent with each new increment of facts.

This bombardment of information is part of a general overstimulation of our senses (the impact of media images, the pace of social change, the transience and novelty of our environment) that has given rise to definite psychosomatic, psychological, and psychosocial pathologies. We are paying a steep price for our way of life. These are the symptoms of extreme wartime tension, society-wide battle fatigue—or future shock.

The problem is one of human adaptation. As Toffler phrases it, "unless man quickly learns to control the rate of change in his personal affairs as well as in society at large, we are doomed to a massive adaptational breakdown."[20] Americans pride themselves on their ability to adjust pragmatically to new problems and circumstances. This boast may not apply to the condition of our psychic state. The observation of René Dubos is directed toward this point: "The limits that must be imposed on social and technological innovations are determined not by scientific knowledge or practical know-how, but by the biological and mental nature of man which is essentially unchangeable."[21] It is undoubtedly true that we can survive as a species within a wide range of situations and under severe pressures. However, our modes of living and thinking are not subject to infinite variety or permanent instability. The maladaptive responses of our body and mind indicate that we cope with the social and psychological hazards of our society only at a cost to our potential development as human beings.

While it is true that on one level—material/physical—the society has been productive and fulfilling of our desires, development as human beings requires that other, higher needs be met. The most basic emotional requirement (beyond physical safety and survival) is that of love and affiliation. This is a vital support for psychic strength, especially in times of stress. Social belonging and affection are getting more difficult to achieve, despite the opportunities of a pluralist society. The following observation attests to this fact.

> In the rush to industrialize we break up communities [physically, culturally and spiritually], so that the controls formerly regulating behavior are destroyed before alternatives can be provided. Urban drift is one result of this process, with a consequent rise in antisocial practices, crime, delinquency, and so on, which are so costly for society in terms both of money and of well-being.[22]

The weakening of personal and geographic ties also has been brought on by the quickening pace of change. Our style of life telescopes relationships with people and places, impeding the formation of bonds of trust and community. For many, the feeling of belonging is both artificial and superficial given the transitory nature of our contacts with others.[23]

More abstract needs remain similarly unsatisfied. People desire some measure of prestige and social esteem; ego satisfaction is a necessary prerequisite for a healthy self-image. Also important is the belief in one's efficacy—control over one's own life and therefore some power over the actions of others with respect to oneself. Likewise, a high value is placed on the needs for creativity and achievement. Social and occupational mobility is the standard tactic for those who want prestigious, powerful, and/or creative positions. However, all societies have provided some opportunities for need-gratification for most of its members. Some evidence, though, suggests that industrial societies generally, and the United States in particular, are noticeably limited in the degree to which these higher needs can be met.

Examining the satisfactions of work situations demonstrates the validity of this claim (although other topics would suffice equally well). Despite the statements of business leaders that technology and automation have eliminated the most routine and mechanical jobs on the assembly line, the factory work environment remains debilitating and dehumanizing. It might be becoming more so; even so-called creative positions are increasingly defined as adjuncts to the machine or "specialties" within a "subfield" of a "discipline." Organizations have grown too large and too complex; workers at all but the top levels are alienated by distant authority operating through depersonalized hierarchies.[24] Industrial psychology has established that a work environment that ignores the nonmaterial needs of the employees risks the loss of productivity and profits. It is significant, therefore, to note the major decline in the motivating power of the work ethic, revealing itself in high absenteeism and turnover rates, carelessness (or perhaps conscious sabotage), and a general resistance to on-the-job authority. The normative mechanisms of industrial cohesion and coordination are breaking down. Other means of insuring job performance and task integration (e.g., higher remuneration, strict oversight coupled with threats of dismissal) require more material resources, are less effective than hoped for, and thus tend to reduce productivity still further. In many respects, the working conditions of Americans remain behind those of their European counterparts, and this has had an impact on comparative economic growth.

When this analysis is applied to society at large, the connection between "style of life" and "quality of life" becomes apparent. The limits of our adaptability to future shock and the inability of institutions to satisfy higher level human needs combine to bring about a host of psychologically related social diseases. Increases in crime and violence, alcoholism and drug addiction, broken marriages, child abuse, etc. are as much social costs of our form of industrialization as is polluted air and water. We face a diminishing of social cohesion, especially in our urban areas, and the creation of a climate of fear and distrust—a garrison mentality. Consequently, society is forced to resort to calculative and/or coercive modes of integration because the moral restraints on antisocial behavior are declining.[25]

To other victims of growth, the loss of social cohesion reveals itself in a nonviolent form—increasing social insensitivity brought about by a turning inward away from the larger group and the larger group's problems. California, in many ways a sociological laboratory of postindustrialism, is an excellent example of the modes of thought and action encouraged by the psychological pressures of change, insecurity, and lost identification with the wider community:

Personal alienation and malaise have also increased among many sectors of California's society. . . . In both Northern and Southern California, the encounter-group mystique, the drug culture, and other loosely organized manifestations of the search for alternative life styles have been sufficiently in evidence to promote a rash of popular commentary. . . . [In addition,] the doctrines of neofundamentalist and mystical religious movements have increased their drawing power.[26]

The growing concern with personal self-awareness (or personal salvation) is in essence a conscious withdrawal from the structural problems of our day. The long-run political implications of this development have been excellently outlined by Edwin Schur in *The Awareness Trap*.[27] To the extent that part of the public is absorbed in self-needs, there will be weakened pressures for social and economic change. These symptoms of social disintegration are the other side of the coin to the violent behavior described above. It is safe to say that both industrial and political cohesion are being threatened by "a creeping paralysis of noncooperation, as expressed in various types of escapism on the part, not only of the oppressed and exploited, but even of highly privileged groups."[28]

Social Breakdown and Limits to Growth

Both of these behavioral responses to psychological stress (and the feelings of alienation, frustration, and insecurity that lie behind them) will inevitably have a negative impact on growth rates: first, by diverting scarce resources, not the least of which is political attention, from other pressing issues to the social problems caused by future shock and need deprivation; second, by creating an atmosphere of justified noninvolvement, making effective, unified action against environmental and economic crises all the more difficult; and third, by directly causing a decrease in worker morale, in identification with corporate goals, and in traditional aspects of economic development. On this last point we note that, along with the decline in the work ethic, we also see less of a willingness to delay gratifications, to be thrifty, to save and invest in order to achieve future rewards. Side by side with this quite materialistic trend is the growth of antimaterialism. Quality-of-life concerns and a desire for existential meaning (voluntary simplicity) have replaced the keeping-up-with-the-Joneses syndrome for some, with important consequences on consumer buying patterns. In addition, faith in the outputs of the private market system has waned. From personnel practices (affirmative action) to investment policies (environmental impact statements) to product quality (seat belts or fire-retardant children's pajamas), more groups are relying on the government to correct the perceived abuses of the private sector. Charles E. Silberman has addressed himself to the economic import, at this point still vague, inherent in the social and psychological developments to which I have alluded:

> Our uncertainties today begin with the probability that Americans may be embracing a set of values so different that they add up to a whole new outlook on life and work and society. . . . The new values could profoundly alter consumer demand, on the one hand, and the growth of productivity of the labor force, hence of the economy's capacity to produce, on the other.[29]

Thus, we can anticipate some drag on our GNP, or on the quality of our lives, from the psychological costs of social change and economic growth.

I would claim that the issue goes deeper than this. We are in a period of transition, of continual transition according to Toffler, leading to the seeming uncontrollableness of social change. We can therefore understand that there is a vital need to buy time in order to find the human resources that will promote personal and social adaptation to the unfolding events of the future. However, our society may be unable or unwilling to reverse the aforementioned trends toward social decay and psychological anguish. In our commitment to consumerism, individualism, and the "now" mentality, we may have lost that sense of national purpose, conviction, hope, and cohesion that is society's most important resource. Social breakdown is a real threat, especially in light of the increased pressures and sacrifices the future will demand of us. How we define our collective destiny, whether we can emotionally identify with the lives of generations yet to be, will dictate the success we have in responding to our long-range economic and environmental ills. In the words of Kenneth Boulding, "there is a great deal of historical evidence to suggest that a society which loses its identity with posterity and which loses its positive image of the future loses also its capacity to deal with present problems, and soon falls apart."[30]

The implications of this statement for the limits-to-growth controversy are self-evident.

The Political Variable

Political Limits

Limits-to-growth advocates often ignore the political aspects of the environmental and economic reality. They slide over the inevitable conflicts of interest among social groups that will mark the way toward reduced economic expansion. Their hope is that some moralistic consensus will arise out of the shock of being on the brink of ecological disaster. Equally confident about the political variable are those who reject the limits argument. Proponents of growth see our physical, social, and economic problems as amenable to careful political control and resolution. The ability of public policy to rectify the environmental wrongs and manage our society with a minimum of delay, conflict, error, or cost to our economic growth rate is never doubted. Both of these positions, in spite of some allusions to politics, basically contain no realistic appraisal of the political prospects of certain changes. By ignoring conflict and uncertainty, they have tried to depoliticize these issues. As Robert Heilbroner has noted, this

> Omission of a political dimension is . . . crippling, even fatal, for a comprehension of the human prospect. For the exercise of political power lies squarely in the center of the determination of that prospect. The resolution of the crises thrust upon us by the social and natural environment can only be found through political action.[31]

We have touched on the political variable in previous sections, but we now examine it directly in order to answer a basic question: Can political decision making be relied upon to overcome, with reasonable efficiency, the various obstacles to continued economic growth, or will it, too, suffer from the crises of the age and thus help to cause, not cure, our future economic ills?

What we are confronting here is the possibility of political limits to growth.

> [Political limits are] set by the already overstrained capacity of human beings to conceive, design, manage, support, and adapt to extremely

complex systems of human interdependence. In short, it is the political limits that are likely to constrain the continuity of physical growth well ahead of all other factors. The United States and other members of the world community are now pressing against their political limits and will find it increasingly difficult to take actions that would be required to assure continuing growth.[32]

This notion of political limits will be tested under fire as our institutions and processes are asked to deal with the problems of resource scarcity, pollution, the loss of social cohesion, contradictions in our political economy, etc. It is my belief that an intensification of policy demands—policy overload—will reveal basic shortcomings in the decision-making capacity of the political system and that these shortcomings will seriously diminish the effectiveness of public policies designed to prolong growth. The remainder of the section examines this hypothesis.

The major source of stress for the political system is the ever increasing and varied demands thrust upon government by an ever increasing variety of groups. Since the New Deal, almost all areas of social life have required (or appear to require) governmental action. The degree and nature of public sector involvement now being called for is a far cry from the public-private distinction premised by Lockean liberalism (and still touted in current political rhetoric). A negative "invisible hand," operating on a number of present crises, requires an enormous increase in collective control of the previously self-regulated private sector and, with more difficulty, the acceptance of a radically new perspective regarding the amount of governmental intervention we must tolerate. Failure in other subsystems (e.g., environment, urban society, international economics) prompts and justifies our turning to politics.

Yet, not all of the demands overloading the system can be attributed to this source. For many groups, the political system has become the new "commons." Every interest seeks a greater share of political largess—tariff considerations, subsidy programs, tax benefits—mindful that the burdens of such interest-specific legislation will be spread throughout society via higher prices, higher taxes, or higher inflation rates stemming from deficit spending. The forces promoting a tragedy of the political commons are formidable.[33] Compounding this new pressure on the political process is government's continued concern with unresolved policy areas; incrementalism does not solve problems so much as defers them. Finally, additional time and energy must now be devoted to the issues posed by the limits crises. Thus, the demands placed upon the system have escalated to threatening levels.

Parallel developments have been taking place with respect to the qualitative nature of these demands. Policy issues have become more complex and interrelated, the variables that need to be considered are more numerous, and the costs associated with delay or error are much greater. Given these difficulties, it is no wonder that the impact of governmental action is often opposite from expectations; policies operate counterintuitively. We still know surprisingly little about the interconnections through which policy outputs (authoritative governmental decisions) are transformed into policy impacts (social consequences). This ignorance is heightened when we focus on issue-areas, such as the environment, about whose internal dynamics even less is known. Policy overload is also related to the gravity of the problems that ask for attention. In an era of backup systems and low-level technology, the consequences of policy mistakes were never irreversible or cataclysmic. Now, however, errors in policy judgment can have severe repercussions upon many other social, economic, and ecological events. As mentioned above, complex interrelated systems and subsystems are more vulnerable. Thus, governmental decisions are filled with immense risk, thereby placing the political system under immense pressure.

Add to these factors the role of time. If we ponder over the problems associated with limits too long, if we do not quickly appreciate the severity of the situation, if our policies are piecemeal and ineffective, matters can only worsen. The immediacy of these crises clashes with a political system prone to delay, obstruction, and non-decision making. It is difficult for us to realize the time pressures we are under. Geometric growth of our energy needs, for instance, means that solutions posited on past requirements might be outdated even as they are being enacted. The pace of change leaves little room for reflection and consultation. In the present context of risk and uncertainty, it is no wonder that policymaking is more stressful.

Unfortunately, the political system has not adapted to the new demand structure of our stressful era. The government is heir to a set of biases that allows it to handle certain types of problems while ignoring or anguishing over others. Thus, the policymaking process, by its very nature, distorts our perception of a given issue and prevents rational approaches toward its resolution. According to Karl W. Deutsch, the procedural and conceptual biases of politics emphasize:

> the near over the far, the familiar over the new, the past over the present, the present over the future. They involve overestimation or overvaluation of the organization compared to the environment, of its past methods and commitments over new ones, and of its current will and inner structure over all possibilities of fundamental change.[34]

The press of elections and the "now" mentality of the electorate discourage long-range time perspectives, especially those that attempt to justify present sacrifices. Simultaneously, fragmentation in the policy-formation process (pluralism and interest-group participation, checks and balances, veto groups, incrementalism, legislative-committee-agency alliances) seriously prevents broad-gauged, systematic approaches. Programs are supported in terms of their immediate and personal political benefits; thus, the tendency is toward symbolic acts that achieve temporary breathing time without antagonizing the powerful interests that would feel threatened by real change. The public is too easily reassured by pseudo policies that, like nondecisions generally, give time the opportunity to aggravate our condition. Without substantive legislation, further deterioration of our physical and human environments is inevitable.

Realize, too, that past affluence (and the illusions of affluence) allowed us the luxury of irrationality and waste. We never had to maximize the utility of every dollar spent. The decision costs of increased policy efficiency outweighed the benefits gained by attention to marginal policy productivity. But in an age of scarcity, economy is a necessarily important aspect of a program's overall objective. Yet, such a concern represents a basic conceptual shift for the public and for policymakers alike. The requirement for optimality increases the decision costs (and thereby decreases the capacities) of the system generally. We can expect political resistance to efficiency reforms from groups that benefit from patterns of waste and ineffectiveness. We cannot ignore the fact that we have reached the present impasse in no small part because of the absence of past political prudence and rationality.

The procedures and institutions of our political system further complicate the task of fashioning an effective response to the limits crises. Is our system an appropriate vehicle for dealing with these new issues? In an interesting article entitled "Clean Rhetoric, Dirty Water," A. Myrick Freeman III and Robert H. Haveman summarize the structural, systemic reasons why current approaches to water pollution abatement (and environmental damage generally) are failing. The authors claim that despite the legislation recently passed, the regulatory strategy being employed to limit pollution "pits the power of public agencies against polluters in a context in which the rules of the struggle and the information available to each party are biased against the government."[35] The economic inducements that public policies offer to companies result in suboptimal measures being taken, with financial benefit going to business but little being gained in water quality. Certain types of pollutants that are less measurable or less visible are de-emphasized in policy because political pressure stresses point source pollution. Thus, feedlot runoff, heavy metal pollution, loss of soil fertility and nutrients, etc. are allowed to continue. Federalism creates cross-pressures that delay solutions and enable one region to shift social costs onto another. The lack of policy coordination and obstacles in the way of implementing legislation are additional causes of failure. Here as elsewhere, the political process distorts policy intentions. Solutions that are technically and economically feasible are not politically viable. Antipollution policy has become another source of governmental funding, another chance to distribute public largess toward oneself. Optimists who are counting on effective, efficient governmental action should consider the conclusion reached by Freeman and Haveman: "the continued spending of taxpayers' money to clean up after polluters—along the lines of current strategy—is going to be an enormously expensive and relatively fruitless venture."[36]

The idea of political limits is a credible addition to the host of other challenges to growth. We may conclude that a synergetic relationship is present. That is, politics may magnify these challenges, distort rational attempts to meet them, prolong costly and debilitating trends, and, in general, achieve minimum salutary effect with maximum misallocation of resources and, therefore, maximum negative impact on growth rates and standards of living.

It is also possible that the political system might be overwhelmed, unable to cope with policy overload. In the process of confronting its own limits, the system might collapse, a pathology best described as political future shock.[37]

The Loss of Legitimacy

The nonphysical limits to growth discussed in this chapter are all indications of the failure of technique, the inability of various specialists to manage the social system. The law of diminishing returns is in effect on a societal scale.

> The more complex the society, the more regulatory functions are required, the more lawyers are needed to argue about inequities, the more administrative personnel are required to plan, supervise, and audit. Most of these people are necessary to manage an extremely complicated society, but they inevitably drain away vast numbers of tax dollars and thus reduce the disposable income of the workers who are producing the goods and rendering the services for which people enjoy spending their disposable incomes.[38]

From a managerial perspective, bigness, centralization, intensive specialization, and interdependence exact their own cost in administrative inefficiency. In both the public and private sectors there are programs of enormous waste, inconsistency, and ineffectiveness. The optimists' expectation of relatively painless managerial cure-alls for our human and physical problems is therefore highly questionable.

Such an expectation provides the momentum for an accelerating cycle of demand-failure-frustration. A heightened level of conflict combines with an added sense of urgency on the part of combatants to improve or maintain their position through the coming economic crisis. However, in the absence of a spirit of compromise, trust, social cohesion, and patience, mutually satisfactory policies may not be found; the system fails to live up to the desires of concerned citizens. This further exacerbates the situation. "The greater the failure of the State to meet the demands made upon it the more the State is overloaded with fresh demands for it to rectify the shortcomings of its performance."[39] Frustration in some circles may take the form of impulsive violence, disruptive terrorism, or well-directed social protest activity. The failure of technique is transformed into a matter for politics: "Our traditional methods of election and management no longer give administrators the skills and capacity they need to handle their complex new burdens and decisions. They become swollen, unresponsive—and repudiated."[40]

This grim prognosis strikes at the heart of our political system. The era of the politicized society foreshadows the end of consensus politics.

> The fragility of the system may be reflected in its declining legitimacy. Many studies suggest that the trendline of support for critical political, economic, and social institutions is down. New forms of conflict and intergroup hostility appear. New groups enter the political process with unprecedented demands that cannot easily be assimilated to established patterns; and ancient cultural and ethnic rivalries are revived, on new terms, with new implications. Some see a growing cleavage between the values and assumptions of elites and mass publics over the desirable direction of change.[41]

This serious observation is not necessarily tied to the fate of any of the previous elements of the limits-to-growth controversy. The squandering of the resource of legitimacy is a separate guarantee that major social and political changes are in the offing.

Conclusions

Chapters 4 and 5 have examined the varied aspects of the limits-to-growth controversy. The argument is clearly not one-sided and will undoubtedly remain on the social agenda until events decide the issue. However, this is no reason to avoid taking a stand. Human choice has a critical role to play: "probably the most important factor in the complex equation of the country's future is the way individuals will respond to crises ahead."[42] So we must choose between the combatants in this debate, knowing that a prudent weighing of the available evidence is always subject to reconsideration. My own analysis leads me to accept the limits hypothesis, not because the expectations of the progrowth position are impossible but because they are improbable.

At first glance, the issue seems to be one of balance; a product or service economy, qualitative versus quantitative growth, a social-versus private-benefit orientation, directed or uncontrolled development—these terms seem to summarize the problems and choices confronting this nation. We need not limit growth, so the argument goes, only reemphasize certain of its components in order to construct a more appropriate and sustainable form of economic growth.[43] Growth advocates hope to avoid major structural change by successfully "tinkering" with (and within) the present system. The concept of technique is at the heart of this position. The economist searches for answers in the careful adjustment of free-market incentives. The scientist and engineer seek relief through the application of their areas of specialized knowledge. And the social scientist relies on the efficient management of effective public policies. Technical "solutions" in this vein can overcome the obstacles to future prosperity without requiring basic and painful alterations in our economic, social, and political systems. Indeed, many contend that the continuing quest of the American Dream is furthered, not obstructed, by coming events: "Most projections of a post-industrial political future have indicated a diminution of conflict. Science and technology have been the benevolent forces that will continue to reshape the physical environment in response to new economic demands."[44]

The curative power of technological "tinkering" to rectify the imbalances of economic growth is, according to the limits position, grossly inadequate to the type of problems we now face. These superficial solutions gloss over the tough battles and major consequences that truly effective policies would entail. More and more observers are impressed with the fundamental nature of the limits crises. What of the claim that we need only adjust the balance in our mode of development in order to successfully handle the disamenities of growth? The "tinkering" that would be required for this endeavor will necessitate basic changes in our political economy. In effect, we will have thereupon accepted a redefinition of growth, and our acting on that new definition will be nothing short of revolutionary. Thus, while technology might ideally alleviate a large part of the economic hardships and dislocations we will experience, its effective use will have major structural consequences.

Limits advocates also point to the factors of politics and power that frequently obstruct a full commitment to the public interest.

The best outcome can hardly be achieved when private interests, the sacrifices of which are a necessary part of the total good, can prevent the passage of desired policy. Conflict will cloud both problems and solutions; in the process, the general lessening of our political capacities will itself become part of the overall crisis. A realistic appraisal would conclude that faith in public policies designed to maintain growth levels is suspect. In an area so fraught with self-interest, social importance, and conflicting opinions, public action will never be swift, clear, cost-effective, and decisive. We will probably continue past trends of neglect, conflict, inconsistency, and waste. The product of our political labors may bring relief, but it will be transitory, costly, and ultimately self-defeating.

The major consequence of the political factor will be on the third variable—time. If technology attempts to buy time for long-range solutions, it is equally accurate to say that politics will often waste time. We need to gradually adjust our structure to a new reality and our minds to new attitudes. A conservational mentality does not develop overnight, nor can it immediately motivate actions and institutions. Yet, we have talked of crises, a term that assumes very little time for such social and psychological shifts. Admittedly, time pressure can encourage the necessary impetus to decision makers, but it does not create a climate conducive to calm deliberation and rational problem solving. This factor seems to be the most crucial and most unknowable in the controversy.

Reviewing the evidence, the most prudent and plausible conclusion is that there will be a long-term drag on our economic growth. At best, this will result in overall stagnation with selective severe distress for many industries, regions, and groups; at worst, economic downturn will significantly lower the standard of living for most Americans.

Those who want to keep people a part of the history-making process, who reject notions of historical imperatives or behavioral inevitability, might object to the determinism implied in my analysis. I share with them the belief that the future is always open to the handiwork of humankind. However, the various historical, ideological, physical, and social forces discussed in Chapters 4 and 5 compose the context within which the subjective factors of technology, politics, and time interact. These structural givens may not determine the future, but they do have a future-shaping role to play. Problems in the physical and human environment are imperatives in the sense that they are the agenda for our discussions and the focus of our energies. As such, they necessarily impede our capacities, divert our attention, divide our collective resources, reduce our options, and, ultimately, prevent an accommodation between further growth and our values as a people. The limits position therefore encompasses both objective and subjective elements in reaching its conclusion. In the words of Robert Heilbroner, *"whether we are unable to sustain growth or unable to tolerate it,* there can be no doubt that a radically different future beckons."[45]

Though events propel us toward limits, our political system hesitates, recoils, and seeks expediency. It is unprepared (or afraid) to accept the possibility of limits, to conceptualize a no-growth society.

> No American politician has ever been able to talk about [problems associated with a no-growth future]; indeed, there is no political language in America—not yet—in which they can be discussed, no language not founded on premises of growth and expansion, and the country desperately needs such a language.[46]

The demands of the transition period are enormous. Just as growth helped to mold our conception of "hope," "success," and "the American way of life," so limits may be equally influential in reconstructing these images. However, if the limits position is correct, we will, we must somehow have to accept our new circumstances. Indeed, even though the political system refrains from confronting the issue of no-growth, many people are slowly awakening to the prospects of limits. But how will society understand and interpret the evolving political economy? The next chapter examines the prospective battle over this question and its implications for the future of U.S. politics.

6

Speculations on the
Future of Politics

Introduction

This chapter speculates on the political questions dominant in a no-growth or slow-growth future. Our initial objective, however, is to examine the process by which society comes to recognize the new economic reality. Conflicts surrounding this process—the politics of awareness—are the first shots in the political battles to come. Attention next turns to forecasting methodology. Biases in current futures research are noted, and the scenarios approach employed in this analysis is introduced. Discussion then focuses on the various scenarios competing for dominance in a future of limited growth. Specifically, we will study the conflicting interpretations of limits vying for popular support, the strategic appeals associated with these interpretations, and, finally, the factors determining the political success or failure of the conflicting images of the future. The conclusion of the chapter probes the implications of limits to growth for the future of democracy in the United States.

The Politics of Limiting Growth

Despite the evidence in favor of the limits-to-growth position and despite the headlines that implicitly warn of its validity, the pressures for change have not built sufficiently to force the creation of a new political system premised on a new set of political issues. This time lag is critical for the analysis that follows. We cannot usefully speculate on the dynamics of a future political situation until we know how that situation will have evolved. Rudolf Klein alludes to this preliminary concern in posing the following question: "What are the social and political processes which will produce a stable society, as distinct from the social and political problems that may be created by the emergence of such a society?"[1] We need to examine the means by which the limits-to-growth problems presented in Chapters 4 and 5 will lead to a general acceptance of economic limits. The future is an outgrowth of the process of economic decline as well as a product of a declined economy; put another way, the politics of limited growth reflects the politics of limiting growth.

Resistance to the Idea of Limits

Creating a limits consciousness will not be easy, so intense has been the support for the growth-as-is position. B. Bruce-Briggs (citing Hudson Institute figures in an article representative of all professional optimists) has proclaimed the present feasibility (read desirability) of a world of fifteen to twenty billion people consuming on average the products and services of a modern U.S. upper-middle-class family—a 100-fold increase in world productive capacity.[2] Additional examples of optimism abound. Even the calendars seem to inspire confidence: "the cultural heritage of millennialism leads to a widespread feeling of hope that rounding the bend of this last thousand-year cycle will usher in a new and better era for man."[3] President Carter has discovered that the energy crisis is not sufficiently warlike in its magnitude, as of yet, to impress upon the public the need for national unity above politics-as-usual. Indeed, the mood of progress infests our attitudes almost in spite of events around us. Individuals, divorcing their own material fortunes from that of the society, expect personal improvement even while acknowledging the troubles of the present.[4]

The public's faith in future growth is further buoyed by business interpretations of the limits debate. The Zero Economic Growth (ZEG) position, according to some business analysts, is planting the seeds of its own success. Fruition depends not upon actual environmental or sociopolitical developments but upon the degree to which such notions as limits create a climate of economic opinion resistant to growth. Gurney Breckenfeld (writing in the *Saturday Review*) believes that current (and future) slow-downs result from business insecurity about the level of social support for growth. Business leaders are hesitant about making an investment in the future because of forces that make their growth plans very risky (e.g., consumerism, environmentalism, labor demands, government interference, an anti-incentive tax structure).[5] Many of our economic ills are therefore "cured" with a healthy dose of optimism. No doubt there is some truth in this observation. A precipitous loss of public confidence would very quickly incite a "run-on-the-banks" mentality and result in a psychologically induced economic collapse. So the maintenance of a positive economic posture, which includes the belief that obstacles can be easily overcome by technological advances or by minor adjustments, is an important cause of business opposition to antigrowth enthusiasts.

International economic and political factors can encourage a "growth-at-any-price" attitude. When future economic expansion is tied to notions of national security, society tends to tolerate the domestic costs of growth. David Amidon states this point clearly:

> There will continue to be virtually irresistible world-wide commitment to growth precisely so long as there is chronic and intense international conflict. In other words, a critical obstacle in the way of antigrowth policies in the most advanced nation-states is the attachment of rival blocs to theories about the relatedness of economics and power and prestige. . . . Every opportunity which seems to afford a chance to increase power is seized upon by the contenders, whether reluctantly or cheerfully, on the grounds that anything that might enable a nation to enhance its power cannot be neglected as a possible advantage in the ongoing conflict. Growth, of course, is generally supposed to contribute fairly directly to increased national power.[6]

Resistance to growth-reducing policies takes on the aura of patriotism. This, however, will not still the debate. Programs will be proposed that, for instance, impose strict regulatory standards on the discharge of industrial wastes. If foreign "enterprises were not subject to similar stringent supervision, they would enjoy relative price advantages in international trading."[7] This would adversely affect our balance of payments, spur the export of investment capital, magnify the economic impact of antipollution policy, and thereby intensify resistance to a limits-to-growth awareness.

A great deal of the popular opposition to the limits position can be attributed to the structural biases in how we perceive indicators of the costs of growth. The gradualness of deterioration in our physical and human environments allows each generation to view the status quo as natural, to accept present levels of social and natural problems as the zero base against which to compare future disamenities. Our past experience with limited growth conjures up in the minds of most Americans the periodic recessions and depressions that have increased unemployment, decreased living standards, and been the source of so much misery. The equations have been burned in the public's consciousness: growth equals affluence, limits equals deprivation. Perceptual bias is also a factor in the weight we give to economic measures of well-being. As a result, people are inclined to overlook any evidence that economic activity may be reducing their standard of living. Communities defend industrial plants that pollute the air and water because of the alleged primacy of monetary considerations. Other examples indicating a similar distortion of values can be found.

Perceptual bias also refers to the way in which signals of decay are conceptually isolated from their economic and political roots. The health hazards imposed by certain types of pollutants are difficult to monitor. Built-in time lags, interactions with environmental processes, and synergistic relationships with other pollutants (as explained in Chapter 4) complicate the task of tracing responsibility for the specific danger to a specific commercial activity. Environmental dangers that manifest themselves by increasing aggregate vulnerability (increasing the likelihood that harm will occur, that a higher percentage of the population will be affected, that the severity will be proportionately greater) perpetuate the idea that *individual* fate and chance, not political and economic structures, lie behind the pollution problem. Continuing along this same vein, many dramatic signs of environmental decay are perceived to arise from diverse and seemingly unrelated sources. As a result, broad demands for basic reform get transformed into weak piecemeal and issue-specific proposals; examples include an air inversion in Los Angeles, unreclaimed, strip-mined land in Ohio, soil erosion in Kansas, cancer deaths and birth defects near nuclear power facilities, massive oil spills off the Texas coast, or a worsening water table in Florida. Viewed as isolated cases, these events could be minimized as the "price of progress" or the "plight of industrial man." A similar form of perceptual evasion occurs regarding the popular understanding of social problems. The tendency here is to place the blame for crime, delinquency, declining social cohesion, etc. on the superstructure (e.g., permissive values) rather than on the substructure (inequality). It is obvious that overcoming these biases and building an awareness of the true import of the growth crisis will be painful and therefore resisted by many.

This resistance is not confined to any one ideological position. Opposition to limits spans the political spectrum. Advertisements by companies favoring growth skirt the fundamental nature of the limits debate. A public service message promoted by the Advertising Council of America (business funding) asks what one person can do to solve the pollution crisis. The suggestions listed (e.g., cleaning spark plugs to get better gas mileage, putting litter in a litter basket) are offered as vital steps toward an effective solution to environmental decay. The piece concludes with a revealing plea: "Above all, let's stop shifting the blame. People start pollution. People can stop it. When enough Americans realize this we'll have a fighting chance in the war against pollution."[8] This approach not only diverts responsibility, it also sets out a hopeful and basically painless means of avoiding the basic growth-environment choice.

Leftists also attempt to deny the limits argument. Claiming that scarcity has been contrived in order to increase corporate prices and profits, Stanley Aronowitz is very much a part of the pro-growth perspective. "I believe that the chance of stemming inflation depends entirely on finding ways to expand production of real goods."[9] Gus Tyler reinforces the same theme.[10] His support for left-liberalism is based upon the expectation that, once in power, its representatives can remove many of the contradictions of capitalism that inhibit the future growth of the economy. Both authors contend that the slow-growth position is elitist and inegalitarian. While there is much substance to their charges that corporate policies lie behind resource scarcity, other elements of the limits argument are less clearly a matter of conscious manipulation. That is, the characterization of the no-growth position as elitist does not ring true. In any case, the progrowth stance taken by most companies and leftists indicates the ideological breadth of the resistance that the limits position generates.

Final mention should be made of the "insider's" assumption

that the pollution issue will follow the usual cycle of public problems and eventually decline in popular attention. This is a common pattern, according to Anthony Downs, but one that is unlikely to occur for this policy area.[11] The author cites a number of reasons why he expects that ecological matters will remain in (perhaps even dominate) the public spotlight, reasons that can also apply to other problem areas we have examined.

This, then, is the dilemma of transition—to reconcile the confrontation between events that will demand increased attention and the massive resistance to the economic implications of these events that can be anticipated. How will this resistance be overcome? The following section discusses the various ways in which the public will accept the validity of limits to growth. This is the politics of awareness.

Transitions to Awareness

Those who already have been converted, who welcome or have resigned themselves to the impending decline in growth rates, do not readily agree amongst themselves on how the public's "awakening" may take place. Some observers believe that society will voluntarily accept the ethics of no-growth, reduce personal and social aspirations, and develop into a form of steady state. The following comment by Erich Jantsch is indicative of this line of thinking:

> The conclusion I draw, and I think it is the only possible conclusion, is that we shall have to get the Western countries not only to prevent their economies from growing, but that the West will have to take several steps backward, lowering the material standard of living of the population, cutting back on consumption and taking a share in a more equitable distribution of the world's resources. This is going to be hard on the Western governments and even harder on the people.[12]

Such a view depoliticizes the process of limits "consciousness raising" and consequently is able to gloss over the conflicts that such a transformation would entail. A variant explanation of the voluntaristic transition is offered by Walter A. Weisskopf.[13] According to Weisskopf, everyone in society is experiencing a profound loss in nonmaterial values by subserving all other definitions of "good" to that of economics. It is clear to him that the steady state is desirable existentially even though it is not yet a physical necessity. I do not doubt the truth of this conclusion, but it is quite another matter to assume that our existential loss applies to all and is seen with similar clarity by everyone.

The obstacles to voluntaristic transition scenarios are both political and conceptual. First, while the stakes that people have in maintaining present arrangements are real, the future remains vague; interests have not yet become concrete. One's losses from change are often obvious, but the future's constituency cannot speak with as firm a voice. Admittedly, some people can identify their interests in a no-growth future and voluntarily accept its constraints. For most others, however, living in a culture that is bent toward the "here and now," a more compelling reason to forego growth will have to be found. Second, the shift to a mentality of economic limits cannot be imagined or intellectualized easily. Awareness can come best only with hard experience (although how "hard" that experience will have to be is open to debate). An interesting demonstration of this point is found in a story told by Jerry Mander on understanding the idea of finiteness.

> I have some friends who about three years ago moved to Hawaii after living most of their lives on the mainland, and who recently wrote me that they are suffering from island sickness (a common syndrome of expatriate mainlanders). They spend weekends driving clear around the island, maybe more than once, thinking that eventually some new direction will appear, but it never does.
>
> The *natives* of Hawaii don't have this problem. . . . They know perfectly well what *finiteness* means and . . . simply don't think about getting off the island.[14]

The limits perspective cannot be internalized by any voluntary effort of will. To some extent we have to live it, experience it, in order to appreciate the change it demands in our outlook and conduct.

A quasi-voluntaristic vision sees the coming decline as a result of the reevaluation of public marginal utilities and a subsequent steady adjustment to a less expansive and more ecologically livable society. The gradual transfer of funds from private material to public or nonmaterial sources of satisfaction is, in fact, what is presently occurring under the notion of personal and social trade-offs: "as environmental quality deteriorates, people will, through voluntary controls and the political process, divert resources from material goods to environmental types of material well-being."[15] Technology helps to buy time to avert the most serious effects of this exchange, to allow for its psychological acceptance, and to insure that the economy and the society can adapt gradually. The growth mentality (and therefore the political influence of growth advocates) slowly loses its pulling power as the high costs and deep contradictions of further growth become self-evident. This last point has been aptly phrased by Lynton K. Caldwell: "As conventional economic assumptions prove inconsistent with emerging ecological realities, 'economistic' thinking loses credibility."[16] This gradualist version of limits awareness places us in the middle or turning point of a classic, S-shaped growth curve. As we approach the "ceiling conditions" imposed by a closed ecological system, the slope *naturally* levels off.[17] The question of how to reduce growth is irrelevant. We would not voluntarily choose a steady-growth policy and repudiate growth; instead, we face the prospect of slowed growth (with some regret, I suspect) as a consequence of policies dealing with other problems that have risen in priority to the "crisis" stage—social breakdown, water pollution, etc.

This vision does have a political element. The incremental anti-growth impacts of numerous, separately contended policies, rather than the conscious mass acceptance of the steady state, more realistically portrays sociopolitical processes. In addition, it does not fall victim to the failing found in much of the ZEG literature. The social values we have lost—community, unalienating work life, authentic personal relationships—cannot be reobtained by simply reducing growth. The current state of our economy, not its continued growth, is the root cause of growth-induced problems, and, as has been often said, ZEG will not change that cause. Yet, the gradualist scenario assumes that the crises we will confront can be overcome through piecemeal programs, that our structural dependence on growth can be withdrawn in stages. This is, in my opinion, not likely. E. F. Schumacher paints a more accurate picture of the difficulty involved: "the present consumer society is like a drug addict who, no matter how miserable he may feel, finds it extremely difficult to get off the hook."[18] Any time gained by technological advances is, like an addict's "one last fix," a reason to believe that limits can be permanently avoided and, therefore, represents a chance to postpone the processes of reform. Gradually "tapering off" is conceivable but not probable.

An effective way of encouraging a limits awareness is by indicating the consequences of ignoring its inevitability. As Frederick Ferré poses the dilemma:

> Either the ending will be involuntary and tragic, through the dooms of starvation and disease, or through widespread pollution catastrophe, or through economic collapse due to exhaustion of nonrenewable resources; or the ending will be voluntary [gradual] and . . . merely horrendously difficult.[19]

The potential of disaster is a popular theme. This quote is indicative of the general "doomsday" approach to no-growth. Ferré offers society no choice regarding limits but a very important choice with respect to when the public recognizes the necessity of reducing growth. Delay brings on disaster. In reality, though, the doomsday literature is aimed not at prediction but at drama. A believable simulation of a major social or environmental crisis may be sufficient inducement for readjustment in growth policy. My own feeling is that such simulations will have negligible effect on long-term trends given the strong resistance to the limits position.

A more realistic and less dramatic version of the disaster thesis ought to be examined. Perhaps our economy, structured for growth rather than for stability, will periodically overshoot its natural limits (whatever they may be at any given time) and then abruptly fall back down to a lower level of economic activity and personal (dis)comfort. Robert Heilbroner posits this bleak sequence of events in his analysis of our awakening to the new order.

> There seems no hope for rapid changes in the human character traits that would have to be modified to bring about a peaceful, organized reorientation of life styles. . . . The myopia that confines the present vision of men to the short-term future is not likely to disappear overnight, rendering still more difficult a planned and orderly retrenchment and redivision of output.
>
> Therefore, the outlook is for what we may call "convulsive change"— change forced upon us by external events rather than by conscious choice, by catastrophe rather than by calculation. . . . A "storm of

crisis problems" . . . may . . . slow down economic growth and give a
necessary impetus to the piecemeal construction of an ecologically
and socially viable social system.[20]

Spasmodic growth thrusts, followed by periods of retrenchment,
depression, and severe hardship, will by degrees alter our psychological and structural inclination toward unbounded, undirected
material growth. A "storm of crisis problems" will provide a sufficient demonstration of the inevitability of limits to force some
reevaluation of personal and social goals.

This examination of the possible transitions to a limits awareness addresses a number of the concerns raised in this chapter.
First, the level of conflict engendered in coming to grips with our
economic fate will carry over into the future. Intense animosities
will hinder consensual no-growth strategies, whereas a spirit of
common sacrifice will be to their benefit. Second, the manner of
our confronting limits will go far to determine the actual level of
sustainable growth we will have achieved, an issue of immense and
obvious importance. Third, the debate over limits will continue
even after the structure has adapted. Expansionist interests want-
ing once more to test the waters of growth will face countergroups
seeking qualitative improvements from further economic retrenchment. The old arguments, muted but not eliminated, will surface
in the politics of the future.

Futures Research

The emergence of a "futures" industry has spawned the kind
of adherence to dogma prevalent in other, more established, disciplines. "Professional predictions" come from academics and
research institutes that contemplate the future from the vantage
point of economic and technological imperatives. Decision making
(and therefore future creating) in the postindustrial society will
be marked, according to this school of thought, by reliance on
specialized knowledge in all spheres of policymaking. Ideological
(value) considerations give way to questions of technique. Increasingly, the rationality of means and ends loses its political element and takes on a deterministic meaning. Although paying lip
service to the idea of value choices and public input, many futurists
support a set of assumptions and criteria that effectively prede-

termine or at least strongly bias the eventual policy selection.

Samuel P. Huntington has observed this bias and comments on it in the following:

> Theorists [e.g. Bell, Kahn and Wiener, Brezezinski] define postindustrial society primarily by its economic, social, and in part, cultural characteristics. They do not give a central role to the nature of its political institutions, political processes, political rulers, or political values. To a considerable degree, in fact, the postindustrial society concept is not at all political.[21]

This omission is somewhat understandable. Like experts in other fields, futures "experts" tend to interpret political input as interference. An acknowledgement of public choice adds a major element of ambiguity to predictions. Therefore, the hope as well as the expectation is that this factor not enter their equations.

However, the conclusion that politics is absent is not entirely accurate. The establishment approach to futures forecasting is as political and strategic as was the "end of ideology" position voiced a generation ago. Perhaps the most lucid statement of this criticism is made by Jan Miles in *The Poverty of Prediction*. On the implications of technical methodology upon futures research generally:

> It is probable that quantitative social science is largely reinforcing rather than challenging an image of a future determined by economic and technological imperatives. Quantitative research can serve a mystifying function in that the high methodology of operational misdefinition and statistical alchemy, offered to computer oracles by a social science priesthood, can convey the impression that only the pronouncements and prescriptions of technical experts have any validity.[22]

Deference to expertise is the encouraged norm. Not only the public and its representatives, but also the researchers themselves may become "mystified" with the supposed certainty of the quantified conclusions. But what are the actual political biases of this antipolitical approach? Miles continues:

> Thus a great deal of current research consists of treating trends as universal laws, of having social predictions solely contingent upon technological and economic forecasting, of technological "fixing" and technological planning, of prescriptions of piecemeal reform to

ensure the adaptability of the *status quo,* and of pouring scorn upon
alternative conceptions of the future.[23]

The dominant futures research paradigm utilizes a methodology
that gives the appearance of objectivity but is, in fact, biased,
reaching conclusions that give the appearance of inevitability
but are, in fact, open to political choice.

Additional bias stems from the irrelevancy of much of the
forecasts coming out of the establishment perspective. Their
projections tend to overemphasize changes in the forms of society.
For example, alterations in the context within which traditional
social forces operate (e.g., presidential-congressional relations,
federalism, the future of our cities) may leave untouched the most
important substantive issues (e.g., degree of control that individuals exercise over life-shaping decisions, changes in the allocation of valued material and nonmaterial resources). The frequently
idealized image of a consumerist future ignores the more basic
question: Will the new gadgets and services of tomorrow improve
our lives, divert our attention, or be a cause for further envy, conflict, and insecurity? Future modes of social organization—the
formal element—may not address our deeper need for more
rewarding social relationships, an increased potential of self-
actualizing life-styles, or more secure and satisfying self-
images. The politics of the future, if it is to have meaning as
a distinct change from the present, must involve some impact
on these most basic of issues. Trends and alternatives must have
a connection with the substance and not just the forms of the
future.

Given the heavy influence of the technofuturist perspective,
it becomes critical to reemphasize the role of people above imperatives. Dennis Gabor states the case well:

> The future will be made less by what is "objectively true" than by what
> people take to be true, how they relate that to their goals, what they
> try to do about it, what they are able to do about it, and what dif-
> ference these efforts make for the kind of society that they will thus
> create.[24]

In this regard, the often-abused word "crisis" is useful in discussing stressful social situations because it is not deterministic

but, on the contrary, leaves room for—indeed, probably necessitates—"political" activity.

> An attention to crisis brings us to focus on the particular issues of
> public choice that emerged at particular points in time, on the policy
> options that were considered and chosen by governing and influential
> elites, and on the way in which the critical resources of contending
> actors were affected.[25]

The future is open—despite the probable constraints of economic
limits—and many alternatives exist from which, presumably, the
people will select. How we view the possibilities, potentials, and
implications of these options (in fact, whether we contemplate
them at all) will determine the shape of our future.

The thought that the public will somehow collectively select
one or another alternative future seems the height of political
innocence. Yet, in a very real sense this will inevitably occur.
Specific issues will of course be handled by those few in positions to make decisions. The public's role will be to provide a
context within which policies are chosen, and in that sense it
will help to predetermine the official evaluation of the potential
alternatives. Wendell Bell and James A. Mau present a model of
social change that incorporates the public choice perspective.[26]
It is schematically represented in Figure 1. According to Bell
and Mau, the decisions that help to shape the future evolve out
of an accepted image of the future. This image is formed (and
continually reformed) from the interaction of our perceptions
of reality and our personal and social values. It, in turn, operates
within the decision-making process to set in motion the individual and collective actions that will construct a new reality.
To be sure, an image is not self-fulfilling. It might be unrealistic
and therefore beyond the system's capacity, it may be short-
sighted and contain the seeds of its own destruction, or it may
be thwarted by outside factors that society can neither anticipate nor control. Generally speaking, however, an appropriate, popular, and dynamic image of the future shapes behavior,
attitudes, and institutions and thereby summons forth its own
realization.

The greatest obstacle to image actualization is the inevitable
conflict that will occur among divergent images of the future.

FIGURE 1
CYBERNETIC-DECISIONAL MODEL
OF SOCIAL CHANGE

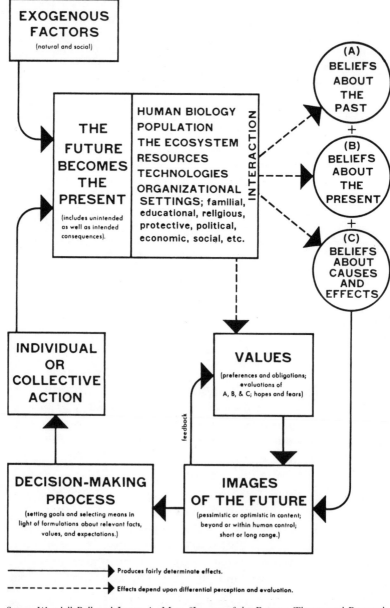

Source: Wendell Bell and James A. Mau, "Images of the Future: Theory and Research Strategies," in *The Sociology of the Future,* eds. Wendell Bell and James A. Mau (New York: Russell Sage Foundation, 1971) p. 21.

The technocratic model is composed of numerous branch alternatives and choices, but it basically conforms to Thomas Kuhn's description of a dominant paradigm.[27] The effort of some interests in society to propagate this image to the exclusion of alternative scenarios indicates the political as well as intellectual nature of paradigm conflicts. Cognizant of this fact and criticizing the narrow perspectives of technocratic planners, Arthur I. Waskow wants to encourage a "politics of imagining" in order to create and publicize a variety of approaches to the future.[28] But, as John McHale states, such a development is already taking place due to the tenor of the times in which we live.

> There are multiple future possibilities in a present replete with rapid change, uncertainty and turbulence, contradictions and seemingly opposed dynamic forces or trends. Divergent theories of the future simply reflect this situation of flux and indeterminacy, indeed they are part of that competitive process of imposing meaning upon human events in a "situation in which no plausible theory has emerged."[29]

The future is fluid and "up for grabs" until such time as a picture of the issues central to limits-to-growth politics captures the continued attention and firm support of the public (or of that segment of the public interested in and capable of having an impact on decision making). What, then, is the future of politics? It cannot be a static vision; rather, politics will be dynamic, reflecting a long-term competition between groups and ideologies that are attempting, through the promotion of a specific image, to set the (biased) ground rules for the next half century of our history. In short, society will be guided not by a collective image of the future but by the balance of political power among contrasting and competing images.

Delineating these specific alternative images is the most futile of undertakings. People's expectations and desires will change as circumstances change. Also, in a real sense we each have our own individual dreams (and fears) for the United States. Finally, many of the better-publicized images are form variations on a single substantive theme. The full scope of possible futures cannot be encompassed within one paradigm. I have chosen to sketch out four alternative images or scenarios, not because they represent all currently viable options for policymaking and future-creating, but because they are sufficiently diverse to include the major perspectives of social theory. These scenarios will be offered as ideal types, indicative of four distinct forms of political/electoral/ psychological appeals. The neo-liberal or pluralist scenario represents, in essence, a continuation of present political, social, and ideological arrangements, modified somewhat to adapt to the fact of economic limits. The radical or neo-Marxist paradigm views limits as an opportunity to create a left-oriented mass constituency demanding basic change in the stratification system. The corporate-conservative or neo-fascist model is primarily a counterimage, designed to thwart leftist influence while continuing to centralize political, economic, and social power in the hands of an elite. The traditional-authoritarian or middle-class conservative position seeks to accept limits by reverting to a more static social system and more controlled forms of economic activity. Within each image, a great deal of disagreement can be found, but it is the differences among these scenarios, not within them, that constitute the broadest—that is, the least self-limiting—conception of future politics.

The strategies associated with each image of the future are also ideal types, to be strategically discarded, readjusted, or combined as social, economic, and political conditions warrant. The success of a strategy will depend upon its ability to convince the public that its expectations, its scenario of future events, and its explanation of the present more realistically and beneficially deal with the new economic situation. If a given image is to garner support, it must respond to a number of pivotal questions. Who is to blame for economic hardship (minorities, foreign powers, capitalists, etc.)? By what measure are we to define our interests (as a nation, a class, a group)? What, if anything, can be done (reform, revolution, resignation, etc.)? The response to these questions will form the crux of any strategy.

The political interaction between the competing scenarios gives the public the opportunity to assess the appropriateness and desirability of each. But this evaluation is not done in isolation. The context determines the relevancy and relative strengths of the various images. Certain variables are vitally important in aiding or hindering the quest of a strategy for popular support by their ability to affect the public's prior perceptions of the situation. This is the core feature of a futurology that has not become depoliticized, in which interacting strategies and socioeconomic developments will combine to shape a new set of normative predispositions and, with them, a new political system.[30]

This is politics in its more dramatic form, a critical battle not over a specific issue but over which of numerous perspectives will mobilize the political loyalties of the nation for the next fifty years. To impose one's perspective upon the political system has enormous consequences on the kinds of conflicts generated, the kinds of policies passed, and the winners and losers in the political wars. It is small wonder that interpretations of the present and images of the future are hotly contested. E. E. Schattschneider describes what is at stake:

> *The definition of the alternatives* [i.e., the dominant prespective] *is the supreme instrument of power*; the antagonists can rarely agree on what the issues are because power is involved in the definition. He who determines what politics is about runs the country, because the definition of the alternatives is the choice of conflicts, and the choice of conflicts allocates power.[31]

The following four scenarios—the strategies that promote them, the values that are implicit in them, and the interests that are favored or disadvantaged by them—all are *potentially* part of the politics of the future.

Liberalism

The Case for Ideological Continuity

The neo-liberal (or liberal capitalist) perspective is a valid point of departure since, despite numerous claims of its imminent demise, liberalism remains the dominant paradigm of our culture. As the historic conceptual context of our political system, it defines, at least initially, both the major policy issues and the terms of debate. The liberal scenario of the future depends for its attractiveness on the ability to parry alternative images while gradually adapting and evolving to the pressures of economic limits. To the extent that the future will be an incremental outgrowth of present trends, a modified form of liberal-capitalism stands a fair chance of maintaining its dominance.

Charles W. Anderson defends the pursuit of ideological continuity.

> The problem is to perceive alternatives that follow from the operating
> rules of the going concern, to find areas of flexibility in what at first
> appears static and final, to see lines of evolution by which we might
> contrive a more desirable future situation out of the materials at hand.
> . . . I would rather look to the possibilities contained in the going con-
> cern than to conjectural scenarios of the future or models of social
> criticism in defining alternatives for public choice.[32]

This is faith in liberal millennialism, in the expectation that
bold, rational policies, prompted by a spirit of sacrifice and cooperation for the public good, will solve our new problems in the
new age. Obviously, liberalism is under attack; the language of
personal and group assertion—"nonnegotiable demands," "totally
unacceptable proposals"—may very well result in nonliberal policies of coercion, a form of institutional counterassertion. But
there is also the possibility that the urgency of the crisis will
sufficiently modify consensus politics to enable the system to endure, to rally public support, and to adequately (in the public's
eyes) respond to emerging social pressures.[33] Aided by the expertise
and technology of the social, natural, and applied sciences, lauded
equally by corporate leaders and union spokesmen, Republicans
and Democrats, this scenario envisions that we will deal with
economic limits within the parameters of our current political
structure. This optimistic claim should not be dismissed lightly.
Because liberalism will most probably continue to control the
policymaking apparatus and dominate the political spotlight for
the immediate future, it falls upon other perspectives to mount a
serious and successful challenge. If the liberal response to limits
proves viable, its electoral strategy effective, and its image of the
future popular, then most of tomorrow's politics has already been
written.

Themes and Policies

A number of themes will most probably be included in the
appeal of this paradigm for support. Not wishing to deny completely the possibility of future growth—that is, still relying on
this means of moderating social conflict—the liberal strategy
would claim that economic progress remains a realizable goal.

Though reduced, regulated, and perhaps redefined, economic expansion could continue and thereby continue its consensual influence; the shadow of growth would serve the same function as growth had served previously. There is always the possibility of overextending ourselves. The risks of major reversals (in social, ecological, and economic terms) would force the government to somehow control the pressures that encourage dangerous and unsustainable levels of growth. Aggrandizing impulses of corporations may have to be reduced; likewise, the destabilizing impact of consumer demands will perhaps decline. But on the whole, the values of competitive striving, consumer orientations, and material progress so central to the liberal-capitalist ethos will not be eliminated, only tempered.

Growth will still be a prime objective of public policy, but the actual nature of growth may be redefined to avoid the environmental pitfalls of industrial expansion. Spending on social services—public investment—would not directly confront the environmental factors limiting industrial growth and additionally would perhaps impact positively on the symptoms and causes of social decline, easing pressures from that quarter. Mass transportation is the most obvious example of this shift, but other forms of collectivist, co-operativist ownership and/or usage is just as indicative (time-sharing arrangements for clothes washers and dryers or vacation homes, multifamily dwellings, community-based entertainment centers such as museums and parks). The (anticipated) continued transition to a service economy, whether publicly or privately funded, will further those dimensions of growth least threatened by environmental repercussions.[34]

The "fly in the ointment" is the lack of economic wherewithal brought on by limits. With industrial profits declining and inflationary pressures making budget deficits even less desirable, the money for the above policy agenda is not easily found. The general belt-tightening will affect government spending levels, perhaps leading to politically explosive cutbacks. Whatever the rationale in terms of growth and efficiency, the familiar pattern of policy retrenchment in times of economic retrenchment will probably recur.

It might be more realistic to expect, at least initially, a change not in definitions of growth but in the means by which growth can be encouraged. Through a deeper understanding of the problems we face and of the most modern techniques of political economy, the government (and by this is meant primarily the federal government) can enable the economy to drastically reduce inefficiencies and contradictions. Public aid to and administration of the private sector, so the argument goes, will be the difference between a spirit of hope or one of despair. Central planning and control can lessen the duplication inherent in competitive capitalism; it can direct production toward ecologically sound goods and services (thus reducing the possibility of adverse impacts on our ecology); it can coordinate our resources on the national level to strengthen our economic position vis-à-vis foreign trade rivals; it can further cooperation between possibly antagonistic elements of the economy; it can promote research and development efforts. In short, planning and control will maximize whatever growth potential is still available to us. Only by this further merging of the economic and political systems can we apply the tools for sound economic recovery. More trust and confidence will be tendered to the political system in order for it to carry out these functions. But this does not reflect a departure from the liberal-capitalist paradigm. The growth in formal governmental power will not be a threat to private business interests since the thrust of policy will take the form of incentives for growth and profits (through use of various subsidies, market-control arrangements, and mechanisms for shoring up consumer demand). The expansion of public responsibility for growth rates represents an adjustment of a second-order value (limited government) in order to protect the viability of a more critical and central value (mass acquiescence to unequal wealth due to the ameliorating effects of economic growth). The fusing of social and scientific technology creates an impressive potential to deal with the problems of limits. The scenario anticipates that liberalism will reassure us spiritually as it attempts to revive us economically.

We need to note that this scenario requires even more economic concentration than presently exists. According to Anderson, central planning as a "technique only worked satisfactorily when 80 percent of the production was concentrated in 20 percent of the firms."[35] In addition, success often required the support of trade unions. This points up another vital element in maintaining the dominance of the liberal paradigm. The effectiveness of this level of centralized, bureaucratic control is dependent upon great amounts of group compliance. Liberalism obtains compliance through co-optation, not coercion. For example, some leaders in Germany attribute that nation's peaceful labor situation to the principle of co-determination, whereby the worker is made partially responsible for the success of the industry.[36] Along a similar vein, reformist representation in the decision-making process (e.g., consumerist, environmentalist, and minority spokesmen on corporate boards) institutionalizes conflict and creates a collective stake in the maintenance of the system. Peter Drucker's observation about union pension plans in *The Unseen Revolution* reveals how deeply the worker's future has been tied to the strength of corporate America.[37] Widespread participation (or pseudo-participation) has the added advantage of dispersing responsibility for policy, always useful if one wants to deflect pointed criticism and demands for structural change. The public, kept out of the processes of economic policymaking, might very well turn on leadership elements, threatening corporate wealth and power. Co-optation (participation) may seem to be a palatable approach to preventing this polarization.

Traditional divisions within the liberal perspective will continue. Left-liberals (reformers) will dispute right-liberals (the "Establishment") over the efficacy of different techniques for handling potential social unrest. Progressive groups would push for broader participation and selective appeasement, noting the recent success in isolating and defusing student/radical activists (primarily by responding to noneconomic issues—drug use liberalization, loosening of sexual standards, abolition of the draft, nationalizing the eighteen-year-old vote, reducing art and media censorship). Student involvement in college and university governance provides an outlet for demands while reducing the economic and political implications of student frustration. The actual impact of formal participation mechanisms on questions of power and policy is open to debate, but on the problem of conflict management the consequences are clear. Broad involvement can give the appearance of unity, create consensus-inducing dependency, and cloud issues of accountability—very useful stratagems for perpetuating control.

One important theme of liberal politics is the issue of economic mobility. Undoubtedly, opportunities for advancement in the public and private sectors will diminish as economic stagnation sets in. Class lines will harden, and the upper classes will become more concerned about passing their advantages on to their children. This is as critical an occurrence as is the existence of limits itself. Economic opportunity and expectations of individual advancement are deeply ingrained in the U.S. mythology. These hopes will not fade away quietly. Instead, what once was a safety valve for lower-class strivings may become a time bomb of frustration, resentment, and political unrest. For this reason, liberalism must continue to press for policies to encourage mobility and maintain opportunity. Education had been the traditional means of promoting an open class system, but other mechanisms and outlets are being tried, with mixed results.[38] An additional reason for keeping the goal of opportunity as a real objective relates to the liberal desire to optimize growth levels, an aim ill-served by a rigid class structure: "the pressures to use human talent efficiently, by rewarding merit, are countered by pressures making for social continuity in the class position of fathers and sons."[39] It is obvious that this policy direction will engender enormous opposition and inspire intense debate. Support for this position (and other reformist and adaptive programs) might entail a mild brand of class consciousness to overcome the formidable power of economic privilege.

Bias, Uncertainty, and the Potential Weakness of Liberalism

Liberalism faces obstacles to continued ideological preeminence. Some of these obstacles arise out of the propensities and biases dominant in the scenario itself. Others stem from the uncertain influence of variable factors that may lessen the appeal of the liberal image. The principal bias is one that we have already discussed. Designed to respond to concentrations of power, liberalism, in either its Republican or Democratic variant, will distribute *unequally* the burdens of economic decline. In so doing, it will incite rather than mute social conflict. For instance, the thrust of regulatory policy allegedly is to control private power for the public good, but the actual impact may be quite another matter. The old laissez-faire views of economic freedom and property rights have been greatly modified by events and policies since the Depression. A redefinition of property rights (e.g., pollution regulation) has already taken place, as noted by Daniel Bell: "property today consists not only of visible things (lands, possessions, titles) but also of claims, grants and contracts. The property relationship is not only between persons but between the individual and the government."[40] But this is not so much the socialization of private property about which conservative ideologues warn us; rather, it represents the privatization of social policy, the extension of private property rights onto selected areas of the public sphere. Private interests use public power for private gain (via grants, subsidies, market guarantees, and other special-interest programs). Politicians defend this policy approach—interest-group liberalism—as democratic, a form of governmental regulation in pursuit of the public interest (e.g., economic growth, industrial stability).[41] However, political "control" of business may lead, through incremental steps, to a major redistribution of wealth from poor and middle to the corporate class. Luther P. Gerlach and Virginia H. Hine back up this analysis: "Critics . . . suggest that if this trend should continue, the public might end up 'owning' more and more of the means of production but without commensurate control over operation or participation in financial rewards."[42] The economic system gains further legitimacy, while the political system has to bear this additional burden on its own freedom of action and on its level of public support.

The emphasis on long-range planning and expertise and the diminution of political standards of rationality might lead liberalism to adopt a very strong elitist position. The limiting of public input by intellectual intimidation and/or manipulation leaves the expert decision maker free to construct and pursue "optimal" policy. Paul Ehrlich and Dennis Pirages attempt to justify this bias of liberalism.

> Long-range planning in a very complex society will require a much higher level of competence in politics. Governing must be transformed into a profession that is reserved for wise and dedicated individuals. . . . In the short run, the critical problem to be faced in transforming politics might very well be to defend existing political institutions against a populist onslaught.[43]

This attitude will strengthen the hand of status quo interests, further inegalitarian policies, and all the time give the appearance of rationality, objectivity, and necessity.

The following quote from *Business Week* highlights the policy directions that result from a liberal scenario biased toward business interests.

> It is inevitable that the U.S. economy will grow more slowly than it has. . . . Some people will obviously have to do with less, or with substitutes, so that the economy as a whole can get the most mileage out of available capital. . . . Indeed, cities and states, the home mortgage market, small business, and the consumer, will all get less than they want because the basic health of the U.S. is based on the basic health of its corporations and banks: the biggest borrowers and the biggest lenders. . . . Yet, it will be a hard pill for many Americans to swallow—the idea of doing with less so that big business can have more.[44]

The line of thinking in the article conforms well with the dominant ideology. Even more important, this may be the only policy direction feasible (passable) within the capitalist, inegalitarian structure of liberal consensus politics. Efforts to induce economic recovery will be justified by updated versions of the "trickle-down" theory. Attempts to reduce feelings of hardship and relative deprivation will be symbolic (psychic reassurance) and status oriented, letting material distributions follow past patterns. In short, many of the claims of privilege, backed up by the power mustered by the privileged, will find a receptive audience in the future liberal perspective. Economic hardship, even more than presently, may be not a national calamity but a burden to be distributed unequally by the political, social, and economic systems.

The biased policy-complex envisioned for postlimits liberalism will kindle demands for a change in distributive arrangements, but only insofar as the public clearly recognizes the interests, institutions, processes, and attitudes responsible for policymaking. The success of liberal strategy is therefore tied to tactics of deflecting blame. In a system of control based primarily on the market, the allocation of benefits and burdens is not perceived to be in the hands of an identifiable social group. Because the market mechanism is so highly impersonal, the power to alter this distribution appears diffused. Inequality seems to evolve out of abstract, quasi-sanctified forces or by purposeless chance. Because responsibility is so hard to pin down, acceptance tends to be the norm.

There are reasons to believe that this reaction will be less pronounced in the future politics of limits. First, the policy load on government will increase in amount and intensity. The politicization of more issues inevitably will lead to more overt conflict between competing interests over vital policy matters. Daniel Bell discusses this point:

> The more planning there is in a society, the more there are open group conflicts. Planning sets up a specific locus of decision, which becomes a visible point at which pressures can be applied. Communal coordination—the effort to create a social choice out of discordance of individual personal preferences—necessarily *sharpens* value conflicts.[45]

Second, as government becomes further involved in the economy, it becomes the legitimate target for economic grievances. The ongoing breakdown of the public-private dichotomy serves to remove a form of conceptual insulation protecting the political process from the distributive ramifications of economic arrangements. Third and most important, the coming economic decline and its impact on political and social structure will have an illuminating effect on public perceptions. "Perhaps the only benefit of a crisis is that the institutions become transparent, that their structure and power relations are visible to the naked eye."[46] If the reward system now appears as the consequence of the purposeful activity of those groups benefiting from public policy the most, its accountability—and the potential for consciously changing the system toward one's own ends—is clearly revealed. Increased economic concentration and government regulation tend to shift blame from immutable market forces to obvious and controllable rules, institutions, and individuals.

Many factors intervene that either underscore or conceal (and deflect) the responsibility of the system. Primary may be the organizational effectiveness of competing scenarios. In the absence of recognized legitimate alternatives to the dominant paradigm, any failure can be interpreted as unavoidable and outside of the system's control, excusable because the objective situation required certain outcomes, unintended in spite of great precautions, etc. However, the probability is that left-liberalism will offer a continual (though not structural) critique of the reigning capitalist ideology. The existence and validity of this reformist alternative is vital, for it offers legitimacy to other forms of leftist criticism and thereby may move the entire tenor of political debate in that direction.

The role of the media is also critical. In an atmosphere of national crisis, the media may help to lower expectations and counsel patience, excuse the failings of government and encourage an apolitical fatalism, caricature extremist positions and dramatize their potential for violence, fragment issues and publicize personal aspects of the problem (scapegoats and success stories), and, in general, may rally around the liberal-capitalist flag. However, in a climate open to some criticism, the coverage might emphasize the structural connections between disparate headlines, highlight corruption and the unevenness of economic sacrifices, illuminate the substance of radical interpretations of events and the alternate policies that follow, and, in general, help to wean the public away from a blind acceptance of liberal politics. Noting the trends of the last decade and the nature of the media's work, Samuel P. Huntington envisions the latter outcome as likely. His comment, directed toward political conflict within the executive branch, applies with even more appropriateness toward politics generally.

> The national media . . . increasingly came to conceive of themselves in an adversary role vis-à-vis the executive government. At stake were not merely conflicting personalities and differing political viewpoints, but also fairly fundamental institutional interests. The media have an interest in exposure, criticism, highlighting and encouraging disagreement and disaffection within the executive branch. The leaders of the executive branch have an interest in secrecy, hierarchy, discipline, and the suppression of criticism. The function of the press is to expand political debate and involvement; the natural instinct of the bureaucracy is to limit it.[47]

The press can reveal or conceal the failings and biases to which the liberal scenario is prone.

Events in the international arena can also improve or hinder the appeal of the liberal scenario in various ways. Generally speaking, "war and the consequent prominence of foreign policy concerns do in fact work toward a reduction of polarization," especially that resulting from class distinctions.[48] This diversion of popular attention and the national unity brought about by the presence of a common enemy is clearly beneficial to liberal strategies. But intense international divisions put additional policy loads upon liberal governments, diverting resources from economic recovery and threatening the level of individual freedom that is the hallmark of liberal philosophy. Such tensions may be inevitable once the true dimensions of the limits crisis are known. For example, a prolonged worldwide economic slump "could force individual nations to pursue their separate interests and breed an international political disaster as well."[49] Foreign and domestic spheres interact in a mutually detrimental relationship. We also cannot overlook the possibility of raw materials cartels forming in the underdeveloped world (parallel to OPEC) that would be in a position to demand a higher price through control of the resource supplies. Third World governments may nationalize Western industries, initiate acts of terrorism and sabotage (e.g., hostages in Iran) against Americans, or in other ways threaten our physical and economic security. While the negative impact of these hypothetical developments may be substantial, their political consequences might actually be system-supportive, directing attention and blame from the domestic to the more unaccountable foreign sphere. A pliable "crisis mentality" may make it easier to pass policies demanding mass sacrifices.

Even on this score, the interpretation of events is not obvious, and therefore there will probably be some disagreement over the implications of international problems. Although direct military threats will almost certainly unify the nation, other types of international tension will prod our patriotism much less. Foreign nationalization of U.S. investments overseas may appear to be a justified reaction to exploitation or a useful end to a corporation's exporting capital and jobs outside of the United States. Foreign nations experiencing similar economic pressures might approach them in a way not in keeping with our liberal framework. The success of these approaches would put into doubt the correctness of our own techniques; their failure would reinforce faith in our system and buttress the belief that nothing more can be done to better our situation. It is therefore uncertain how events overseas will affect the viability of liberal strategies.

Conclusions

The diversionary potential of any variable is critical in estimating the staying power of liberalism. If accountability can be deflected, if efforts to institute left-liberal reforms confront not clear opposition but the structural quicksand of consensus politics, and if the severity of the crisis does not give credence to ideological criticism, the probability is that liberalism will hold as an image of the future.

But there are too many tensions within the paradigm. The dominance of right-liberal forces may lead reformists to embrace the ideology (and the class-oriented strategies) of leftism in order to further the ideals of liberalism. On the other hand, the institutions, procedures, and power relations of capitalist democracy tend to block reformist goals and to fulfill conservative objectives. Can liberalism contain those forces that are polarizing the society? The pressures of limits to growth may make leftist images and neofascist counterstrategies more effective at mobilizing support. Incapacity on the part of the dominant paradigm clearly represents increased options and political resources for those interests and ideologies intent on competing with and supplanting liberalism. Halfhearted policies will not remedy the imbalances and strains of the economic crisis; rather, it is reasonable to expect that they will intensify both the problems and the public's frustration with governmental failure. How liberalism weakens, in which direction it leans, will determine the alternative images that vie for center stage and will also shape the battle for preeminence between liberalism and its challengers. Even in failure, liberalism sets the agenda for politics, the context of the debate. If the power structure prevents reformist policies, structural criticism from the Left is more appealing. If left-liberalism appears to be gaining influence and success, a corporate-conservative counter-image will more likely arise. A polarization of some sort is probable, either by the growth of a set of forces opposed to the liberal middle or by the fading of liberalism and the increasing confrontation between policy extremes. The most effective strategy will be the one most favored by events and the one most able to mobilize the public to appreciate its image of the political future.

Neo-Marxism

Positive and Negative Dimensions of Radical Images

The drawing power of leftist or neo-Marxist images of the future have been successfully dampened under consensus politics. Admittedly, egalitarian values have had some influence, and class consciousness has not always been submerged as a political force. Still, as a thoroughgoing critique of and major alternative to the liberal-capitalist paradigm, it has been quite ineffective within the political arena. The awareness and impact of economic limits can potentially enhance the intellectual appeal of leftist policies and create the emotional climate within which leftist strategies will flourish.

As noted in the previous section, much depends upon the fate of the liberal response to limits. The dominance of Republican, Establishment, or probusiness forces pursuing their objectives with narrow, self-serving policies may leave left-liberalism with no reformist and consensual options. There is little reason to believe that the hardship imposed by limits is a burden that powerless and powerful will share equally. Indeed, logic (and past practice) compel us to accept a different conclusion: the costs associated with economic limits, and with attempts to overcome those limits through public policy, will be as unequally distributed as have been the benefits of growth. Obvious economic injustice will make it more difficult for liberalism to maintain the legitimacy and social cohesion necessary for its survival.

Additional drains on these vital resources can be expected from the increasing ineptness of public policy. The political system, even with a surfeit of information and broad administrative control, is unable to handle the problems that threaten growth rates. The issues have become too complex and interrelated to be dealt with through incremental and pluralist processes; the liberal-capitalist paradigm may no longer be appropriate to the tasks of environmental protection, social integration, political stability, etc. Political failure and further deterioration will give credibility to the argument that patchwork repairs cannot mend this most recent and serious damage to the social and economic fabric. Radical change is required.

Finally, liberalism itself tends to give sanction to leftist critiques of the system, a fact noted by Herman Kahn and B. Bruce-Briggs.

> Conflict between revolutionaries and the status quo will be promoted
> if there is a continued tendency toward a lack of assurance on the part
> of the established forces in dealing with "progressive" and/or humanis-
> tic revolutions, agitation, and criticisms of the existing system. The
> principal cause of this factor is that the Western "Establishment" is
> to a large extent motivated by the same values expressed by its critics.
> Since the Western leadership itself believes in peace, justice, freedom,
> etc., it is vulnerable to claims that these ideals have not been achieved.[50]

We might have some reservations regarding the system's real
commitment to these ideals. However, the rhetoric of liberalism
helps to instill in the public the values that form the basis of the
neo-Marxist image of the future.

This alternative to the liberal perspective sketches out a highly
and perhaps necessarily vague picture of the future. Undoubtedly,
included within the publicized image would be provisions for a
more egalitarian stratification system, a more democratic society,
and more humanistic social relationships (all hallmarks of radicalism's idealistic appeal). But along with this positive alternative
attracting support is a negative component critiquing present
arrangements. This is a matter of tactical necessity, as David C.
Schwartz indicates. "It is often easier to attract support by being
against something rather than for something. . . . Stressing what
one is against increases one's coalition potential. Thus, very disparate groups can converge on the one agreed on point, overthrow
of the hated regime."[51] The class bias of governmental policy,
increased and visible economic inequality, exploitation anxieties
(job security, occupational safety), etc. are sufficiently onerous
prospects to spur pressures for radical change. These negative
expectations, and the positive image of the future provided by
the neo-Marxist alternative, highlight the crux of the radical
strategy.

This strategy receives encouragement from the social tensions
produced by limits to growth. Economic distress opens up enormous opportunities for polarizing society along class lines, the
traditional strategy of the Left. The immediacy of the economic
crisis also eliminates the major tactic that had previously been the

route to radicalize the working class—gradualism, education, single issues—the "politics of the long haul."[52] The dominant mood of cynicism, powerlessness, and loss of trust and faith in institutions leads to a marked receptivity to new outlooks and a notable expectation of radical change. The Left cannot ignore this opportunity without foreclosing on its future potential for power: a turning point, by definition, cannot be returned to.

Leftist interpretations will also benefit from a changed attitude toward the system in general, and toward the business elite in particular. The generation whose political socialization encompassed the years 1960-1974 has been exposed to and therefore is cognizant of an undercurrent of structural criticism unlike most previous generations. The idea that something is basically wrong and in need of change will not be too unique or difficult to accept. Then, too, there is a growing realization that our corporate economy is not all-beneficent. This recognition weakens the defense of the economic status quo based on the positive outcomes of the system. Daniel Bell refers to this trend.

> A feeling has begun to spread in the country that corporate performance has made the society uglier, dirtier, trashier, more polluted, and noxious. The sense of identity between the self-interest of the corporation and the public interest has been replaced by a sense of incongruence.[53]

The loss of corporate stature cannot help but give aid and comfort to political strategies designed to reduce corporate power.

An additional possible advantage to the neo-Marxist cause hinges on the nature of the economic decline we will experience. If it appears that the hardships of limits are not equally felt among all social groups, that the wealthy have been able to protect their resources and even take advantage of the situation, resentment and pressures for redistributive policies will build.[54] Publicizing both the affluence of the economic elite and the deterioration of the living standards for most other Americans will make stratification more visible and irritating. This is especially true if the classlessness myths discussed in Chapter 3 remain a formidable element of liberal ideology and popular culture. David Potter's examination of the dysfunctions of these equality myths is doubly relevant in an era of economic limits:

When living in a society that [preaches and] practices outward unifor-
mity, [an individual] . . . finds himself the object of class discrimina-
tions imposed at close quarters and based upon marginal, tenuous criteria, . . . then the system of classes itself, no longer natural, no longer
inevitable, begins to seem unjust and hateful. . . . By diminishing the
physical differentials, the social diversity, and the real economic disparities that once separated classes, it has made any class distinction or
class stratification seem doubly unfair and discriminating . . . ; by eliminating class diversity without being able to abolish class distinctions,
abundance has only made subjective differentials more galling, while
making objective differentials less evident.[55]

There is a strong possibility that power relationships between economic groupings will become as explicit and repugnant as other
class distinctions. As generalized job anxieties increase, employers
acquire extra bargaining leverage in proposing work speedups,
poorer working conditions, the arbitrary removal of "trouble-
makers," tighter work regulations, etc. The perception of class differences is a critical precondition for a viable class-oriented strategy. In the past, the differences within the broad middle class were
seen as more important, but such distinctions as blue or white
collar, regionalism, urban or suburban residency, even race and age,
may not be able to cloak the unity of class interests. And this is
especially likely if economic limits make material needs and distinctions more central and salient.

Radicalization and Polarization

Michael P. Lerner in "The Future of the Two-Party System in
America" sets out a scenario along leftist lines. Lerner anticipates
that rates of economic growth will decrease drastically due to the
inability of U.S. monopoly capital to continue the exploitation
of Third World nations or the domination of the international
economic system (the "end of imperialism" argument). In the
past, a small part of the surplus skimmed off the top by U.S.
corporations trickled down to the lower classes, providing some
benefits and an apparent coincidence of interests. However,

In the period ahead, monopoly capital will have less room to maneuver,
and this will progressively decrease its ability to buy off American
workers. As a result, there will be an increase in class consciousness,
which will be expressed first through labor agitation, second through

existing party mechanisms, and last through the likely emergence of an explicitly socialist party.[56]

Lerner's assumption, not so unreasonable given the above-mentioned biases of liberal politics, is that the powerful will pass any hardships of limits onto weaker, poorer groups. A divide-and-conquer strategy whereby ethnics and poor/minority/inner-city elements are played off against each other is used to deflect attention away from structural criticism. However, this strategy cannot succeed in weakening class unity since it does not address the major issues of the 1970s and beyond. The author does not claim that a socialist victory is inevitable, but, in keeping with a realistic vision of the future, he does expect that the focus of political debate in this country will shift farther to the left. The issue of inequality will finally be put on the political agenda.

Lerner's vision is perhaps that of a true believer seeing possible converts wherever he looks. Yet, analyses of relative deprivation and revolution give a strong measure of support to the neo-Marxist scenario. An examination of revolution is highly appropriate to this study. It will underscore those two factors that heighten social unrest and channel it toward political action: a conceptual rejection of existing reality and organized efforts to bring to realization a different image of the future.

The work of James C. Davies is perhaps the most cogent and relevant of any attempt to grasp the aspiration-frustration-aggression relationship central to leftist scenarios. The following summary quote of Davies's thesis has been graphically represented in Figure 2.

> Revolutions are most likely to occur when a prolonged period of objective economic and social development is followed by a short period of sharp reversal. The all-important effect on the minds of people in a particular society is to produce, during the former period, an expectation of continued ability to satisfy needs—which continue to rise—and, during the latter, a mental state of anxiety and frustration when manifest reality breaks away from anticipated reality.[57]

The J-shaped curve in economic capacities occurs over a time span too short to allow for adjustments in expectations. When "people are made aware of not having what they have been brought to

188

FIGURE 2
NEED SATISFACTION AND REVOLUTION

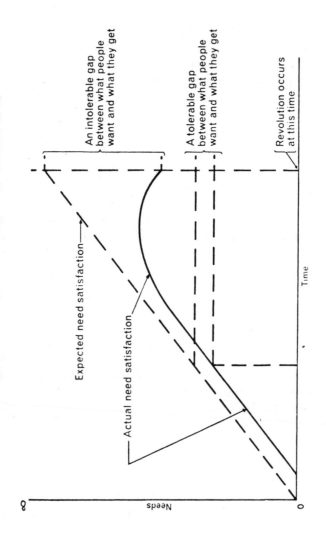

Source: James C. Davies, "Toward a Theory of Revolution," in *When Men Revolt and Why*, ed. James C. Davies (New York: Free Press, 1971), p. 135.

think it feasible or proper or necessary that they should have," tensions and the search for blame result.[58] If government and other institutions (e.g., capitalism) can be blamed for this gap, desire for a radical alternative builds.

An increase in relative deprivation (and the corollary of perceptions of downward mobility) is the major motivational impetus behind leftist appeals. As the gap between needs and satisfactions widens, the feeling grows that one is falling behind, losing ground. Relative to one's expectations, deprivation seems to worsen, whatever the real levels of need satisfaction. In addition, actual (as opposed to felt) downward mobility may be an unavoidable consequence of the economic dislocations brought on by our approach to limits. What intensifies this problem are the numbers experiencing such mobility and their probable grouping among certain precarious sectors of the economy. In this situation, a reevaluation of the entire social system may take place. Structural interpretations of one's predicament tend to predominate, as do collective strategies for improving one's chances: "If an entire stratum, craft, or profession is declining, there is more chance of unity in misery and a collective protest."[59]

Vulnerable segments of the working class, middle class aspirants to professional and managerial positions, rural and middle America generally, and elements of the intelligentsia may seek redress of their condition through revolutionary change. These groups will be hurt by the economic and social transformations to come, and therefore they will probably provide support and leadership resources for the leftist cause. And where the normal channels for collective action are blocked and the policies offered to these groups do not seem to measure up to their desires and to the vastness of the problems, then protest will take a radical turn. The pivotal role of liberal policies attempting to keep open the class system is more clearly apparent. If these efforts are not made or are thwarted after passage, the potentially explosive situation of downward mobility beckons.

The overarching educational strategy of the Left is to increase an awareness of class unity and the role of economic position on one's life. Social protest that rests on occupational, cultural, philosophical, regional, and racial bases can be used instrumentally to further leftist causes, but their long-range usefulness is slight because of the ultimately divisive class-cutting nature of their outlook. Limits can allow people to appreciate the similarities in their *economic* condition and therefore to overcome the separations imposed by alternate self-definitions of interest. The gap between blue-collar and clerical or service occupations will be lessened, increasing perceptions of a common *working-class* interest.[60] Similarly, other challenges to the dominant culture (neo-nostalgia and primitivism, back to nature, inner-awareness and personality development, new family arrangements, antiscience and antitechnology, sensitivity) are individualistic and apolitical in their long-range goals but contain the seeds of a radical social critique with neo-Marxist dimensions. The Left anticipates a transformation of the Ecology movement toward less reformist aims, and this can be a catalyst for an overlapping coalition of issue-based movements connected by a class analysis of U.S. politics.

Along these lines, Michael Mann's study, "The Social Cohesion of Liberal Democracy," indicates that while the ideological principles of the Establishment paradigm are accepted (or at least repeated) by working-class members, regarding positions on specific issues and policies, *class* interests are accurately expressed. Mann believes that social stability is the result of the socialized inability of the lower classes to connect their awareness of particular interests with a broader delegitimizing interpretation of society.[61] Hard times will notably raise the priority of concrete issue conflicts, perhaps to the point at which the dominant liberal abstract beliefs will seem less and less relevant. In effect, economic limits will undermine the cohesive impact of socialization and provide a conceptual bridge linking particular class interests with a thoroughgoing class critique.

In a related development we can anticipate a rise in the importance of ideology generally. People will be under immense pressure from a multifaceted crisis in coming decades. They will need to assimilate and understand the often inconsistent information and behavioral signals that they receive. At the same time, the dominant explanatory framework may have been discredited and rejected. Searching for an interpretation of events and acting within a politicized environment (movements, threats to one's interests, calls for participation, high emotions), people may ignore the explanations of established leaders and seek some security through consciously chosen ideological constructs.

Short of a major ideological commitment, a group-oriented

reformist posture (e.g., trade-union consciousness) may leave room for strong pressure placed sporadically and for narrow ends. However, its ability to inspire generalized and intense dissent or to encompass a broader view of politics and society is severely restricted. Anthony Giddens has demonstrated that relative deprivation and resentment, alienation and social disorganization cannot in and of themselves bring about a change in consciousness. A major perceptual leap must be made. Revolutionary consciousness "involves a recognition of the possibility of an overall *reorganization in the institutional mediation of power . . . , and a belief that such a reorganization can be brought about through class action.*"[62] Offering an alternative image of social order and fostering the popular (political) support in furtherance of that image are the necessary tasks of a leftist political party. The existence of an acknowledged organ of leftist aspirations is vital in the politicization-polarization process. Among the functions of the mass-based, neo-Marxist party is providing political cues for those who are sympathetic to a class analysis but lack the ideological awareness to recognize their class interests on abstract or distant issues.[63] A certain threshold is reached where the organization's size and strength enable it to effectively address its political cues to a noticeably enlarged audience. The credibility of its anti-establishment message is increased as well, allowing people to *switch* ideological allegiances rather than asking them to take the more difficult step of rejecting the previous model of political rationality without having been offered a substitute. The movement, once legitimized by numbers and prominence, can promote the very conditions most favorable to its maintenance and growth: sensitizing members to deprivation, increasing social disorganization, inciting establishment repression. The dynamics of movements allows people to make the conceptual leaps required for revolutionary change.[64] The gap between ideals and reality becomes the wedge with which the Left can encourage individuals to loosen and eventually break their attachment to the current economic system.

The existence of a viable Antisystem movement might also lead Establishment forces to reactions that would intensify the drift to social polarization. If liberalism is itself pushed to the right in order to counter egalitarian strategies, reformists will find it increasingly difficult to differentiate themselves from the more critical Left. In an effort to quell the movement, dissent is labeled disloyalty, with counterintuitive results. "Where the existing regime tends to force (ascribe) a revolutionary or illegitimate status onto a reformist group, the revolutionary fervor of the group may markedly increase."[65] Radical action becomes the only option as the society continues to polarize. The recruitment of reformist groups and other disillusioned and resentful members of the old order (e.g., elements of the national bourgeoisie embittered over the economic and political power of multinational corporations) offers a broader constituency for the Left (but one that will be a future source of tension as well). In summary, the strengthening of neo-Marxist forces and the realization of the leftist scenario is possible on its own (Davies) and is downright plausible if certain actions are taken by liberal forces and by radical organizations that would heighten class consciousness and mass receptivity to revolutionary change.

Defects in the Leftist Scenario

The weaknesses in this scenario, and therefore the causes of its potential failure to dictate the image of the future, are many and varied. The first category concerns contradictions within neo-Marxist ideology. The strategy of the Left is to incite resentment against inequality. This appeal reinforces the materialist ethic of liberal capitalism and divides the public on the basis of that ethic. Both of these effects run counter to the advertised image of an egalitarian future, a transcendent social unity beyond materialist strivings and jealousies. The notion that the Antisystem movement, once in power, can help society to meet the blocked material expectations of the movement's adherents conflicts with the aim of creating a structure with nonbourgeois values and aspirations. Can a moral and compassionate society be achieved through a politics of conflict, envy, and probably some violence? The authoritarianism of the traditional Left is juxtaposed to the imagery of the humanistic Left; the means to gain power conflict with the broad ends for which that power is sought. Consumeristic envies provide a power base but undercut long-range ideological goals. The "solution" is not pleasant. Either the goal is pursued authoritatively and the initial strategy is merely manipulative (e.g., the Russian Revolution's slogan of land followed by Stalin's collectivization campaign), or the goal is abandoned as the Left experiences deradicalization.

Deradicalization is probable if the scenario is allowed to develop without coup or civil war. It can take a number of forms. The distinction made above between the form versus the substance of social change is appropriately returned to here. The typical leftist policy bias toward nationalization of private property is an ineffective means of changing the nature of economic relationships in society. This constitutes part of a modified, inadequate definition of the radical perspective. As E. F. Schumacher has noted, it is often the scale of ownership that is most at fault. A more substantial (and more radical) approach is needed in fostering a humane relationship between the worker, his work, and his world.

Perhaps the major form that deradicalization takes is in the switch in emphasis from economic equalization to equal opportunity and social welfare, primarily because the latter two goals will travel on the path of least political resistance. Frank Parkin discusses this tendency:

> Insofar as countries with a record of socialist rule could be said to differ from others in patterns of rewards, it is in the relative openness of their class system. . . . In other words, Social Democrats appear to have been more able or willing to broaden the social base of recruitment to privileged positions than to equalize rewards attached to different positions.[66]

The role of political expediency is central. Parkin continues:

> Whether or not socialist approaches to inequality become politically acceptable depends on whether or not they confer advantages on the dominant class, or at least an important section of it. Welfare and meritocratic reforms do carry such advantages. . . . Egalitarian reforms designed to change the rules of distribution and ownership do not.[67]

Deradicalization will occur if the middle class is satisfied with the gains made in opening up the class system. However, according to the neo-Marxist scenario, such groups will have been thoroughly immersed in the leftist image of the future, including the critical concept of equality. This points up one of the most damaging weaknesses of the scenario. Many people will give support to radical positions without ever accepting their ideological underpinnings. Still materialist and individualistic, their attraction to the Left stems from narrow self-interest, not a cooperativist or socialist mentality. This somewhat cynical observation is well stated by Lopreato and Hazelrigg, paraphrasing Pareto.

> People . . . do not engage in "class behavior" for abstract reasons. They do so because it is in their selfish interest. People do not wish equality. They are merely "bent on escaping certain inequalities not in their favour, and setting up new inequalities that will be in their favour, this being their chief concern." In the process, they will support those parties that offer the greatest promise, but will offer whatever explanations are "fashionable" for their actions.[68]

An instrumental commitment to neo-Marxism is almost a guarantee of declining popular influence with increased policy success. It is thus doubtful whether a determined leftist coalition operating within the confines of pluralist electoral politics can hold together long enough and fervently enough to truly revolutionize the stratification system.

The assumption of policy success is itself one of the weakest links in the leftist scenario. Many of the administrative problems facing liberal programs will also diminish the effectiveness of radical efforts. Indeed, overreliance on central planning—a hallmark of socialism in power—may tend to strengthen trends toward political instability and managerial incompetence discussed in the previous chapter. Lest we think that a clear ideology somehow allows us to apply simple solutions to complex human problems, the plight of England (prior to the discovery of oil in the North Sea) should demonstrate the handicaps under which all systems must operate. A Labour government, sympathetic to the material demands that its strategy had helped to promote, had found it difficult to institute effective action versus the limits crisis while at the same time maintain both a semblance of national unity and a spirit of egalitarian reform. Economic distress and the confrontations spawned by leftist ideology encourage anger, resentment, and even violence, diverting scarce political resources toward conflict resolution and away from economic recovery. There is reason to believe that, in the context of limits to growth, democratic neo-Marxism is not a viable and stable approach. Given the potential conflicts of a limits society, some form of authoritarian control, *either by or against the most embittered*, may be inevitable. Class may indeed become a central political issue, as some contend, but the ability of leftist parties to handle class conflict within nonauthoritarian structures can sincerely be questioned.

The major obstacle to the success of this image is not those mentioned above. Rather, unlike its liberal-capitalist counterpart, radicalism must compete with other images in a structural situation that is not favorably disposed to its message. Our political culture has socialized us to oppose radicalism instinctively, to suspect its idealism and reject the substance of its arguments. This cultural and ideological bias means that a heavier burden of proof rests on the leftist position than on other approaches to the limits crisis. While conservative scenarios play on established patterns of belief, radicalism requires mass acceptance of new ideas and new modes of organization at variance with past experience. The neo-Marxist image also carries a heavier burden of organization. Present forms and levels of public participation help to maintain present power relationships. The dominant cultural attitudes of deference, resignation, parochialism, and top-down communication, conservative in their influence, can be overcome only by organized mass involvement in the political process. Such a commitment, difficult to achieve in any era, is even more difficult today. Walter Dean Burnham has documented the trend toward voter disaggregation, which is reducing both voter participation and the ideological potential inherent in electoral politics.[69] The directed passion, party loyalty, and total mobilization underlying the leftist scenario may be almost impossible to nurture. Conversely, other strategies that demand less of their adherents' time, attention, loyalty, etc. would stand a better chance.

The blind optimism (read material determinism) of the Left as it contemplates economic decline ignores the political conflicts to come. Hard times are not necessarily or inevitably opportunities for the building of an egalitarian constituency. Quite the contrary,

> Times of depression are conservatizing. It is in the affluent periods when people can afford to demonstrate and rebel and worry about their identity crises. In times like these, they become more square, less interested in Consciousness III, more worried about three meals a day, more job-oriented and the hell with liberal arts.[70]

If economic and social collapse occurs, a survivalist mentality might be the dynamic motor force behind political behavior. The most basic needs draw and preoccupy our attention; the most narrow definitions of self-interest have currency. We can be certain that an attempt to stimulate these perceptions will be made by groups bent on undercutting leftist strategies. Corporate-conservatism represents the counterimage to neo-Marxism, and it is to this scenario that I now turn.

Corporate-Conservatism

The corporatist-conservative scenario reflects a *qualitative* refinement of the strategies and policies pursued by conservative business interests within the liberal paradigm. More conscious of its own interests, more intent on long-range control, more subtle and effective in its use of power, the business elites formulate a Machiavellian strategy that is not accompanied by any clearly positive image of the future. An outgrowth as well as a challenge to the dominant liberal framework, this scenario is a reaction to the potential inability of liberalism to ward off the threat from the political Left. Fearing the rise of class consciousness, class-based resistance to economic privilege, and a radical restructuring of the stratification system, corporate conservatives devise a counter-strategy. The personal frustrations of nonelites who are painfully facing the new reality of economic limits might be deflected and/or redefined to actually *stabilize* the system of control and even to further the interests of the economic elite.

This strategy is obviously Hobbesian in its conception of power, conflict, authority, and human nature. A centrally inspired and controlled "state of nature," a "war of all against all" among *nonelite forces* allows for unchallenged power by industrial, commercial, and financial elites. The past inappropriateness of the Hobbesian vision in explaining U.S. politics was due in large part to the mitigating circumstances of economic growth that cushioned the impact of self-interest and muted the frustrations of subordination. Economic limits lend relevance to the discarded vision. But the new leviathan will not necessarily suppress conflict; instead, it will remove its system-destabilizing and egalitarian ramifications. Numerous social divisions, skillfully manipulated, will displace class conflict and create an atmosphere of structural insecurity. This is the perfect context for corporate groups to achieve political hegemony and for the wealthy to reap economic advantage. Kenneth E. Boulding alludes to this scenario in a discussion of the steady-state society.

> In the stationary state, there is no escape from the rigors of scarcity. If one person or group becomes richer, then the rest of society becomes poorer. Unfortunately this increases the pay offs for successful exploitation—that is, the use of organized threat in order to redistribute income. . . . In the stationary state, unfortunately, investment in exploitation may pay better than in progress [i.e. economic growth]. Stationary states, therefore, are frequently mafia-type societies in which government is primarily an institution for redistributing income toward the powerful and away from the weak.[71]

In its own way, corporate-conservatism would politicize the distribution system as surely as neo-Marxism would, but with totally different consequences.

Bertram Gross has laid out the extreme version of this image of the future in an article entitled "Friendly Fascism: A Model for America."[72] The author suggests that the growth of a fascist state is plausible given certain trends unless the drift is recognized and consciously thwarted. Under the guise of democratic and patriotic slogans, the governing elite will defuse the forces of social change and covertly direct social, economic, and political activity for its own benefit. Democratic symbols and institutions will survive, but only in form. Substantial (and pervasive) control, according to Gross, will be concentrated in relatively few hands, immune from the constraints of pluralist politics.

> A managed society rules by a faceless and widely dispersed complex of warfare-welfare-industrial-communications-police bureaucracies caught up in developing a new-style empire based on a technocratic ideology, a culture of alienation, multiple scapegoats, and competing control networks.[73]

Attempts to inspire division, diversion, and despair and to manipulate these attitudes toward support of elite-maintaining programs underscore the long-range implications of corporate-conservative strategy.

Complementing Gross's picture of "Friendly Fascism" is a

scenario of the future that stresses international dynamics and variables. Nurtured perceptions of leftist threats to national security, either from within or outside our borders, lead to demands for a buildup in our external and internal military capabilities in order to insure the United States' stability and survival. Real threats (terrorism and sabotage, expropriation of overseas investments, resource embargoes), when combined with a well-orchestrated series of implied dangers (economic breakdown, fifth-column insurrections), will yield an agreed-upon justification for increased surveillance, suppression, ideological vigilance, a state of military preparedness, and perhaps the diversions of brushfire wars. This image of a garrison state, developed by Harold Lasswell,[74] is an obvious corollary to other elements of corporate-conservatism. It is especially related to the desire to submerge class as a political issue.

> The acceptance of any goals, aims, or ends cutting across class lines serves to stress inter-class agreement and inhibit class consciousness. Nationalism, particularly in wartime, focusses and sharpens the perceptions of members of all classes on a common enemy and common object of loyalty, thereby blurring the perception of objective class differences or making it a fringe, subsidiary consideration.[75]

Events in the international sphere can be expected to influence greatly the application and effectiveness of corporate-conservative strategies.

In terms of the domestic dynamics of this scenario, there are numerous cleavages along which the working class, broadly defined, can be divided. To explore and exploit the internal disunity among the Left's potential constituency is a central task of corporate-conservative tactics. Racial and ethnic distinctions are traditional points of weakness, perhaps made more vulnerable during times of economic transition. In an article on vertical mobility and bias, Joseph Greenbaum and Leonard I. Pearlin conclude that mobility, up or down, tends to increase prejudice toward Jews, blacks, and, by inference, other ethnics as well. Feelings of prestige insecurity, during the process of downward mobility especially, encourage the stereotyping reactions associated with prejudice.[76] Inter-ethnic scapegoating assures an almost unbridgeable gap between similarly situated working-class groups.

Regional differences provide additional sources of division, as revealed in the continuing battles over energy policy between oil-rich and oil-dependent states. Even age differences can be exploited to advantage. For instance, the student protest movement has been greatly defused by ignoring its broad critical messages and instead treating it as a generational and cultural conflict. Isolated from potential allies, student radicalism could then be handled as simply another case of group pressure within a pluralist system. A more telling example can be found in Richard Nixon's 1968 and 1972 presidential election campaigns. Playing on racial, welfare, and cultural images through such symbolically loaded issues as crime, drugs, abortion, radicalism, and patriotism, Nixon combined corporate funding and a Middle America constituency to fashion victory. Such an approach, consciously pursued over a number of campaigns, could optimally encourage members of the middle class to view themselves in opposition to welfare poor, assertive minorities, liberals, planners, humanists, and other images of the Left. Obviously, corporate-conservatives must firmly direct this movement so that their own interests and maneuverability are not threatened by these newly salient issues.

The overarching economic ethos of this image divides individuals and groups and, in the process, further diverts their attentions from the true causes of their condition. Materialism remains a dominant feature of social behavior; indeed, as social organization degenerates, unfulfilled social and personal needs increasingly become a source of misplaced consumer demand. Amitai Etzioni notes how far this process has already progressed:

> The American way of life may well have been founded on the notion that obtaining products is a main route to obtaining greater affection (from spouse and children), higher prestige (respect from one's fellows), and even self-actualization (in the command of machines, the power of money, and the like).[77]

Limits to growth heighten consumerist desires and, with them, competition between people for the fewer rewards. The aggression arising from frustrated expectations is turned against competitors or against oneself, not against the system. The zero-sum game of limits, played for a reduced slice of the pie, pits blacks against whites, sunbelt versus Northeast, suburbanites against city dwellers. The business elite need not play, for it has already taken its share off the top. As long as the structure fosters this game, as long as economic tensions produce a culture of alienation rather than one of common perceptions and purposes, the corporate-conservative strategy can enjoy political success.

In this regard, the development of a two-tiered economic system is especially conducive to the sort of social cleavages most supportive of corporate-conservatism. Multinational giants lead a top sector of major companies whose successful operation is securely maintained through market control arrangements with would-be "competitors." Small companies or companies in peripheral economic sectors are prone to the cyclical dislocations of the economy and receive a reduced share of production. Economic power maintains this division. In the labor sphere, unions affiliated with dominant companies or industries, and who recognize and accept managerial prerogatives, obtain a fair return for their labors. Likewise, technological skills are rewarded whatever the industry or company. On the lower rungs, the poor, the unskilled, minorities, small businesses, subsistence farmers, migrants, etc. form a permanent underclass without opportunity or hope. The fear that this group, which bears the brunt of the costs in the transition to a limits economy, will challenge the relatively secure position of the bulk of the working class guarantees the support of the middle-class population for the system and against egalitarianism. A large and visible underclass also provides a reference group with which those workers "making it" can favorably compare themselves, thus reducing feelings of relative deprivation. Finally, the existence of this depressed group gives rise to a survivalist mentality for others a few rungs up; the fear of falling to such a state is impetus for directing all attention and energies to individual needs, narrow self-interest, and the pursuit of material security.

Policy in the corporate-conservative scenario would follow one major pattern. Programs will be devised that, while purportedly responding to public demands, serve as vehicles for the redistribution of funds toward the wealthy and powerful. Antipollution efforts will take the form of subsidies, tax credits, and governmental supports in an infinite variety, assuring us a dime's worth of antipollution "bang" for every dollar of public and consumer monies spent. Increases in spending for social welfare, health care, housing needs, or manpower development will help to funnel money to representatives of the corporate elite, leaving the social needs still glaringly apparent. Part of the reason for the public's tolerance of this charade is the intimidating weight of technocratic expertise used to buttress policy choices. The masses defer to the government's judgment, aware of probable policy failure but impressed by the rationality behind the attempts.[78] Amitai Etzioni comments on the individual and political ramifications of this policy pattern in his article on basic human needs. Given a governmental structure that is unresponsive to human needs, symbolic assurances of responsiveness will lead a person to direct his aggression not against a known obstacle (i.e., the "Establishment") but inward toward himself. To internalize frustration is to depoliticize it and in the process to create a climate in which rational analysis of one's situation cannot take place. As Etzioni makes clear, this is not merely a hypothetical concern.

> World War II . . . may mark the initiation of a new period, post-industrial or post-modern, in which inauthentic elements are arising. . . . It is a mark of the post–World War II industrialized societies that they devote a major part of their endeavors to "front" activities.[79]

Inauthenticity is an aspect of politics generally, but it is central to the corporate-conservative strategy.

Even decentralization, which has long been thought of as a radical departure from current structural arrangements, can be construed in ways that are perfectly acceptable to this scenario. The sociopolitical implications of decentralization may be highly supportive of conservative interests. Decentralization is a means of (1) reducing relative deprivation by reducing contacts across communal-class lines that would otherwise accentuate class distinctions; (2) deflecting attention from central structures and similarly disadvantaged people—potential allies—while emphasizing local issues, local distinctions, etc.; (3) structurally (ideologically and institutionally) inhibiting support for social policies dealing with collectively conceived of problems (e.g., stratification); (4) insulating and limiting the impact of local radical tendencies; (5) encouraging the acceptance of locally imposed social and political controls, ignoring the structural roots underlying local conditions (e.g., high unemployment); (6) co-opting local leaders by offering them limited power and status in exchange for acquiescence in the national status quo; and (7) promoting noneconomic paths to individual satisfaction (e.g., local political mobility), thus undercutting the strategic use of envy, deprivation, and resentment in fomenting radical discontent. Other policies can also be devised that, while radical in form, are conservative in substance.

As to the problem of economic limits, the corporate-conservative scenario, more so than the other alternatives, is likely to continue progrowth policies while tolerating the high environmental and social costs that this development entails. A progrowth and consumerist ethic is facilitated by the organized ideological and institutional power of big business. Political efforts to restrict either economic expansion or corporate prerogatives bring on threats by companies to export their capital investment to friendlier cities, counties, states, or nations. This form of blackmail is used on all governmental levels to obstruct any attempts to impose profit-reducing controls on business operations. As to the unwanted environmental side effects of postindustrial development, costs can be transferred from the public at large to those segments of the public least able to defend their interests. Unavoidable costs (higher resource prices) can be handled through the price system, thus becoming a regressive excise tax falling most heavily on the poorest. Social stability can be imposed by conditioning welfare benefits to "good behavior," increasing police power (wiretapping, stop-and-frisk laws), maintaining control over the communications network, and by the judicious use of selective coercion. Growth will be sought to the limits allowed, but these limits and the view of what costs are tolerable for the sake of growth are greatly extended under the corporate-conservative scenario.

This scenario might signal the end of politics, or at least the end of representative government. Surely that is the theme behind Gross's "Friendly Fascism" cited above. This theme is echoed by Christopher Lasch, who fears a number of politically restrictive postindustrial trends.

> The tendency of political grievances to present themselves as personal grievances, the tendency for repressive authority to assume the guise of benevolence, the substitution of psychology for politics, and the pervasiveness of the managerial mode of thought help prevent conflicts

from coming to the surface and contribute to the illusion that ideology has exhausted itself.[80]

Both subtle and overt forms of authoritarianism benefit from the developments that Lasch presents. Without any ideological contrast model, this image will have free reign to shape our political destiny according to its own values and interests.

Corporate-conservatism, however, is not immune to the numerous potential pitfalls and complications that will obstruct any of the various images from gaining absolute dominance. With reference to this scenario in particular, the degree of policy comprehensiveness and elite coordination is probably beyond the system's capacity. Even with increased centralization, it is highly unlikely that any plan can be initiated without the unintended consequences and errors of design that weaken its ability to operate. There is also the need to simulate representativeness in order to maximize voluntary compliance. Finally, the problem of policy effectiveness is compounded for authoritarianism, as it is for liberals and radicals, by the complications of economic limits and the pressures of policy overload.

Effectiveness aside, the corporate-conservative strategy must make its appeals in competition with other strategies, each relevant in its way to the reality of limits. The politics of the future prohibits any easy victory for neo-fascism. The efforts to submerge the class issue and to cloak the injustice of widening inequality must overcome the vocal opposition of left-liberalism and radical elements. Previous discussions of these two scenarios indicate the strong forces behind the question of relative shares. This is an issue that will not simply fade away. Thus, there definitely will be contrast models challenging this image. They can be concealed only by our relinquishing even the appearance of an open society. Short of this outcome, we can expect that the corporate-conservative strategy will have a role to play in the politics of the future but one the importance of which will depend upon the interplay of events and competing strategies.

Traditional-Conservatism

The final scenario, Durkheimian in its idealization of a static social order, harkens back to an age in which growth and the

narrow material strivings that accompany a growth ethic were not
the central dynamics of life. Traditional-conservatism, more remi-
niscent of feudalism than of postindustrialism, is a plausible model
of the future because, despite the intrusions of modern economies
and social patterns, it has remained an attractive way of life. A
study of the impact of no-growth on selected metropolitan areas
reveals that there are potentially very desirable consequences to be
achieved within a static setting.

> The stability of the no-growth communities seemed to have positive . . .
> aspects in some of the case study areas. Church, family, and ethnic ties
> were strong. The incidence of stress diseases was low. They were rela-
> tively safe from crime. . . . The reluctance of so many people to leave
> was not perhaps irrational, but a reflection of a particular set of values
> in which these qualities outweighed the possible material gain associated
> for some of them with moving to a more prosperous area.[81]

In our prospective no-growth situation, the public's decision
would be not one of limiting personal mobility (as in the above
quote). Rather, it would be whether to adopt public policies that
emphasize nonmaterial values within a less stressful social setting.
According to this scenario, support for the old verities (God,
family, community) rather than the old enmities (race, class,
culture) will tone down the level of intrasocial conflict and provide noneconomic outlets that prove more important to an individual's self-image than the satisfaction of consumerist material
desires.

Indeed, a major aspect of the traditional-conservative strategy
is an attack on materialism and the social deterioration brought on
by modernity. Thus, limits-to-growth policies would be more con-
scientiously promoted, and they would be tied to a structural and
ideological reconditioning of man and society more in keeping
with a no-growth economy. The principal reconditioning goal
would be to lower expectations of material progress and thereby
to prevent the growth of class consciousness and frustration-
aggression tendencies. Morris Rosenberg states this theme in the
following quote.

> We would expect class consciousness to be least where the indi-
> vidual's past and anticipated future position accords with his present

condition. This is particularly likely to occur in a static society, in which a view into the past or future is not likely to produce perceptual distortion of class position.[82]

Positions in such a system are allocated via a *highly modified* meritocracy, without the degree of divisive competitiveness associated with the notion of equal opportunity. Low mobility expectations have other advantages for society. They bring about lower levels of insecurity and frustration (the psychic costs of competition and failure), reduced fragmentation of the social order arising from mobility, and renewed interest in the worth of the work one is presently doing.[83]

The task of reducing expectations is also handled by calls for the stoic acceptance of the end of growth. The process of accepting limits will transform man's acquisitive appetites and allow him to rediscover nonconsumerist life-styles. Personal living habits will be made less complex, more simplified, fulfilling basic psychological needs but without many of the frills (goods and services) that society has come to demand as necessities. The belief is encouraged that these cutbacks in one's standard of living are inevitable, ought not to be resisted but, on the contrary, ought to be the impetus for the creation of a new social order.

Further lowering of aspirations can be anticipated by readjustments in types of reference groups that determine levels of relative deprivation. The ironic truth is that "a decline in prosperity, if not too violent, can restrict the sense of relative deprivation by inhibiting comparisons with more fortunate groups."[84] Whereas radicals attempt to revise our comparisons upward, thereby hoping to heighten feelings of resentment, conservatives point to those below or those in other countries who are worse off, thus promoting feelings of satisfaction and perhaps even gratitude. In this regard, it is important to note the role played by advertising in increasing expectations and perpetuating relative deprivation. Advertising intensifies dissatisfaction and taps elements of our personality (ambition, vanity, greed) not appropriate to a limits economy or a nonmaterial perspective. Presently, the trend is for more "hard sell" (the role of sexual images in product promotion, commercials directed at children), and this will probably continue as the economic situation worsens. It is obvious that this scenario will involve controls on advertising (and other reference-group-determining mechanisms) as part of a general policy of reducing economic expectations.

The description of the social structure proposed by traditional conservatives also serves to elicit acceptance of the consequences of limits to growth. Society is viewed as an organic whole composed of interrelated roles, institutions, and groups. By upgrading the status of lower-class occupations and by highlighting the functional and social importance of all positions, the interdependence of the various parts of the structure is demonstrated and accentuated. A well-nurtured spirit of national unity and a transcendent faith in the whole system prevent people from seeing their roles in isolation or in purely self-interested terms.

In this light, inequality is justified and tolerated as part of the natural order of things. Hardship and unequal opportunity go unresented. To the extent that limits to growth are taken to be unavoidable, the inequities of the social structure will acquire a similar cast and a like-minded measure of resigned acceptance. Efforts to question material stratification will be interpreted as threats to the equilibrium of the system and to the nonmaterial benefits the system provides.

The quest for stability is basic not only to this image of social structure but also for the ascending ecological perspective as well. The conservative implications of environmentalism dovetail nicely with the political implications of the traditionalists' limits-to-growth scenario:

> Although [the ecological perspective] has radical implications—it forces us to regard the structure of a system as a whole—it is also quite conservative. It suggests that changes should be made with extreme care because even the most well-meaning and constructive action can have deadly consequences. To view the environment as a system, then, immediately imposes a certain constraint on the outlook of economic and political decision-makers.[85]

Traditional-conservatism thus presupposes a philosophy that limits the actions of the power holders along with the hopes of the powerless.

An examination of the source of this scenario, its social basis, and the circumstances required for its strength will help to differentiate it from the corporate-conservative strategy mentioned previously. This brand of conservatism is a counterstrategy, not to a resurgent leftism but to a degenerative liberalism. The dominant liberal paradigm is unable to cope with the demands and pressures of the limits crisis. Its coalitional, nonauthoritarian procedural biases prevent effective policies from being formulated or initiated. Liberalism flounders, but its failure is not a catalyst for leftist mobilization or countermobilization by the corporate Right. Power is maintained by a top-bottom coalition of forces that fails to represent the interests of the "great middle."[86] Middle populism organizes in response, gaining conservative strains and allies along with some liberal-reformist supporters. However, it remains basically unsubverted by either side, being anti-big-business as well as anti-liberal-leftism. Seen as a prime constituency for numerous strategies, once organized on their own terms, they are viewed suspiciously by both the corporate elite and traditional radicals.

Herman Kahn and B. Bruce-Briggs cite the possibility of "ideological renewal governments" dedicated to preserving traditional values against intrusions by Left revolutionaries and the Right business leadership.[87] Populist in the sense of sincerely attempting to further the interests of the common man, this alternative form of authoritarianism has a rural and traditionalist base. However, in this nation other elements of the population may be drawn to traditional-conservatism. Its neo-nostalgic, antigrowth, and anti-technology appeals have a strong attraction for segments in the environmental movement who see the problem of no-growth as that of social integration rather than class conflict. Frustrated by the petty debates of incremental politics, these supporters seek to further policies for broad social and ecological regeneration while paying a price in terms of liberal (individualistic) freedom and democratic (pluralistic) procedures. Faced with social and environmental Armageddon, people may readily renounce voluntaristic approaches and opt instead for authoritarianism. Robert Heilbroner makes a strong argument along these lines:

> The passage through the gantlet ahead may be possible only under governments capable of rallying obedience far more effectively than would be possible in a democratic setting. If the issue for mankind is survival, such governments may be unavoidable, even necessary.[88]

The many problems constituting the limits crisis as well as the problems associated with maintaining stability in a no-growth situation strengthen the belief that such authoritarian structures will be not only condoned but also welcomed.

In addition to an authoritarian bias, other elements of this scenario make it similar in appeal to corporate-conservatism. The stress placed on unifying values, including patriotism and nationalism, inclines this image toward militarism and interventionism (although a reverse reaction, a turning inward, cannot be dismissed). Attitudes toward social dissent, social unrest, and many forms of social deviance are comparable in the appeals of both strategies. An emphasis on the traditional values of the work ethic, frugality, etc. may result in a conservative backlash against welfare programs and an insensitivity toward segments of the poor. Indeed, a major strategic goal will be the repression of class conflict, seen as the prime obstacle to group integration and social cohesion. Members of the business community may therefore create tactical alliances with the leaders of this scenario for the pursuit of common objectives. However, despite this overlap caused by practical political considerations, traditional-conservatism represents a distinct alternative image.

This is quite evident when we examine other trends that give this scenario ties to left-liberal and radical political forces. Political controls on investment decisions, advertising, and other aspects of corporate policy will be necessary to insure social stability but will be detrimental to business profits. The discouragement of consumerism, materialism, and mobility strivings and the emphasis placed on environmental and spiritual regeneration and on non-economic outlets for self-definition are clearly not the goals of a corporate-dominated ruling elite. In fact, they reflect part of the cultural critique of advanced capitalism prevalent in New Left writing (and largely absent from working-class radical analysis). A strategy that has in view the lowering of levels of class and group conflict will attempt to smooth the roughest edges of the stratification system. Funds may be directed toward labor-intensive industries and projects to garner support from that sector for the economic status quo. In short, depending on circumstances, choices, and threats, this scenario can align with or offer the same appeals as any of the others, gaining temporary tactical advantages in the process of furthering long-range strategic objectives. If the leadership of traditional-conservatism can maintain its political independence, this image stands a chance of gathering broad-based support. We witnessed the beginnings of this response in the initial attractiveness of California governor Jerry Brown and President Jimmy Carter.

The critical phase in the prognosis of this scenario is the transition stage. Like liberalism, this brand of conservatism is built around consensual forms of political interaction and gradualistic forms of social change. But stability is a prized and perhaps rare commodity in a market stocked with tension and strife. It can be argued that, of the different images we have examined, the attitudes and behavioral patterns of traditonal-conservatism are best suited to a future no-growth society. The dilemma lies in trying to habituate ourselves to the self-constraints of limits to growth while enduring the traumas of economic crises. The nonmaterial, communal, and spiritual values that this scenario hopes to protect and promote may not survive the potentially explosive pressures and conflicts ahead. It is possible that a politics of drift and estrangement, coupled with the slow decline of our economy toward a state of permanent sluggishness, might ease the transition to traditional-conservative ideological, political, and social structures. On the other hand, a precipitous drop in economic well-being might give rise to a host of domestic and international confrontations. In such a setting, this image of the future would find it difficult taking hold in the public consciousness. It is therefore obvious that the popular receptivity of this scenario's appeal, the effectiveness of its strategy, is in large measure determined by the events of the moment.

Conclusions

One of the major themes running through this chapter is that the future is open to choice. Most of the meaning behind so-called technological, economic, or environmental imperatives is an attempt to limit the perception of possibilities. Such futurologists define as inevitable what is in fact quite problematical in order to create a general acceptance of their own opinion of events. But in truth, the reality of choice is not open to dispute; only the number of people aware of and involved in the choosing is what is at issue.

This tactical ploy—the claims of necessity—is part of the politics of the future, being fought over now in the present. This irony is perfectly understandable once we accept the fact that the future is rarely a break with the past (except in severe cases of catastrophe); rather, it is part of an evolutionary development, only a portion of which is visible. Long-term changes in attitudes and values often come about through a slow process of *predispositioning.* Political appeals help to create *conceptual and perceptual biases* that rise to the surface when confronted with catalytic events or circumstances. A crisis triggers these evolving political-ideological propensities. What passes for a major turning point in political and social history is thus the result of groundwork prepared years and decades previously. In subtle and not-so-subtle ways, our view of the future is being predetermined, much as past socialization processes correspond to our present attitudes and behavior.

This is not to say that our future freedom to persuade or to be persuaded by others is illusionary. We will face various conflicting messages, and our eventual mental state, our receptivity to one or another of the images and strategies of limits-to-growth politics, will reflect this confusion. In addition, the preconditioning signals of present political appeals must hope for favorable circumstances whenever the crisis situation will demand public input. If the role of the press, events in foreign affairs, and the nature of the economic decline are not advantageous for a given perspective, the public will likely side with a more appropriate scenario. Yet, our definition of "appropriateness" is quite subjective because these variables (circumstances) are themselves subject to the politics of predispositioning. In the end, paradigm disputes (of which the conflict among these four images of the future is a case in point) are decided by the interaction between evidence (events, variables, circumstance) and values, the role of present political disputes being a central factor in the future definition and application of either criterion.

Normal politics is designed to work on mundane matters with incremental tools. However, the anomalies of normality build up to crisis proportions; the structure of our system is less and less able to cope. Incremental, equilibrium-maintaining policies, the sum and substance of consensus politics, are futile remedies for the imbalances and strains of the evolving crisis. Though perhaps successful as temporary adjustments to system stress, their continued application intensifies both the basic condition and mass frustration. Many people take comfort in a flight from freedom—the search for a strong leader, personal withdrawal from political involvement and responsibility, regression into antisocial attitudes and behavior. Our worsening political-social-economic-environmental-existential problems may simply make these paths more attractive.

Maybe, however, the depth of the coming challenge to consensus politics does not allow for such easy evasions. The record of U.S. political history speaks to the potential democratizing opportunity represented by the crisis of limits to growth. The debate among proponents of each of these scenarios (or the confrontation between their more realistically created intermixtures) and the conflicting appeals made by the different images of the future are the signs of a critical era in U.S. politics; a series of electoral confrontations addressing vital issues in an ideologically charged and polarizing fashion may reverse trends toward voter disaggregation and apathy. It would bring the electorate back into the political process, as was the case periodically in our nation's history, by offering the public a choice on the general direction of the polity for the next thirty to fifty years. Critical elections socialize conflict as nothing else in normal politics can.[89] And limits to growth is a cause, *par excellence,* for a critical election. The fear that democracy will end and that an antidemocratic dictatorship will somehow seize control is not to be lightly dismissed; the potential is there for such an occurrence. But I would suggest that a different future beckons. The politics of the future may mean the regeneration of our political process, the reintroduction of citizen input. Perhaps it signals not the end of democracy, but its rebirth.

7
Conclusions

All systems contain feedback mechanisms enabling them to maintain stability in the face of incremental changes. Readjustments in a system's peripheral, secondary elements allow it to preserve its central character. These mechanisms obviously operate best when the upsetting exogenous or endogenous changes do not directly threaten the system's primary supports. However, when such threats do occur, normal patterns of self-regulation may no longer suffice. The system must then either adjust by transforming itself, reaching a new equilibrium diverging more or less markedly from what had previously existed, or collapse entirely. A complete examination of this process ought to be highly instructive regarding the nature of the prior system, the dynamics of the transitional state, and the basic outlines of the future structure.

This study has attempted to apply such an examination to political change in the United States. It has been argued in Chapter 2 that the ideological biases, power relationships, and institutional arrangements that together constitute the political structure conspire to inhibit the formation of redistributive demands and to blunt the redistributive nature of those economic demands that do reach the political agenda. Current patterns of political interaction—consensus politics—prevent the issue of economic inequality from enlivening our political discourse. A web of conceptual and procedural givens insulates the political system from the potentially unsettling consequences of economic stratification and material deprivation. Reference was made to two areas of social conflict (party politics and labor-management relations) that might otherwise have become scenes of intense battles over relative shares were it not for the success of consensus politics in nullifying any

egalitarian impulses. Issue avoidance is the key goal in the operation of consensus politics. The traditional ability of the political
system to divert social energies away from the tensions arising
from economic stratification rests on the existence of economic
growth. Perceptions of growth counterbalance and conceal perceptions of inequality. Chapter 3 indicated the ways in which economic expansion has promoted a set of attitudes and activities
that is quite system-supportive. In its impact both on our hope for
personal upward mobility and on our belief in a future of shared
prosperity, a high and steady rate of economic growth serves to
moderate the politically disruptive potential inherent in a stra-
tified society. Growth is the crucial variable strengthening the feedback cycles of consensus politics. Once these cycles are broken,
other perceptions, structures, and stabilizing mechanisms will
inevitably fill the political vacuum thus created. Questions regarding the permanence of economic growth therefore go to the heart
of the future of consensus politics.

Chapters 4 and 5 explored the controversy surrounding limits
to growth. Various arguments were summoned to support or refute the prime contention—that this nation will be unable and/or
unwilling to sustain economic growth of a kind and at levels that
typified its previous history. Interrelated problems involving both
physical and social trends threaten to remove this central pillar
of consensus politics. Claims have been made that the development and application of technology (scientific, economic, managerial) will overcome the most troubling obstructions to further
economic growth. Yet, as I have tried to demonstrate, the inevitable role of politics in the problem-solving process will impede
our ability to find and utilize efficient and effective policies. In
fact, politics will more likely compound the growth-reducing problems we will confront. Finally, the element of time lends an air
of urgency to the controversy, creating serious consequences for
decision makers who wish to follow their natural inclinations and
delay action. The conclusion I draw from this analysis is that expectations of reduced growth rates are plausible, indeed probable,
and are made ever more undeniable the longer we ignore the issues
raised by the limits-to-growth debate.

The previous four chapters were preliminary to the speculative
task that this study had undertaken. They have presented the outlines of our present political system, noted the crucial function of

a central variable, and surveyed the numerous forces that threaten this primary support and, with it, the stability of the system. Such an analysis of the dynamics of system stability is a necessary prelude to any examination of future political trends. But it is hardly sufficient. Knowing how an important factor in a complex social system will change is not equivalent to knowing how the system itself will be transformed in adapting to this initial change.

In social systems, the future is not preordained through immutable laws of cause and effect. The human element impels us to focus on the choices open to society and the historical context within which they will be made. Present futures research all too often succumbs to an apolitical posture. The language of scientific predictability rather than of public choice frames our conclusions. While certain static images of the future seem to plot out the inevitable direction of change (e.g., steady-state, no-growth, space-ship economy), they have ignored the politics of choice in society's future-creating, direction-determining activities. These time-fixed pictures of a hypothetical future society serve a heuristic function, illuminating the values and policy objectives associated with a given image and mobilizing political support around those values and objectives. However, they cannot act as guides for tactics and strategies in the all-important transitional phase, for they do not address the problems of coping with the lost stability of a growth-oriented society.

Chapter 6 aimed at creating a model for the study of political futures that would overcome the predictive emphasis of most futurology. The four scenarios presented here have avoided this difficulty by stressing the ongoing interaction of power and purpose in order to reveal more concretely the politics of the future. In this regard, it is significant to note that each scenario, each image of the future, has reference to a traditional body of social philosophy that gives credibility to its specific expectations of political development. My belief is that the classic confrontation among diverse theoretical perspectives does have relevance in a no-growth future. Political ideologies, recast to address the issues of the day, help to structure our awareness of events and to motivate our political actions. Undoubtedly, the specifics of the conflicts over equality, freedom, community, and well-being will be shaped by numerous situational variables (e.g., the actual nature of our economic decline). For this reason, analysts would do well to explore the probability of alternative futures within various hypothetical (possible) supportive and inhibiting settings. In any case, this recognition of competing perspectives and public choices is an intrinsic part of the speculative enterprise. Chapter 6 sought to illustrate this approach to futures research and to convey the unavoidable uncertainty that accompanies it.

One final comment concerns the content of the competing images of the future. Researchers must somehow incorporate the notion of political change into the alternative futures they construct. These images, like the society they reflect, must be dynamic, containing within them internal contradictions and necessities for choice, and thus conceived as transitional stages in the development of even more distant futures. An image of the future that is devoid of politics, that fails to embrace the idea of change, has implicitly posited an end to human history.

In this light, we can conclude that an analysis of the political future ought to be closely akin to an analysis of political history. This is true on two accounts. First, the need to analyze political behavior, to assess the impact of change, to evaluate, interpret, assume, and imagine binds both the historian and the futurologist to a common intellectual endeavor. Second, the object of investigation is the same—political man operating within a political context. The values and philosophies of the past and present will still motivate partisans of the future; various interests and factions will still combine, confront one another, then recombine in quest of relative advantages; the claims of power and self-interest and the pull of reason and ideals will, like always, form the sum and substance of political debate. A study of future political behavior, by including the human element in its analysis, allows us to view forecasting in its proper *historical* light. Stated simply, past, present, and future intermingle and merge in perpetual drama, the continuing story of human experience.

Notes

Chapter 1

1. Bertrand de Jouvenel, *The Art of Conjecture,* quoted in *Politics and the Future of Industrial Society,* ed. Leon N. Lindberg (New York: McKay, 1976), pp. 1-2.

2. Daniel Bell, "The Future as Present Expectation," *Daedalus,* Summer 1967, p. 258.

Chapter 2

1. The basis for this taxonomy can be found in Mostafa Rejai, "Political Ideology: Theoretical and Comparative Perspectives," in *The Decline of Ideology,* ed. Mostafa Rejai (Chicago: Aldine, 1971), p. 14.

2. Robert Michels, *Political Parties* (New York: Free Press, 1966).

3. Louis Hartz, *The Liberal Tradition in America* (New York: Harcourt, Brace and World, 1955).

4. Christopher Jencks, *Inequality* (New York: Basic Books, 1972), p. 3.

5. Jerome Mileur, *The Liberal Tradition in Crisis* (Lexington, Mass.: Heath, 1973), p. 25.

6. James Madison, "Federalist 10," in *American Government,* 3d ed., ed. Peter Woll (Boston: Little, Brown and Company, 1969), pp. 126-27.

7. Hartz, *Liberal Tradition,* p. 223.

8. Theodore Lowi, *The End of Liberalism* (New York: Norton, 1969), pp. 289-90.

9. Charles Lindblom, "The Science of 'Muddling Through,'" *Public Administration Review* 19 (Spring 1959): 86.

10. James P. Young, *The Politics of Affluence* (Scranton, Pa.: Chandler, 1968), p. 51.

11. Frank Parkin, *Class Inequality and the Political Order* (New York: Praeger, 1971), p. 90.

12. Jack Newfield, "The Death of Liberalism," *Playboy Magazine,* April 1971, p. 246.

13. David Reisman, *The Lonely Crowd* (New Haven, Conn.: Yale University Press, 1961), pp. 177-87.

14. As quoted in Hartz, *Liberal Tradition,* p. 265.

15. Robert Haber, "The End of Ideology as Ideology," in *The End of Ideology Debate,* ed. Chaim I. Waxman (New York: Funk and Wagnalls, 1968), p. 183.

16. Edward A. Shils, *The Torment of Secrecy* (Glencoe, Ill.: Free Press, 1956), p. 226.

17. Peter Bachrach, *The Theory of Democratic Elitism* (Boston: Little, Brown and Company, 1967), p. 93.

18. Young, *Politics of Affluence,* p. 204.

19. E. E. Schattschneider, *The Semi-Sovereign People* (New York: Holt, Rinehart and Winston, 1960), p. 35.

20. Seymour Martin Lipset, *Political Man* (Garden City, N.Y.: Doubleday, 1960), p. 439.

21. Peter Bachrach and Morton Baratz, *Power and Poverty* (New York: University of Oxford Press, 1970), p. 44.

22. Aaron Wildavsky, *The Politics of the Budgetary Process* (Boston: Little, Brown and Company, 1964), p. 12.

23. André Gorz, *A Strategy for Labor* (Boston: Beacon Press, 1964), p. 5.

24. Howard P. Tuckman, *The Economics of the Rich* (New York: Random House, 1973), p. 28.

25. Philip Taft and Philip Ross, "American Labor Violence: Its Causes, Character, and Outcome," in *The History of Violence in America,* eds. Hugh Davis Graham and Ted Robert Gurr (New York: Bantam, 1969), p. 281.

26. Charles M. Rehmus and Doris B. McLaughlin, eds., *Labor and American Politics* (Ann Arbor, Mich.: University of Michigan Press, 1967), p. 4.

27. Ronald Radosh, "The Corporate Ideology of American Labor Leaders from Gompers to Hillman," in *Beyond Liberalism: The New Left Views American History,* ed. Irwin Unger (Waltham, Mass.: Xerox College Publishing Company, 1971), p. 214.

28. William Appleman Williams, *The Contours of American History* (Chicago: Quadrangle Books, 1966), pp. 445-86.

29. Stanley Aronowitz, *False Promises* (New York: McGraw-Hill, 1974), p. 7.

30. Daniel Bell, *The End of Ideology* (New York: Free Press, 1961), pp. 214-15.

31. Aronowitz, *False Promises,* p. 95.

32. Adolf Sturmthal, *Comparative Labor Movements* (Belmont, Calif.:

Wadsworth Publishing Company, 1972), p. 43.

33. Walter Fogel and Archie Kleingartner, eds., *Contemporary Labor Issues* (Belmont, Calif.: Wadsworth Publishing Company, 1966), p. 186.

34. William Serrin, *The Company and the Union: The "Civilized Relationship" of the General Motors Corporation and the United Automobile Workers* (New York: Knopf, 1973).

35. Murray Edelman, "The Conservative Political Consequences of Labor Conflict," in *Essays in Industrial Relations Theory*, ed. Gerald G. Somers (Ames, Iowa: Iowa State University Press, 1969), pp. 164-65.

36. Aronowitz, *False Promises*, p. 14.

37. Jack Newfield and Jeff Greenfield, *A Populist Manifesto* (New York: Warner Books, 1972).

38. Gorz, *Strategy for Labor*, p. 20.

Chapter 3

1. John Kenneth Galbraith, *The Affluent Society* (New York: Mentor Books, 1958), p. 72.

2. Werner Sombart, "American Capitalism's Economic Rewards," in *Essays in the History of American Socialism*, eds. Seymour Martin Lipset and John H. M. Laslett (Garden City, N.Y.: Anchor Press, 1974), p. 599.

3. Irving Louis Horowitz, "Another View From the Bridge," in *The End of Ideology Debate*, ed. Chaim I. Waxman (New York: Funk and Wagnalls, 1968), p. 173.

4. Noam Chomsky, "Interview 42," in *On Growth*, ed. Willem L. Oltmans (New York: Capricorn Books, 1974), p. 285.

5. Committee for Economic Development, Program Committee, *Economic Growth in the United States* (New York: Committee for Economic Development, 1969), p. 7.

6. Louis Hartz, *The Liberal Tradition in America* (New York: Harcourt, Brace and World, Inc., 1955), p. 17.

7. Richard A. Easterlin, "Does Money Buy Happiness?" *Public Interest* 30 (Winter 1973):3.

8. For two diverse views on this subject, see Walter Heller, "Coming to Terms with Growth and the Environment," in *Energy, Economic Growth and the Environment*, ed. Sam H. Schurr (Baltimore: Johns Hopkins Press, 1972), pp. 10-11; and Walter A. Johnson, "The Guaranteed Income as an Environmental Measure," in *Toward a Steady-State Economy*, ed. Herman Daly (San Francisco: W. H. Freeman, 1973), p. 180.

9. Denis Goulet, "The United States: A Case of Anti-Development," in *Up the Mainstream*, ed. Herbert G. Reid (New York: David McKay Company, 1974), p. 176.

10. John Curtis Raines, *Illusions of Success* (Valley Forge, Pa.: Hudson Press, 1975), p. 12.

11. Francis X. Sutton, et al., *The American Business Creed* (Cambridge, Mass.: Harvard University Press, 1956), p. 49.

12. Richard C. Edwards, Michael Reich, and Thomas E. Weisskopf, eds., *The Capitalist System* (Englewood Cliffs, N.J.: Prentice-Hall, 1972), p. 363.

13. Arthur B. Shostak, Jon Van Til, and Sally Bould Van Til, *Privilege in America* (Englewood Cliffs, N.J.: Prentice-Hall, 1973), p. 14.

14. Michael H. Best and William E. Connolly, "Market Images and Corporate Power: Beyond the 'Economics of Environmental Management,' " in *Public Policy Evaluation,* ed. Kenneth Dolbeare (Beverly Hills, Calif.: Sage Publications, Inc., 1975), p. 57.

15. Jencks, *Inequality,* p. 5.

16. André Gorz, *Strategy for Labor* (Boston: Beacon Press, 1964), p. 91. See pp. 80 passim; individual needs now demand social means of fulfillment. This relates not only to the fact that, as city dwellers most of us must purchase our food rather than grow it ourselves. Also, caring for aging parents, in the past a normal function of the extended family, is now a purchasable service (nursing homes, old-age homes) because our life-styles have eliminated for many the previous alternative. Also note Best and Connolly, "Market Images," pp. 56-58 on the increased profitability of the new range of goods and services from which to choose. It is this and not merely changes in demand patterns that prompt a more expensive selection of necessary consumables.

17. E. F. Schumacher, *Small Is Beautiful: Economics as if People Mattered* (New York: Harper and Row, 1973), p. 46.

18. Erich Fromm, "The Alienated Consumer," in *Capitalist System,* eds. Edwards et al., pp. 267-68.

19. Robert E. Lane, *Political Ideology* (New York: Free Press, 1962), p. 80.

20. Theodore Prager, "On the Political Compulsions of Economic Growth," in *Socialism, Capitalism and Economic Growth,* ed. C. H. Feinstein (Cambridge: Cambridge University Press, 1967), p. 206.

21. Peter Jenkins, "The Indian Summer of Democracy," *The Manchester Guardian,* 20 September 1975, p. 4.

22. David M. Potter, *People of Plenty* (Chicago: Phoenix Books, 1954), p. 92.

23. Ibid., p. 97.

24. See R. Richard Wohl, "The 'Rags to Riches' Story: An Episode of Secular Idealism," in *Class, Status, and Power,* eds. Seymour Martin Lipset and Reinhard Bendix (Glencoe, Ill.: Free Press, 1953), p. 394.

25. Raines, *Illusions of Success,* p. 78.

26. Joseph Lopreato and Lawrence E. Hazelrigg, *Class, Conflict, and Mobility* (San Francisco: Chandler Publishing Company, 1972), p. 442.

27. Seymour Martin Lipset, *Political Man* (New York: Doubleday, 1960), p. 257. Also see James Alden Barber, Jr., *Social Mobility and Voting Behavior* (Chicago: Rand McNally, 1950); "The influence of mobility on the political system would seem . . . to be a moderating one: lending flexibility to the electoral process, reducing the stakes involved in elections, and diluting the class content of politics" (p. 267).

28. Ralf Dahrendorf, *Class and Class Conflict in Industrial Society* (Stanford, Calif.: Stanford University Press, 1959), p. 222.

29. Potter, *People of Plenty*, p. 95.

30. Seymour Martin Lipset and Reinhard Bendix, *Social Mobility in Industrial Society* (Berkeley: University of California Press, 1967), p. 280.

31. C. Wright Mills, *White Collar: The American Middle Classes* (New York: Oxford University Press, 1951). Many accept the view that the "managerial revolution" has resulted in an increase in mobility for groups outside of the traditional economic elite. While this is a common theme, it is not altogether proven; see Anthony Giddens, *The Class Structure of Advanced Societies* (New York: Harper Torchbooks, 1973), pp. 167-71.

32. Frank Parkin, *Class Inequality and Political Order* (New York: Praeger Publishers, 1971), p. 56. See also Giddens, *Class Structure*, p. 181.

33. Lipset and Bendix, *Social Mobility*, pp. 76-77.

34. See Anselm L. Strauss, *The Contexts of Social Mobility* (Chicago: Aldine Publishing Company, 1971), pp. 41-44. The Turner Thesis is sound in its appreciation of the perceptual though perhaps not the physical effect of the frontier in muting class consciousness.

35. Lane, *Political Ideology*, p. 79.

36. John H. Schaar, "Equality of Opportunity, and Beyond," in *Up the Mainstream*, ed. Reid, p. 240.

37. Strauss, *Contexts of Social Mobility*, pp. 250-51.

38. Lipset and Bendix, *Social Mobility*, p. 4. See also Vilfredo Pareto, *The Mind and Society, Vol. IV*, ed. Arthur Livingston, trans. Andrew Bongiorno, Arthur Livingston, with James Harvey Rogers (New York: Brace and Company, 1935), p. 1516.

39. Raines, *Illusions of Success*, p. 16.

40. Hartz, *The Liberal Tradition*, p. 135.

41. Harold L. Wilensky, "Class, Class Consciousness, and American Workers," in *Labor in a Changing America*, ed. William Haber (New York: Basic Books, 1966), p. 27.

42. Wilbert E. Moore, "Changes in Occupational Structures," in *Social Structure and Mobility in Economic Development*, eds. Neil J. Smelser and Seymour Martin Lipset (Chicago: Aldine Publishing Company, 1966), p. 205.

43. Morris Rosenberg, "Perceptual Obstacles to Class Consciousness," *Social Forces* 32 (October 1953):26-27.

44. We have reason to suspect the reality of "upgrading" when we dis-

cover that occupations such as janitor, newsboy, cook, typist, etc. are classified as non–blue collar. The lower levels of the service and clerical occupational hierarchies are no less alienating or better paid than is the base of the blue-collar (or manual) pyramid.

45. This "status" mobility raises one's position with reference to one's past, not necessarily in comparison with society as a whole. The fact that it is so frequently practiced indicates that an employer accepts job reclassification as a relatively painless way of placating employees and responding to their desire for mobility.

46. Strauss, *Contexts of Social Mobility,* pp. 211-13. Age phasing refers to career ladders in which progress to the next stages is to a large extent guaranteed after a fixed period of training, probation, seasoning in the previous position, etc.

47. Ibid., pp. 203-5.

48. Bruce C. Johnson, "The Democratic Mirage: Notes Toward a Theory of American Politics," in *Up the Mainstream,* ed. Reid, p. 219n.

49. Gino Germani, "Social and Political Consequences of Mobility," in *Social Structure,* eds. Smelser and Lipset, p. 380.

50. Not mentioned at all are noneconomic paths for mobility aspirations that a dynamic pluralist society offers. From captain of the bowling team to head of a local charity drive to elder of the church, civic and community activities provide outlets for the socially ambitious and compensate for losses of self-respect stemming from one's economic disappointments.

51. See W. G. Runciman, *Relative Deprivation and Social Justice* (Berkeley: University of California Press, 1966), pp. 90, 193. Indeed, there are indications that workers are totally unaware of just how much better off some members of society are.

52. Lane, *Political Ideology,* p. 61.

53. Aronowitz, *False Promises,* p. 81.

54. Lipset and Bendix, *Social Mobility,* pp. 262-63.

55. See Lane, *Political Ideology,* p. 75.

56. Schaar, "Equality of Opportunity," p. 241.

57. Milton Friedman, *Capitalism and Freedom* (Chicago: Phoenix Books, 1962), p. 166.

58. Schaar, "Equality of Opportunity," p. 241.

59. There are chronological and structural places for each of the two general mechanisms described in this chapter. The young, initially hopeful about raising themselves out of their class environment, will increasingly identify with their class fate as years pass and hopes fade. Structurally, unionism is most common in blue- and white-collar professions that have obvious, inherent limitations on mobility aspirations. Teachers and lower-level civil servants, for example, realize the limited height of their respective opportunity

ladders. They thus have organized in order to benefit from collective action. In this regard, it is interesting to note how the belief that better opportunities are available to low-echelon office personnel (the mail-clerk-to-company-president story) inhibits white-collar unionization efforts.

60. Henry C. Wallich, "Zero Growth," *Newsweek*, 24 January 1972, p. 62.

61. Johnson, "The Democratic Mirage," p. 190.

62. Easterlin, "Does Money Buy Happiness?" pp. 3-10.

63. Stephan Thernstrom, "The Myth of American Affluence," in *Up the Mainstream*, ed. Reid, p. 173.

64. Stephan Thernstrom, "Class and Mobility in a Nineteenth Century City," in *Class, Status and Power*, 2d ed., eds. Lipset and Bendix (New York: Free Press, 1966), p. 609.

65. Lipset and Bendix, *Social Mobility*, p. 109.

66. Ibid., p. 106. See also Giddens, *Class Structure*, p. 216.

67. Raines, *Illusions of Success*, p. 100.

68. T. B. Bottomore, "The Persistence of Ideology," in *Up the Mainstream*, ed. Reid, p. 160.

69. Johnson, "The Democratic Mirage," pp. 199-200.

70. Philip Taft, "The Philosophy of the American Labor Movement," in *Labor*, ed. Haber, pp. 134-35.

71. William Pfaff, as quoted in Jonathan Cobb and Richard Sennett, *Hidden Injuries of Class* (New York: Alfred A. Knopf, 1972), pp. 4-5.

72. Sutton et al., *American Business Creed*, p. 19.

73. Jerome G. Manis and Bernard N. Meltzer, "Attitudes of Textile Workers to Class Structure," *American Journal of Sociology* 60 (July 1954): 35.

74. Lopreato and Hazelrigg, *Class Conflict, and Mobility*, pp. 186-89.

75. Sutton et al., *American Business Creed*, p. 46, quoted from an advertisement approved by the Public Policy Committee of the Advertising Council and appearing in *Woman's Home Companion*, November 1948 as a public service.

76. Kenneth E. Boulding, "The Economics of Human Conflict," in *The Nature of Human Conflict*, ed. Elton B. McNeil (Englewood Cliffs, N.J.: Prentice-Hall, 1965), p. 187.

77. W. H. Hutt, *The Strike-Threat System* (New Rochelle, N.Y.: Arlington House, 1973), p. vii.

78. Jeffrey D. Strauss, "Technological Counsel and Societal Change," in *Politics and the Future of Industrial Society*, ed. Leon N. Lindberg (New York: David McKay Company, 1976), p. 154.

79. Ibid., p. 155 as quoted from Clark Kerr, *Marshall, Marx in Modern Times: The Multidimensional Society* (London: Cambridge University Press, 1969).

80. Potter, *People of Plenty,* p. 118.

81. Dennis Pirages, *Managing Political Conflict* (New York: Praeger Publishers, 1976), p. 119.

82. Anatol Rapoport, "Game Theory and Human Conflict," in *Human Conflict,* ed. McNeil, p. 210.

83. Morton D. Davis provides this example in *Game Theory: A Non-Technical Introduction* (New York: Basic Books, 1970), p. 81.

84. Giddens, *Class Structure,* p. 206.

85. Strauss, *Contexts of Social Mobility,* p. 142.

86. Robert Lindsey, "Young Women, Blacks Still Have High Hopes," *New York Times,* 27 October 1975, pp. 1, 51; quote on p. 51. Also see "Economy Mars Belief in the American Dream," *New York Times,* 26 October 1975, pp. 1, 48.

87. Committee for Economic Development, *Economic Growth,* p. 56.

88. Robert L. Heilbroner and Lester C. Thurow, *Understanding Macroeconomics* (Englewood Cliffs, N.J.: Prentice-Hall, 1975), p. 277.

Chapter 4

1. Donella H. Meadows, Dennis L. Meadows, Jørgen Randers, and William W. Behrens III, *Limits to Growth* (New York: Universe Books, 1972), p. 23.

2. Pirages, *Managing Political Conflict,* p. 116.

3. John Maddox, *The Doomsday Syndrome* (New York: McGraw-Hill, 1972), p. 279.

4. Our ability to comprehend danger is tied to our time perspective. Most people cannot think very much beyond the problems immediately facing them. Their space and time framework involves primarily family, business, and neighborhood on the spacial dimension and the next few years on the time dimension. Only when problems in these ranges are eased can people be concerned with the broader picture. This analysis raises three important points:

1. Often, the impact of larger events, undermining more immediate hopes and efforts, is ignored. People are left out of the big decisions because they are not sensitive to the consequences these matters have on personal and immediate events;

2. People suffering financial hardship will ignore long-range planning, preoccupied with the need merely to survive. This has consequences on the psychological receptivity of some to seeing the utility of broad alternatives, long-range goals, and collective action;

3. Inevitably, however, long-term trends will have immediate consequences. The dominant approach in dealing with immediate and disembodied (isolated) problems—incrementalism—is a hallmark of

our polity. It has resulted in highway expansion without an overall transportation policy, urban and suburban development without an overall housing or land-use policy, etc.

5. Stewart L. Udall, "Limits: The Environmental Imperative of the 1970's," in *Agenda for Survival: The Environmental Crisis—2,* ed. Harold W. Helfrich, Jr. (New Haven, Conn.: Yale University Press, 1970), p. 230.

6. Ira Sharkansky, *The United States: A Study of a Developing Country* (New York: D. McKay, 1975), p. 138.

7. Allen L. Hammond, William D. Metz, and Thomas H. Maugh II, *Energy and the Future* (Washington, D.C.: American Association for the Advancement of Science, 1973), p. 127.

8. Edmund Faltermayer, "The Energy 'Joyride' Is Over," *Fortune* 86 (September 1972):99.

9. Peter Passell, Marc Roberts, and Leonard Ross, review of Meadows et al., *Limits to Growth,* in *New York Times Book Review,* 2 April 1972, p. 1.

10. V. E. McKelvey, "Mineral Resource Estimates and Public Policy," in *Perspectives on Energy: Issues, Ideas and Environmental Dilemmas,* eds. Lon C. Ruedisili and Morris W. Firebaugh (New York: Oxford University Press, 1975), pp. 37-38.

11. Lee Schipper and Allan J. Lichlenberg, "Efficient Energy Use and Well-Being: The Swedish Example," *Science,* 3 December 1976, p. 1012.

12. Maddox, *Doomsday Syndrome,* p. 104.

13. National Academy of Science, National Research Council, *The Earth and Human Affairs* (Scranton, Penn.: Camfield Press, 1972), p. 83.

14. Joseph L. Fisher and Hans H. Landsberg, "Resources on 1980," in *America 1980,* ed. Robert L. Hill (Washington, D.C.: Graduate School, U.S. Department of Agriculture, 1965), pp. 47-48.

15. René Dubos, from an interview conducted by Paul London entitled "Change and the Future," *Current* 171 (March 1975):40.

16. Part of the resistance may stem from the image of extracting corporations as greedy and insensitive to the needs of rural America. However, a much more likely scenario would be the arousal of regional enmity. The resource-bearing states would object to seeing their wealth shipped to the population concentrations of the Northeast at cutrate prices while they are forced to bear the brunt of the social costs of extraction. Recent battles over the erection of high-tension power lines hints at the coming confrontation. The fight to develop our domestic energy resources will require as much political as technical savvy.

17. Wilfred Beckerman, *Two Cheers for the Affluent Society* (New York: St. Martin's Press, 1974), p. 126.

18. H. C. Wallich, "How to Live with Economic Growth," *Fortune* 86 (October 1972):121.

19. Rufus E. Miles, Jr., *Awakening from the American Dream* (New York:

Universe Books, 1976), p. 30.

20. Edward J. Mishan, ' Growth and Antigrowth: What Are the Issues?" in *The Economic Growth Controversy,* eds. Andrew Weintraub et al. (White Plains, N.Y.: International Arts and Sciences Press, 1973), p. 9.

21. Barry Commoner, *The Closing Circle* (New York: Knopf, 1971), p. 39.

22. Claude F. Anderson and William Ramsay, *Managing the Environment: An Economic Primer* (New York: Basic Books, 1972), p. 25.

23. Maddox, *Doomsday Syndrome,* p. 156.

24. Beckerman, *Two Cheers,* p. 96.

25. This is not the only solution; different approaches should be considered on a case-by-case basis. However, it should be noted that a proposal with high decision costs (high political risk) for executive, legislator, and administrator will likely not be passed, implemented, or enforced effectively. Yet, given the nature of the problem, these are the solutions most apt to work.

26. William F. Baxter, *People or Penguins: The Case for Optimal Pollution* (New York: Columbia University Press, 1974), p. 75. It must be admitted that these conclusions assume a high elasticity of demand brought on by the existence of readily affordable substitutes, a condition that will not be true for all cases.

27. Ibid., p. 9.

28. Cy A. Adler, *Ecological Fantasies* (New York: Delta Books, 1973), p. 35. This notion of a threshold level is not altogether accurate for certain pollutants. For instance, radiation exposure at any level carries some risk.

29. See H. E. Stokinger, "Sanity in Research and Evaluation of Environmental Health," *Science,* 12 November 1971, pp. 662-65.

30. Forward, by René Dubos, in John S. Williams, Jr., et al., *Environmental Pollution and Mental Health* (Washington, D.C.: Information Resources Press, 1973), p. iv.

31. For various opinions on this subject, see Reid A. Bryson, " 'All Other Factors Being Constant . . .'—Theories of Global Climatic Change," in *Man's Impact on Environment,* ed. Thomas R. Detwyler (New York: McGraw-Hill, Inc., 1971), pp. 167-74.

32. Adler, *Ecological Fantasies,* p. 150. Of course, some basic principles must be followed; dumping should be done far offshore and in water currents in order for the cleansing properties of the ocean to be adequately utilized.

33. Graham J. Smith et al., *Our Ecological Crisis: Its Biological, Economic and Political Dimensions* (New York: Macmillan, 1974), p. 97.

34. Commoner, *The Closing Circle,* p. 153.

35. Brian J. Skinner, *Earth Resources* (Englewood Cliffs, N.J.: Prentice-Hall, 1969), p. 130.

36. *The Earth and Human Affairs,* p. 10. The author continues his disquieting analysis: "dissolved salt can be an insidious and ubiquitous con-

taminant of our water supplies. Nearly every human activity tends to increase the concentration of salt in our surface and underground water reservoirs. The accumulation of salt will inevitably continue and increase over the coming decades. . . . Fresh water has thus become another one of our dwindling natural resources" (p. 13).

37. Ibid., p. 72.

38. Fisher and Landsberg, "Resources," p. 39.

39. Anderson and Ramsay, *Managing the Environment,* p. 209.

40. Mishan, "Growth and Antigrowth," p. 19.

41. Commoner, *The Closing Circle,* p. 261.

42. Ibid., p. 176.

43. Gerald Garvey, *Energy, Ecology, Economy* (New York: W. W. Norton, 1972), p. 193.

Chapter 5

1. Richard C. Edwards, Michael Reich, and Thomas E. Weisskopf, eds., *The Capitalist System* (Englewood Cliffs, N.J.: Prentice-Hall, 1972), p. 462.

2. Richard C. Edwards, "The Logic of Capitalist Expansion," in *The Capitalist System,* eds. Edwards et al., p. 104.

3. James O'Connor, *The Corporations and the State* (New York: Harper Colophon Books, 1974), p. 114. The comment about "huge government liabilities" should be examined in conjunction with the upcoming discussion on the growth in consumer debt.

4. Arnold A. Rogow, "The Revolt Against Social Equity," in *Up the Mainstream,* ed. Reid, p. 252.

5. John Kenneth Galbraith, *The Affluent Society* (New York: Mentor Books, 1958), p. 125; see pp. 124-130.

6. Potter, *People of Plenty,* p. 115.

7. France, West Germany, Italy, Japan, United Kingdom, USSR—according to Albert Syzmanski in "The Decline and Fall of the American Eagle," in *Economics: Mainstream Readings and Radical Critiques,* ed. David Mermelstein (New York: Random House, 1973), pp. 65-70.

8. This statement ought to be qualified by noting a trend toward services demanded from us, the revenues from which do not show up in balance-of-trade figures (dividends, fees, royalties, etc.) but go to more than off-set our deficit. "The U.S. also has a strong lead in the exporting of services, from banking and accounting to food handling, franchising and management consulting. . . . They can be expected to grow increasingly important as the U.S. economy becomes less focused on physical production and more attuned to services" (Ann C. Scott, "Can the U.S. Compete?" *Newsweek,* 24 April 1972, p. 66).

9. Jason Epstein, "Capitalism and Socialism: Declining Returns," *New*

York Review of Books, 17 February 1977, p. 37; see also, William D. Nordhaus, "The Falling Share of Profits," in *Brookings Papers on Economic Activity,* vol. 11, eds. Arthur M. Okum and George L. Perry (Washington, D.C.: Brookings Institute, 1974), pp. 169-208.

10. See John Curtis Raines, *Illusions of Success* (Valley Forge, Penn.: Judson Press, 1975), pp. 31-41.

11. Ibid., p. 46.

12. Fred Hirsch, *The Social Limits to Growth* (Cambridge, Mass.: Harvard University Press, 1976).

13. Lester R. Brown, quoted in Leonard Silk, "Economics 1—The Summit: Chautauqua, Babel or Consensus?" *The New York Times Magazine,* 22 September 1974, p. 96.

14. Richard J. Barnet and Ronald Müller, "The Negative Effects of Multinational Corporations," in *Economics,* ed. Mermelstein, p. 153.

15. C. A. Pérez, "What the Third World Wants," *Business Week,* 13 October 1975, p. 56.

16. For an example of this line of reasoning, see Michael P. Lerner, "The Future of the Two-Party System in America," in *1984 Revisited: Prospects for American Politics,* ed. Robert Paul Wolff (New York: Knopf, 1973).

17. Leon N. Lindberg, "Strategies and Priorities in Comparative Research," in *Politics and the Future of Industrial Society,* ed. Leon N. Lindberg (New York: David McKay, 1976), p. 271.

18. Alvin Toffler, *Future Shock* (New York: Bantam Books, 1970).

19. Address by Bruno Bettelheim, given at the Institute on Futurology Conference at the College of Mount St. Joseph, Cincinnati, Ohio, 28 June 1976.

20. Toffler, *Future Shock,* p. 2.

21. René Dubos, "The Limits of Adaptability," in *The Environmental Handbook,* ed. Garrett De Bell (New York: Ballantine Books, Inc., 1970), p. 28.

22. Edward Goldsmith et al., *Blueprint for Survival* (Boston: Houghton Mifflin, 1972), p. 16.

23. See Toffler, *Future Shock,* pp. 74-123.

24. See E. F. Schumacher, *Small Is Beautiful: Economics As If People Mattered* (New York: Harper and Row, 1975), pp. 50-53, 142-45.

25. This decline is in some measure caused by the events surrounding us that undermine our attempts at self-control: publicity of political corruption in high places, the atrocities of a questionable war, public service unions on strike, etc.

26. Todd La Porte and C. J. Abrams, "Alternative Patterns of Postindustria: The California Experience," in *Politics,* ed. Lindberg, pp. 44-45.

27. Edwin Schur, *The Awareness Trap* (New York: Quadrangle/The

New York Times Book Co., 1976).

28. Schumacher, *Small Is Beautiful*, p. 29. Also see Martin Pawley, *The Private Future: Causes and Consequences of Community Collapse in the West* (New York: Random House, 1974), for a discussion of many of the themes presented in this section.

29. Charles E. Silberman, "The U.S. Economy in an Age of Uncertainty," *Fortune* 83 (January 1971):75.

30. Kenneth Boulding, "The Economics of the Coming Spaceship Earth," in *Environmental Quality in a Growing Economy*, ed. Henry Jarrett (Baltimore: Johns Hopkins Press, 1966), p. 11.

31. Robert L. Heilbroner, *An Inquiry into the Human Prospect* (New York: Norton, 1974), p. 100.

32. Rufus E. Miles, Jr., *Awakening from the American Dream: The Social and Political Limits to Growth* (New York: Universe Books, 1976), p. 2.

33. Justifications of using government as a political commons are analyzed in Theodore Lowi, *The End of Liberalism* (New York: Norton, 1969). The author does not use the "commons" terminology in describing this behavior.

34. Karl W. Deutsch et al., *The Nerves of Government* (New York: Free Press, 1963), pp. 229-30.

35. A Myrick Freeman III and Robert H. Haveman, "Clean Rhetoric, Dirty Water," *Public Interest*, no. 28 (Summer 1972):52.

36. Ibid., p. 56.

37. See Toffler, *Future Shock*, pp. 124-51 on causes and symptoms of managerial incapacity and societal ungovernability.

38. Miles, *Awakening from the American Dream*, p. 55.

39. Peter Jenkins, "The Indian Summer of Democracy," *Manchester Guardian*, 20 September 1975, p. 4.

40. John Platt, "What We Must Do," *Science*, 28 November 1969, p. 1116.

41. George W. Anderson, "Public Policy and the Complex Organization: The Problem of Governance and the Further Evolution of Advanced Industrial Society," in *Politics*, ed. Lindberg, p. 192.

42. John Hamer, "America's Next Century," in *Editorial Research Reports on the American Future*, eds. Editorial Research Reports Staff (Washington, D.C.: Congressional Quarterly, 1976), p. 8.

43. See Thomas E. Jones, "Toward a Future of Selective Growth," in *The Next Twenty-Five Years: Crisis and Opportunity*, ed. Andrew A. Spekke (Washington, D.C.: World Future Society, 1975), pp. 72-89.

44. Pirages, *Managing Political Conflict*, p. 116.

45. Heilbroner, *An Inquiry*, p. 94.

46. Peter Schrag, "America Needs an Establishment," *Harpers*, no. 251 (December 1975):58.

Chapter 6

1. Rudolf Klein, "The Trouble with a Zero-Growth World," *New York Times,* 2 June 1974, p. 81.

2. B. Bruce-Briggs, "Against the Neo-Malthusians," *Commentary* 58 (July 1974):25-29.

3. Elise Boulding, "Futurology and the Imagining Capacity of the West," in *Search for Alternatives,* ed. Franklin Tugwell (Englewood, Cliffs, N.J.: Winthrop, 1973), p. 96.

4. Albert Cantril and Charles Roll, *Hopes and Fears of the American People* (New York: Universe Books, 1971), pp. 29-30.

5. Gurney Breckenfeld, "The Perilous Prospects of a Low-Growth Economy," *Saturday Review,* 12 July 1975, pp. 35-41; also see Bruce-Briggs, "current energy problems are the result not of scarcity but of bad government and bad business policy" (p. 26).

6. David Amidon, "Discussion of the Papers," in *The Economic Growth Controversy,* eds. Andrew Weintraub et al. (White Plains, N.Y.: International Arts and Sciences Press, 1973), p. 183.

7. Richard England and Barry Bluestone, "Ecology and Social Conflict," in *Toward a Steady-State Economy,* ed. Herman Daly (San Francisco: W. H. Freeman, 1973), p. 196.

8. Quoted in Cy A. Adler, *Ecological Fantasies: Death from Falling Watermelons* (New York: Green Eagle Press, 1974), p. 306.

9. Stanley Aronowitz, *Food, Shelter and the American Dream* (New York: Seabury Press, 1975), p. 160.

10. Gus Tyler, *Scarcity* (New York: Quadrangle/The New York Times Book Company, 1976).

11. Anthony Downs, "Up and Down with Ecology—the 'Issue Attention' Cycle," *Public Interest* 28 (Summer 1972):38-50.

12. Erich Jantsch, interviewed by G. R. Urban, "For a Science of Man," in *Futurists,* ed. Alvin Toffler (New York: Random House, 1972), pp. 216-17.

13. Walter A. Weisskopf, "Economic Growth Versus Existential Balance," in *Toward a Steady-State Economy,* ed. Daly, pp. 240-51.

14. Jerry Mander, "The Meaning of Limits," in *The Failure of Success,* eds. Theobald and Stephanie Mills (Indianapolis: Bobbs-Merrill Co., Inc., 1973), p. 102.

15. Roland N. McKean, "Growth vs. No Growth: An Evaluation," in *The No-Growth Society,* eds. Mancur Olson and Hans H. Landsberg (New York: Norton, 1973), p. 209.

16. Lynton K. Caldwell, "1992: Threshold of the Post-Modern World" (Paper delivered for Franklin Lectures in Science and Humanities, Auburn University, Auburn, Alabama, 1 November 1972, revised 31 January 1974), p. 18.

17. Daniel Bell examines and disputes the S-curve hypothesis in *Coming of Post-Industrial Society: A Venture in Social Forecasting* (New York: Basic Books, 1973), pp. 181-85.

18. Schumacher, *Small Is Beautiful*, p. 144.

19. Frederick Ferré, *Shaping the Future: Resources for the Post-Modern World* (New York: Harper and Row, 1976), p. 7.

20. Heilbroner, *An Inquiry*, pp. 131-33.

21. Samuel P. Huntington, "Postindustrial Politics: How Benign Will It Be?" *Comparative Politics* 6 (January 1974):164.

22. Jan Miles, *The Poverty of Prediction* (Lexington, Mass.: Lexington Books, 1975), pp. 179-80. Also note E. Boulding, "Futurology," on the conservative influence of most futures research.

23. Miles, *Poverty of Prediction*, p. 7.

24. Dennis Gabor, *Inventing the Future* (Westminster, Md.: Knopf, 1969), p. 239.

25. Leon N. Lindberg, "Strategies and Priorities for Comparative Research," in *Politics*, ed. Lindberg, p. 234.

26. Wendell Bell and James A. Mau, "Images of the Future: Theory and Research Strategies," in *The Sociology of the Future*, eds. Wendell Bell and James A. Mau (New York: Russell Sage Foundation, 1971), pp. 6-44. Their theory on images of the future is derived in large part from the groundbreaking work of Frederik Lodewijk Polak, *The Image of the Future* (Dobbs Ferry, N.Y.: Oceana Publications, 1961).

27. Thomas Kuhn, *The Structure of Scientific Revolutions* (Chicago: University of Chicago Press, 1962). Also see Luther P. Gerlach and Virginia H. Hine, *Lifeway Leap* (Minneapolis: University of Minnesota Press, 1973).

28. Arthur I. Waskow, "Towards a Democratic Futurism," in *Futurists*, ed. Toffler, p. 86. See also Toffler, *Future Shock*, p. 460.

29. John McHale, *The Future of the Future* (New York: Braziller, 1969), p. 238.

30. For an interesting analysis of the elements of value changes that lead to sociopolitical changes, note Nicholas Rescher, "What is Value Change? A Framework for Research," in *Values and the Future*, eds. Kurt Baier and Nicholas Rescher (New York: Free Press, 1971), p. 69.

31. Schattschneider, *The Semi-Sovereign People*, p. 66.

32. Charles W. Anderson, "Public Policy and the Complex Organization: The Problem of Governance and the Further Evolution of Advanced Industrial Society," in *Politics*, ed. Lindberg, p. 195.

33. See T. H. Marshall, *Citizenship and Social Class* (New York: Cambridge University Press, 1963); also see Lopreato and Hazelrigg, *Class, Conflict and Mobility* (New York: Chandler, 1972), p. 66.

34. Daniel Bell disputes this point: "The expansion of the service sector— a significant feature of post-industrial society—had become a drag on pro-

ductivity" (*Coming of Post-Industrial Society,* p. 463).

35. Anderson, "Public Policy," p. 212.

36. Peter Jenkins, "Diagnosis for the English Sickness," *Manchester Guardian,* 11 October 1975, p. 11.

37. Peter Drucker, *The Unseen Revolution: How Pension Fund Socialism Came to America* (New York: Harper and Row, 1976).

38. The pluralists' penchant for avoiding class definitions of need, using region, race, occupation, and age as targets of many welfare programs, is especially noticeable in some aspects of Affirmative Action. As a means of opening up the class system, its long-strategic term impact is perhaps more deleterious than desirable. See Nathan Glazer, *Affirmative Discrimination: Ethnic Inequality and Public Policy* (New York: Basic Books, 1976).

39. Frank Parkin, *Class Inequality and Political Order: Social Stratification in Capitalist and Communist Societies* (New York: Praeger, 1971), pp. 58-59.

40. Daniel Bell, *Coming of Post-Industrial Society,* p. 362.

41. The most lucid statements of this view are Theodore Lowi, *The End of Liberalism* (New York: Norton, 1969); and Grant McConnel, *Private Power and American Democracy* (New York: Random House, 1970).

42. Gerlach and Hine, *Lifeway Leap,* p. 23.

43. Dennis Pirages and Paul R. Ehrlich, *Ark Two: Social Responses to Environmental Imperatives* (New York: Viking Press, 1974), pp. 164-65. Note the authors' desire for weighted voting to benefit the *informed* and active citizen.

44. John Carson-Parker, "The Options Ahead for the Debt Economy," *Business Week,* 12 October 1974, p. 120.

45. Daniel Bell, "Notes on the Post-Industrial Society," in *Search for Alternatives,* ed. Tugwell, p. 271.

46. Aronowitz, *Food, Shelter, and the American Dream,* p. 5.

47. Huntington, "Postindustrial Politics," pp. 184-85.

48. Philip E. Converse, "Shifting Role of Class in Political Attitude and Behavior," in *Readings in Social Psychology,* 3d ed., eds. Eleanor E. Maccoby et al. (New York: Holt, Rinehart and Winston, 1958), p. 396.

49. Leonard Silk, "Economics 1—The Summit: Chautauqua, Babel or Consensus?" *New York Times Magazine,* 22 September 1974, p. 97.

50. Herman Kahn and B. Bruce-Briggs, *Things to Come: Thinking About the Seventies and Eighties* (New York: Macmillan, 1972), pp. 142-43.

51. David C. Schwartz, "A Theory of Revolutionary Behavior," in *When Men Revolt—And Why,* ed. J. C. Davies (New York: Free Press, 1971), p. 124.

52. Peter Clecak, "A Grim Vision of the Future," *Dissent,* Winter 1975, p. 32.

53. Bell, *Coming of Post-Industrial Society,* p. 272. Also note Ian H. Wilson, "Business and the Future: Social Challenge, Corporate Response,"

in *The Next Twenty-Five Years: Forty-Four Papers,* ed. Andrew A. Spekke (Washington, D.C.: World Future Society, 1975), pp. 143-52.

54. This is highly probable since the upper classes, often safely positioned within large and stable organizations, are less vulnerable to market fluctuations, experience less downward mobility, and are able to protect their capital investments. Great wealth was (in the Depression for instance) and still is secure wealth. Surely one of the advantages of privilege and power is the structural protection of position, just as one of the disadvantages of lower-class status is economic insecurity.

55. Potter, *People of Plenty,* pp. 102-3.

56. Michael P. Lerner, "The Future of the Two-Party System in America," in *1984 Revisited,* ed. Wolff, p. 114.

57. James C. Davies, "Toward a Theory of Revolution," in *When Men Revolt,* ed. Davies, p. 136.

58. Runciman, *Relative Deprivation,* p. 22.

59. Harold L. Wilensky, "Measures and Effects of Mobility," in *Social Structure and Mobility,* eds. Smelser and Lipset, p. 127. See also Strauss, *Contexts of Social Mobility,* p. 179.

60. See Andrew Levison, *The Working Class Majority* (New York: Penguin, 1975).

61. Michael Mann, "The Social Cohesion of Liberal Democracy," *American Sociological Review* 35 (June 1970):423-39.

62. Giddens, *Class Structure,* p. 113.

63. See Phillip E. Converse, "The Nature of Belief Systems in Mass Publics," in *Ideology and Discontent,* ed. D. E. Apter (New York: Free Press, 1964), p. 216.

64. See Gerlach and Hine, *Lifeway Leap,* pp. 149-62.

65. Ted Gurr, "A Causal Model of Civil Strife: A Comparative Analysis Using New Indices," in *When Men Revolt,* ed. Davies, pp. 121-22.

66. Parkin, *Class Inequality,* p. 121.

67. Ibid. Liberal policies to maximize growth potential will inevitably blend with radical appeals for redistribution. The underdeveloped areas of the South, the skills lying unused in minorities, women, the aged, and the handicapped, growth potential in previously ignored public services sectors, all are (or can be) both growth-inducing and redistributive. Radicals, if they are to respond to legitimate demands for growth from developing sectors of society, must redefine economic growth to take advantage of its redistributive thrust. Their strategy will be not to reject growth but to change its impact and direction. And the liberal position regarding growth is the tactical wedge to legitimize this emphasis.

68. Lopreato and Hazelrigg, *Class, Conflict, and Mobility,* p. 474.

69. Walter Dean Burnham, *Critical Elections and the Mainsprings of American Politics* (New York: Norton, 1971).

70. Walter Dean Burnham, quoted in Robert J. Donovan, "Conservatism Thrives in Bad Economy," *Capital Times,* Madison, Wis., 29 December 1975, p. 14.

71. Kenneth E. Boulding, "The Shadow of the Stationary State," in *The No-Growth Society,* eds. Olson and Landsberg, p. 95.

72. Bertram Gross, "Friendly Fascism: A Model for America," in *Search for Alternatives,* ed. Tugwell, pp. 287-301.

73. Ibid., p. 290.

74. Harold D. Lasswell, "The Garrison State," *American Journal of Sociology* 46 (January 1941):455-68; Lasswell, "The Garrison-State Hypothesis Today," in *Changing Patterns of Military Politics,* ed. Samuel P. Huntington (New York: Free Press, 1962), pp. 51-70.

75. Morris Rosenberg, "Perceptual Obstacles to Class Consciousness," *Social Forces* 32 (October 1953):26.

76. Joseph Greenbaum and Leonard I. Pearlin, "Vertical Mobility and Prejudice: A Socio-Psychological Analysis," in *Class, Status and Power,* eds. Lipset and Bendix, pp. 480-91.

77. Amitai Etzioni, "A Creative Adaptation to a World of Rising Shortages," in *Adjusting to Scarcity, Annals of American Academy of Political and Social Science,* vol. 420, ed. Marvin E. Wolfgang (July 1975), p. 104.

78. See Murry Edelman, "On Policies That Fail," *Progressive* 39 (May 1975):22-23.

79. Amitai Etzioni, "Basic Human Needs, Alienation and Inauthenticity," *American Sociological Review* 33 (December 1968):882-83.

80. Christopher Lasch, "Toward a Theory of Post-Industrial Society," in *Politics in the Post-Welfare State,* eds. M. Donald Hancock and Gideon Sjoberg (New York: Columbia University Press, 1972), p. 46.

81. Edger Rust, *No-Growth: Impacts on Metropolitan Areas* (Indianapollis: Heath, 1975), p. 218.

82. Rosenberg, "Perceptual Obstacles," p. 27.

83. Melvin M. Tumin, "Some Unapplauded Consequences of Social Mobility in a Mass Society," *Social Forces* 36 (October 1957):32-37.

84. Runciman, *Relative Deprivation,* p. 25.

85. Graham J. Smith et al., *Our Ecological Crisis: Its Biological, Economic, and Political Dimensions* (New York: Macmillan, 1974), p. 3. Also note this quote from Kenneth E. Boulding, "New Goals for Society?" in *Energy, Economic Growth and the Environment,* ed. Sam H. Schurr (Baltimore: Johns Hopkins Press, 1972), p. 149: "The Spaceship Earth image of the future . . . implies a high value on modesty rather than grandeur. There is no room for 'great societies' in the spaceship. . . . It implies a high value on taking things easy, on conflict management. . . . Everything must be directed toward the preservation of precarious order rather than experimentation with new forms."

86. See Burnham, *Critical Elections,* pp. 159-66.

87. Kahn and Bruce-Briggs, *Things to Come,* pp. 104-7.

88. Heilbroner, *An Inquiry,* p. 110.

89. Schattschneider, *Semi-Sovereign People;* and Burnham, *Critical Elections.*

Bibliography

Books

Adler, Cy A. *Ecological Fantasies: Death from Falling Watermelons*. New York: Green Eagle Press, 1974.

Anderson, Claude, and Ramsay, William. *Managing the Environment: An Economic Primer*. New York: Basic Books, 1972.

Apter, David E., ed. *Ideology and Discontent*. New York: Free Press, 1964.

Aronowitz, Stanley. *False Promises*. New York: McGraw-Hill, 1974.

Aronowitz, Stanley. *Food, Shelter and the American Dream*. New York: Seabury Press, 1975.

Bachrach, Peter. *The Theory of Democratic Elitism*. Boston: Little, Brown and Company, 1967.

Bachrach, Peter, and Baratz, Morton. *Power and Poverty*. New York: University of Oxford Press, 1970.

Baier, Kurt, and Rescher, Nicholas. *Values and the Future*. New York: Free Press, 1971.

Barber, James Alden, Jr. *Social Mobility and Voting Behavior*. Chicago: Rand McNally, 1950.

Baxter, William F. *People or Penguins: The Case for Optimal Pollution*. New York: Columbia University Press, 1974.

Beckerman, Wilfred. *Two Cheers for the Affluent Society*. New York: St. Martin's Press, 1974.

Bell, Daniel. *The Coming of Post-Industrial Society: A Venture in Social Forecasting*. New York: Basic Books, 1973.

Bell, Daniel. *The End of Ideology*. New York: Free Press, 1961.

Bell, Daniel, ed. *Toward the Year 2000*. Boston: Beacon Press, 1969.

Bell, Wendell, and Mau, James A., eds. *The Sociology of the Future*. New York: Russell Sage Foundation, 1971.

Brown, Harrison. *The Challenge of Man's Future*. New York: Viking Press, 1954.

Brown, Harrison et al. *The Next Hundred Years.* New York: Viking Press, 1963.

Bundy, Robert, ed. *Images of the Future: The Twenty-First Century and Beyond.* Buffalo, N.Y.: Prometheus Books, 1976.

Burnham, Walter Dean. *Critical Elections and the Mainsprings of American Politics.* New York: Norton, 1971.

Burns, James MacGregor. *The Deadlock of Democracy.* Englewood Cliffs, N.J.: Prentice-Hall, 1967.

Cantril, Albert, and Roll, Charles. *The Hopes and Fears of the American People.* New York: Universe Books, 1971.

Cobb, Jonathan, and Sennett, Richard. *The Hidden Injuries of Class.* New York: Knopf, 1972.

Cole, H.S.D. *Models of Doom.* Cambridge, Mass.: MIT Press, 1974.

Committee for Economic Development, Program Committee. *Economic Growth in the United States.* New York: Committee for Economic Development, 1969.

Committee on Geological Sciences, Division of Earth Sciences, National Research Council, National Academy of Sciences. *The Earth and Human Affairs.* San Francisco: Canfield Press, 1972.

Commoner, Barry. *The Closing Circle.* New York: Knopf, 1971.

Dahrendorf, Ralf. *Class and Class Conflict in Industrial Society.* Stanford, Calif.: Stanford University Press, 1959.

Daly, Herman, ed. *Toward a Steady-State Economy.* San Francisco: W. H. Freeman, 1973.

Davies, James C., ed. *When Men Revolt and Why.* New York: Free Press, 1971.

Davis, Morton D. *Game Theory: A Non-Technical Introduction.* New York: Basic Books, 1970.

DeBell, Garrett, ed. *The Environmental Handbook.* New York: Ballantine Books, 1970.

Detwyler, Thomas R., ed. *Man's Impact on Environment.* New York: Mc-Graw-Hill, 1971.

Deutsch, Karl W. et al. *The Nerves of Government.* New York: Free Press, 1963.

The Economic Impact of Pollution Control: A Summary of Recent Studies. Prepared for the Council on Environmental Quality, Department of Commerce, and the Environmental Protection Agency. Washington, D.C.: U.S. Government Printing Office, March 1972.

Editorial Research Reports Staff, eds. *Editorial Research Reports on the American Future.* Washington, D.C.: Congressional Quarterly, 1976.

Ehrlich, Paul, and Ehrlich, Anne H. *The End of Affluence.* New York: Ballantine Books, 1974.

Ehrlich, Paul, and Ehrlich, Anne H. *Population, Resources, Environment: Issues in Human Ecology.* San Francisco: W. H. Freeman, 1972.

Ferré, Frederick. *Shaping the Future: Resources for the Post-Modern World.* New York: Harper and Row, 1976.

Feinstein, C. H., ed. *Socialism, Capitalism and Economic Growth.* New York: Cambridge University Press, 1967.

Fogel, Walter, and Kleingartner, Archie, eds. *Contemporary Labor Issues.* Belmont, Calif.: Wadsworth, 1966.

Gabor, Dennis. *Inventing the Future.* Westminister, Md.: Knopf, 1969.

Garvey, Gerald. *Energy, Ecology, Economy.* New York: Norton, 1972.

Gerlach, Luther P., and Hine, Virginia H. *Lifeway Leap.* Minneapolis: University of Minnesota Press, 1973.

Giddens, Anthony. *Class Structure of the Advanced Societies.* New York: Harper Torchbooks, 1973.

Goldsmith, Edward et al. *Blueprint for Survival.* Boston: Houghton Mifflin, 1972.

Gorz, André. *Strategy for Labor.* Boston: Beacon Press, 1964.

Graham, Hugh Davis, and Gurr, Ted Robert, eds. *The History of Violence in America.* New York: Bantam, 1969.

Haber, William, ed. *Labor in a Changing America.* New York: Basic Books, 1966.

Hammond, Allen L. et al. *Energy and the Future.* Washington, D.C.: American Association for the Advancement of Science, 1973.

Hancock, M. Donald, and Sjoberg, Gideon, eds. *Politics in the Post-Welfare State.* New York: Columbia University Press, 1972.

Hartz, Louis. *The Liberal Tradition in America.* New York: Harcourt, Brace and World, 1955.

Heilbroner, Robert L. *An Inquiry into the Human Prospect.* New York: Norton, 1974.

Heilbroner, Robert L., and Thurow, Lester C. *Understanding Macroeconomics.* Englewoods Cliffs, N.J.: Prentice-Hall, 1975.

Helfrich, Harold W., Jr., ed. *Agenda for Survival.* New Haven, Conn.: Yale University Press, 1970.

Hill, Robert L., ed. *America 1980.* Washington, D.C.: Graduate School, U.S. Department of Agriculture, 1965.

Hirsch, Fred. *The Social Limits to Growth.* Cambridge, Mass.: Harvard University Press, 1976.

Hofstadter, Richard. *The American Political Tradition.* New York: Random House, 1954.

Hoos, Ida. *Systems Analysis in Public Policy: A Critique.* Berkeley: University of California Press, 1972.

Hutt, W. H. *The Strike-Threat System.* New Rochelle, N.Y.: Arlington House, 1973.

Jencks, Christopher. *Inequality.* New York: Basic Books, 1972.

Johnson, Cecil E., ed. *Eco-Crisis.* New York: John Wiley and Sons, 1970.

Kahn, Herman, and Bruce-Briggs, B. *Things to Come: Thinking About the Seventies and Eighties.* New York: Macmillan, 1972.

Kahn, Herman, and Wiener, A. J. *The Year 2000.* New York: Macmillan, 1967.

Karp, Walter. *Indispensable Enemies*. Baltimore: Penguin Books, 1974.
Kuhn, Thomas. *The Structure of Scientific Revolutions*. Chicago: University of Chicago Press, 1962.
Kuhns, William. *Post-Industrial Prophets*. New York: Harper and Row, 1971.
Lane, Robert E. *Political Ideology*. New York: Free Press, 1962.
Lasswell, Harold D. "The Garrison-State Hypothesis Today." In *Changing Patterns of Military Politics*, edited by Samuel P. Huntington. New York: Free Press, 1962, pp. 51-70.
Levison, Andrew. *The Working Class Majority*. New York: Penguin, 1975.
Lindenfeld, Frank, ed. *Radical Perspectives on Social Problems*. New York: Macmillan, 1973.
Lindberg, Leon N., ed. *Politics and the Future of Industrial Society*. New York: McKay, 1976.
Lipset, Seymour Martin. *Political Man*. New York: Doubleday, 1960.
Lipset, Seymour Martin, and Bendix, Reinhard, eds. *Class Status, and Power*. Glencoe, Ill.: Free Press, 1953, 1966.
Lipset, Seymour Martin, and Bendix, Reinhard. *Social Mobility in Industrial Society*. Berkeley: University of California Press, 1967.
Lipset, Seymour Martin, and Laslett, John H. M., eds. *Failure of a Dream? Essays in the History of American Socialism*. Garden City, N.Y.: Anchor Press, 1974.
Lopreato, Joseph, and Hazelrigg, Lawrence E. *Class, Conflict, and Mobility*. San Francisco: Chandler Publishing Company, 1972.
Lowi, Theodore. *The End of Liberalism*. New York: Norton, 1969.
Maccoby, Eleanor E. et al., eds. *Readings in Social Psychology*. 3rd ed. New York: Holt, Rinehart and Winston, 1958.
McConnel, Grant. *Private Power and American Democracy*. New York: Random House, 1970.
McHale, John. *The Future of the Future*. New York: Braziller, 1969.
McNeil, Elton B., ed. *The Nature of Human Conflict*. Englewood Cliffs, N.J.: Prentice-Hall, 1965.
Maddox, John. *The Doomsday Syndrome*. New York: McGraw-Hill, 1972.
Marshall, T. H. *Citizenship and Social Class*. New York: Cambridge University Press, 1963.
Meadows, Donella H. et al. *Limits to Growth*. New York: Universe Books, 1972.
Mermelstein, David, ed. *The Economic Crisis Reader*. New York: Vintage Books, 1975.
Michels, Robert. *Political Parties*. New York: Free Press, 1966.
Miles, Jan. *The Poverty of Prediction*. Lexington, Mass.: Lexington Books, 1975.
Miles, Rufus E., Jr. *Awakening from the American Dream: The Social and Political Limits to Growth*. New York: Universe Books, 1976.

Mills, C. Wright. *White Collar: The American Middle Classes.* New York: Oxford University Press, 1951.

Mishan, E. J. *Technology and Growth: The Price We Pay.* New York: Praeger, 1970.

National Bureau of Economic Research. *Economic Growth.* New York: Columbia University Press, 1972.

National Goals Research Staff. *Toward Balanced Growth: Quantity with Quality.* Washington, D.C.: U.S. Government Printing Office, 1970.

Newfield, Jack, and Greenfield, Jeff. *A Populist Manifesto.* New York: Warner Books, 1972.

O'Connor, James. *The Corporations and the State.* New York: Harper Colophon Books, 1974.

Olson, Mancur, and Landsberg, Hans H., eds. *The No-Growth Society.* New York: Norton, 1973.

Oltmans, Willem L., ed. *On Growth.* New York: Capricorn Books, 1974.

Ophuls, William. *Ecology and the Politics of Scarcity.* San Francisco: W. H. Freeman, 1977.

Parkin, Frank. *Class Inequality and the Political Order: Social Stratification in Capitalist and Communist Societies.* New York: Praeger, 1971.

Passell, Peter, and Ross, Leonard. *The Retreat from Riches: Affluence and Its Enemies.* New York: Viking Press, 1973.

Pawley, Martin. *The Private Future: Causes and Consequences of Community Collapse in the West.* New York: Random House, 1974.

Pirages, Dennis. *Managing Political Conflict.* New York: Praeger, 1976.

Pirages, Dennis, and Ehrlich, Paul R. *Ark Two: Social Responses to Environmental Imperatives.* New York: Viking Press, 1974.

Polak, Frederik Lodewijk. *The Image of the Future.* Dobbs Ferry, N.Y.: Oceana Publications, 1961.

Potter, David. *People of Plenty.* Chicago: Phoenix Books, 1954.

Raines, John Curtis. *Illusions of Success.* Valley Forge, Penn.: Judson Press, 1975.

Rehmus, Charles M., and McLaughlin, Doris B., eds. *Labor in American Politics.* Ann Arbor: University of Michigan Press, 1967.

Reid, Herbert G., ed. *Up the Mainstream.* New York: McKay, 1974.

Rejai, Mostafa, ed. *The Decline of Ideology.* Chicago: Aldine, 1971.

Runciman, W. G. *Relative Deprivation and Social Justice.* Berkeley: University of California Press, 1966.

Rust, Edger. *No Growth: Impacts on Metropolitan Areas.* Indianapolis: Heath, 1975.

Schattschneider, E. E. *The Semi-Sovereign People.* New York: Holt, Rinehart and Winston, 1960.

Schumacher, E. F. *Small Is Beautiful: Economics as if People Mattered.* New York: Harper and Row, 1975.

Schur, Edwin. *The Awareness Trap.* New York: Quadrangle/The New York Times Book Company, 1976.

Schurr, Sam H., ed. *Energy, Economic Growth and the Environment.* Baltimore: Johns Hopkins Press, 1972.

Seneca, Joseph, and Taussig, Michael. *Environmental Economics.* Englewood Cliffs, N.J.: Prentice-Hall, 1974.

Serrin, William. *The Company and the Union: The "Civilized Relationship" of the General Motors Corporation and the United Automobile Workers.* New York: Knopf, 1973.

Sharkansky, Ira. *The United States: A Study of a Developing Country.* New York: David McKay, 1975.

Shostak, Arthur B. et al. *Privilege in America.* Englewood Cliffs, N.J.: Prentice-Hall, 1973.

Skinner, Brian J. *Earth Resources.* Englewood Cliffs, N.J.: Prentice-Hall, 1969.

Smelser, Neil J., and Lipset, Seymour Martin, eds. *Social Structure and Mobility in Economic Development.* Chicago: Aldine, 1966.

Smith, Graham J. et al. *Our Ecological Crisis: Its Biological, Economic and Political Dimensions.* New York: Macmillan, 1974.

Somers, Gerald G., ed. *Essays in Industrial Relations Theory.* Ames: Iowa State University Press, 1969.

Somit, Albert, ed. *Political Science and the Study of the Future.* Hinsdale, Ill.: Dryden Press, 1974.

Spekke, Andrew A., ed. *The Next Twenty-Five Years: Forty-Four Papers.* Washington, D.C.: World Future Society, 1975.

Strauss, Anselm L. *Contexts of Social Mobility: Ideology and Theory.* Chicago: Aldine, 1971.

Sturmthal, Adolf. *Comparative Labor Movements.* Belmont, Calif.: Wadsworth, 1972.

Sutton, Francis X. et al. *The American Business Creed.* Cambridge, Mass.: Harvard University Press, 1956.

Theobald, Robert, ed. *Futures Conditional.* New York: Irvington, 1972.

Theobald, Robert, and Mills, Stephanie, eds. *The Failure of Success.* Indianapolis: Bobbs-Merrill, 1973.

Toffler, Alvin. *Future Shock.* New York: Bantam Books, 1971.

Toffler, Alvin, ed. *Futurists.* New York: Random House, 1972.

Tuckman, Howard P. *The Economics of the Rich.* New York: Random House, 1973.

Tugwell, Franklin, ed. *Search for Alternatives.* Englewood Cliffs, N.J.: Winthrop, 1973.

Tyler, Gus. *Scarcity.* New York: Quadrangle, 1976.

Unger, Irwin, ed. *Beyond Liberalism: The New Left Views American History.* Waltham, Mass.: Xerox College Publishing Company, 1971.

Waxman, Chaim I., ed. *The End of Ideology Debate.* New York: Funk and Wagnalls, 1968.

Weintraub, Andrew, ed. *The Economic Growth Controversy.* White Plains, N.Y.: International Arts and Sciences Press, 1973.

Westoff, Charles et al. *Toward the End of Growth: Population in America.* Englewood Cliffs, N.J.: Prentice-Hall, 1973.

Williams, John S., Jr., et al. *Environmental Pollution and Mental Health.* Washington, D.C.: Information Resources Press, 1973.

Williams, William Appleman. *The Contours of American History.* Chicago: Watts, 1966.

Wolff, Robert Paul, ed. *1984 Revisited: Prospects for American Politics.* Westminister, Md.: Knopf, 1973.

Wolfgang, Marvin E., ed. American Academy of Political and Social Science, Annals. *Adjusting to Scarcity.* Vol. 420. July 1975.

Wolfgang, Marvin, E., ed. American Academy of Political and Social Science, Annals. *The Future Society: Aspects of America in the Year 2000.* Vol. 408. July 1973.

Wolozin, Harold, ed. *The Economics of Air Pollution.* New York: Norton, 1966.

Young, James P. *The Politics of Affluence.* Scranton, Penn.: Chandler, 1968.

Articles

Best, Michael H., and Connolly, William E. "Market Images and Corporate Power: Beyond the 'Economics of Environmental Management.' " Dolbeare, Kenneth, ed. *Public Policy Evaluation.* Beverly Hills, Calif.: Sage Publications, 1975, pp. 41-74.

Boulding, Kenneth. "A Twenty-First Century Politics." *Current,* October 1976, pp. 36-45.

Breckenfeld, Gurney. "The Perilous Prospects of a Low-Growth Economy." *Saturday Review,* 12 July 1975, pp. 35-41.

Bruce-Briggs, B. "Against the Neo-Malthusians." *Commentary,* July 1974, pp. 25-29.

Bugler, Jeremy. "The Left and the Environment." *New Statesman,* 16 April 1976, pp. 500-2.

Caldwell, Lynton. "Nineteen Ninety Two: Threshold of the Post-Modern World." Paper delivered for Franklin Lectures in Science and the Humanities, Auburn University, Auburn, Alabama, 1 November 1972, rev. 31 January 1974.

Carson-Parker, John. "The Options Ahead for the Debt Economy." *Business Week,* 12 October 1974, p. 120.

Clecak, Peter. "A Grim Vision of the Future." *Dissent* 22 (1975), pp. 27-33.

Downs, Anthony. "Up and Down with Ecology—the 'Issue-Attention Cycle.' "

Public Interest 28 (1972), pp. 38-50.

Easterlin, Richard A. "Does Money Buy Happiness?" *Public Interest* 30 (1973), pp. 3-10.

Epstein, Jason. "Capitalism and Socialism: Declining Returns." *New York Review of Books,* 17 February 1977, pp. 35-39.

Etzioni, Amitai. "Basic Human Needs, Alienation and Inauthenticity." *American Sociological Review* 33 (1968), pp. 870-85.

Faltermayer, Edmund. "The Energy 'Joyride' is Over." *Fortune,* September 1972, p. 99.

Freeman, A. Myrick, III, and Haveman, Robert B. "Clean Rhetoric, Dirty Water." *Public Interest* (1972), pp. 51-65.

Hardin, Garret. "Life Boat Ethics: The Case Against Helping the Poor." *Congressional Digest* 54 (1975), p. 205.

Holden, Constance. "Futurism: Gaining a Toehold in Public Policy." *Science,* 11 July 1975, pp. 120-24.

Huntington, Samuel P. "Postindustrial Politics: How Benign Will It Be?" *Comparative Politics* 6 (1974), pp. 163-91.

Jenkins, Peter. "Diagnosis for the English Sickness." *Manchester Guardian,* 11 October 1975, p. 11.

Jenkins, Peter. "The Indian Summer of Democracy." *Manchester Guardian,* 20 September 1975, p. 4.

Klein, Rudolf. "The Trouble with a Zero-Growth World." *New York Times,* 2 June 1974, Sec. 6, p. 14.

Lane, Robert E. "The Politics of Consensus in an Age of Affluence." *American Political Science Review* 59 (1965), pp. 879-95.

Lasswell, Harold D. "The Garrison State." *American Journal of Sociology* 46 (1941), pp. 455-68.

Lindblom, Charles. "The Science of 'Muddling Through.' " *Public Administration Review* 19 (1959), pp. 79-88.

Lindsey, Robert. "Economy Mars Belief in the American Dream." *New York Times,* Sec. 1, 26 October 1975, p. 1.

Lindsey, Robert. "Young Women, Blacks Still Have High Hopes." *New York Times,* 26 October 1975, sec. 1, p. 1.

London, Paul, interview of René Dubos. "Change and the Future." *Current* 171 (1975), pp. 34-44.

Manis, Jerome G., and Meltzer, Bernard N. "Attitudes of Textile Workers to Class Structure." *American Journal of Sociology* 60 (1954), pp. 30-35.

Mann, Michael. "The Social Cohesion of Liberal Democracy." *American Sociological Review* 35 (1970), pp. 423-39.

Newfield, Jack. "The Death of Liberalism." *Playboy Magazine,* April 1971, p. 98.

Passell, Peter, and Ross, Leonard. "Don't Knock the $2-Trillion Economy." *New York Times,* 5 March 1972, Sec. 6, p. 14.

Pérez, C. A. "What the Third World Wants." *Business Week,* 13 October 1975, pp. 56-8.

Platt, John. "What We Must Do." *Science,* 28 November 1969, pp. 1115-21.

Rosenberg, Morris. "Perceptual Obstacles to Class Consciousness." *Social Forces* 32 (1953), pp. 22-27.

Schelling, Thomas C. "The Strategy of Conflict: Prospectus for a Reorientation of Game Theory." *Journal of Conflict Resolution* 2 (1958), pp. 230-64.

Schipper, Lee, and Lichlenberg, Allan J. "Efficient Energy Use and Well-Being: The Swedish Example." *Science,* 3 December 1976, pp. 1001-13.

Schrag, Peter. "America Needs an Establishment." *Harpers,* December 1975, p. 51.

Scott, Ann C. "Can the U.S. Compete?" *Newsweek,* 24 April 1972, p. 63.

Silberman, Charles E. "The U.S. Economy in an Age of Uncertainty." *Fortune,* January 1971, p. 72.

Silk, Leonard. "Economics 1—The Summit: Chautauqua, Babel or Consensus." *New York Times,* 22 September 1974, sec. 6, p. 16.

Taft, Philip, and Ross, Philip. "American Labor Violence: Its Causes, Character and Outcome." Graham, Hugh Davis, and Gurr, Ted Robert, eds. *The History of Violence in America.* New York: Bantam Books, 1969.

Tumin, Melvin M. "Some Unapplauded Consequences of Social Mobility in a Mass Society." *Social Forces* 36 (1957), pp. 32-37.

Wallich, Henry C. "How to Live with Economic Growth." *Fortune,* October 1972, p. 121.

Wallich, Henry C. "Zero Growth." *Newsweek,* 24 January 1972, p. 62.

Index